Culture in Christian Perspective

Culture in Christian Perspective

A Door to Understanding & Enjoying the Arts

LELAND RYKEN

MULTNOMAH · PRESS
Portland, Oregon 97266

The following publishers have given permission to quote the following copyrighted works: Liveright Publishing Corporation for permission to reprint "in Just-" from TULIPS AND CHIMNEYS by E. E. Cummings. Copyright 1923, 1925 and renewed 1951, 1953 by E. E. Cummings. Copyright 1973, 1976 by the Trustees for the E. E. Cummings Trust. Copyright 1973, 1976 by George James Firmage.

Harcourt Brace Jovanovich, Inc., "anyone lived in a pretty how town" by E. E. Cummings. Copyright 1940 by E. E. Cummings; renewed 1968 by Marion Morehouse Cummings. Reprinted from COMPLETE POEMS 1913-1962, by E. E. Cummings by permission of Harcourt Brace Jovanovich, Inc.

Unless otherwise indicated, all Scripture references are from the Revised Standard Version of the Bible copyright 1946, 1952,© 1971, 1973, Division of Christian Education, National Council of the Churches of Christ in the USA. Used by permission.

Scripture references marked KJV are taken from the King James Version of the Bible.

Cover design and illustration by Britt Taylor Collins
Edited by Rodney L. Morris

Portland, Oregon 97266

Printed in the United States of America

Library of Congress Cataloging-in-Publication Data

Ryken, Leland.
Culture in Christian perspective.

Bibliography: p.
Includes index.
1. Christianity and the arts. I. Title.
BR115.A8R95 1986 261.5'7 86-1442
ISBN 0-88070-115-3

86 87 88 89 90 91 – 10 9 8 7 6 5 4 3 2 1

For Jo

Contents

Preface

The arts belong to the Christian life. We sometimes think of them as an extraneous luxury, but they have a strange way of asserting themselves in the most threatening of circumstances. When our humanity is in danger, the artistic spirit suddenly lives. The arts give us something indispensable to life.

When missionary Bruce Hunt was imprisoned, he found relief by composing hymn verses. During Corrie ten Boom's prison experiences, her spirit was revived by such seemingly trivial artistic manifestations as the red wrapping of cookies from home, the beauty of the sky and woods, and her sister Betsie's dream of turning the concentration camp into a rehabilitation center with green walls "like springtime." When kidnapped by Ethiopian terrorists, missionary Debbie Dortzbach wrote poems in her journal, embroidered Bible verses, and drew pictures of plants in her notebook.

This is a book about literature, art, and music, both as they are in themselves and as they relate to the Christian faith. My aim is to open the door to understanding and enjoying the arts.

My cherished goal is that ministers, Sunday school teachers, Bible study leaders, and Christians in general will come to value the arts as conveyors of truth and examples of beauty. The arts can enhance both our personal lives and our understanding of our culture. All we need to do is be receptive.

I am happy for this opportunity to record my gratitude to the people whose assistance helped make the book possible: to Dr. John Walford, Chairman of the Wheaton College Art Department, who did what he could to prevent me from plunging myself into disgrace with my comments about art; to Mary Ryken, who proofread the manuscript; to the Wheaton College Alumni Association for a grant; and to Rod Morris, editorial manager of Multnomah Press, who helped tailor the book for the series of which it is a part.

Introduction: Thinking Christianly about the Arts

Christians and Their Culture

> One cannot keep on evangelizing the world without interfering with the world's culture. . . . In Christ man is restored to God as cultural creature to serve his Maker in the world and as ruler over the world for God's sake.
>
> Henry R. Van Til, *The Calvinistic Concept of Culture*

In its broadest reaches, this is a book about culture. My focus will be on art, music, and literature, but what I say about these particular cultural manifestations usually applies to culture more generally.

My concern throughout the book will be to relate culture to a Christian world view. The big question that I have attempted to answer is, How can Christians relate human culture to their faith? This is obviously a task of integration—of bringing two things together.

I have no doubt that such an integration is both possible and necessary for every thoughtful Christian; it may even be the most pressing issue facing the Christian church in the immediate future. If Christians are to be a force in shaping the contours of their society and evangelizing people in it, they will have to come to grips with the culture in which they inevitably live and move and have their being. They will also have to know where to draw the line against becoming assimilated into a secular culture, lest they lose the quality of being separate that the Bible attributes to true believers.

Cultural involvement is something the Bible enjoins in the very first chapter of Genesis. We read there that God gave the human race a mandate to rule the earthly order in his name and for his glory. This is the cultural mandate, and it is the starting point for thinking Christianly about culture.

The question that has perennially engaged Christians is not whether culture requires their attention, but how it does. Christian thinking on the question has moved between the poles of total rejection and total affirmation of culture. If this book has a unifying theme, it is that neither extreme does justice to the biblical data.

To think Christianly about culture and the arts means to look at them through the "lens" of biblical doctrine. The purpose of this introduction is to provide just such a lens. My aim is to outline the biblical doctrines that touch most directly upon the arts. In connection with each doctrine, I have listed a few of the questions that require an answer and that the rest of the book will explore. Subsequent chapters in the book will relate individual topics to this opening framework, which I envision as an "umbrella" for the whole book.

A Doctinal Framework for Considering the Arts

> If we commit ourselves to saying that the Christian revelation discovers to us the nature of all truth, then it must discover to us the nature of the truth about Art among other things.
>
> Dorothy L. Sayers, "Towards a Christian Aesthetic"

Scripture or Special Revelation

Christianity is a revealed religion. The foundation for its beliefs is the Bible. The Bible is also the starting point for a Christian aesthetic ("philosophy of the arts"). It contributes to such a theory by both its example and its doctrine.

By its own example the Bible establishes the importance of literature, since it is largely a work of literature. It affirms the importance of literary form (not simply content), and it answers questions of literary theory and practice. Is realism a legitimate technique? Can there be Christian tragedy? The form of the Bible provides answers.

Biblical doctrine is equally important. Scripture makes comments about all of the arts, as well as culture in general. It is the source of the doctrines in this initial list of principles that I propose to apply to the arts. Furthermore, the Bible is the ultimate source of truth by which a Christian judges the viewpoints espoused in works of art, literature, and music.

There are some corresponding questions. Exactly what does the Bible say about a given aspect of the arts or about the theme of a given work of art? When the Bible makes reference to one of the arts, how do we know when it is simply describing a practice and when we should regard it as being prescriptive? Since the Bible does not contain everything we need to know about the arts, at what point does the Bible cease to be the final authority on questions of aesthetic theory? How overtly or completely must the content of a work of art adhere to the biblical view in order to be considered true?

Natural or General Revelation and Common Grace

God reveals truth not only in the Bible but in creation, including culture and human reason. God's common grace endows all people, believers and unbelievers alike, with a capacity for truth, goodness, beauty, and creativity.

It follows from this that not all truth about aesthetic issues will be contained in the Bible. This means that we should expect many of the principles underlying the arts to come from the arts themselves, just as our knowledge of the laws of science comes from science itself. Furthermore, if God's truth and beauty permeate the work of non-Christian artists as well as Christian ones, Christians are free to relish truth and artistry wherever these appear. We should be prepared to find truth and grace incognito (hidden or indirectly expressed) in writers who are not themselves Christian.

There are, of course, some accompanying questions. As we wrestle with problems of aesthetic theory, where does special revelation (the Bible) cease to be the authority, and where does general revelation (the arts as human disciplines) begin to function as an autonomous authority? Exactly how incognito should we expect to find Christian truth in works of art? And how enthusiastic should a Christian really be about the frequently superficial level at which works of art correlate with biblical revelation?

Creation

The Bible teaches that God created all that exists, including both the natural creation and people. No other doctrine has such far-reaching implications for the arts.

At least five major principles follow from the biblical doctrine of creation. (1) The fact that God made earthly reality and set the human race over it means that the artist's and critic's preoccupation with human experience and culture is God-ordained. (2) Since God made a world that is beautiful as well as functional, we know that the concern of the creative artist and the critic with beauty, form, and artistic delight is legitimate. (3) God's separateness from creation means that culture cannot be equated with God; the artistic endeavor is God-approved but is not something that is inevitably Christian or even religious. (4) The fact that humans are created in God's image provides a sanction for human creativity and a theological explanation of why people create. (5) The doctrine of creation *ex nihilo* has given Christians a model for regarding artists as capable of creating, through their imagination, works for which there are no existing models that fully account for them, and it allows Christians to revel in originality—in God's doing a new thing.

Along with all these "givens," the doctrine of creation poses some questions that remain difficult to answer. Is all human creativity good? If not, what further criteria allow us to differentiate good from bad manifestations of the creative impulse? What are the limits beyond which creativity ceases to be God-glorifying? If people are to subdue creation and culture to God's glory, what are the precise forms that such control will take for the Christian artist or critic? Exactly where does a Christian artist or critic draw the line between making religious use of the arts and making the arts a surrogate religion or even a substitute for God? When do enthusiasm for the arts and immersion in them become idolatry?

Beauty and Pleasure

The Bible affirms the related ideas of beauty and pleasure. Scripture teaches that God is the ultimate source of beauty, that it is one of his perfections, that God values it and offers it as a gift to the human race. The Bible also affirms pleasure and enjoyment, treating them as good in principle (though capable of being perverted). This endorsement of beauty and pleasure opens the way for enjoying the arts and valuing them for the enrichment they add to life.

Some related questions will continue to exercise thoughtful Christians. How can we distinguish between the good and perverted uses of beauty? How can we distinguish between the enriching and trivial types of pleasure? When does pleasure become depraved and therefore debasing to a person? When does one's pursuit of beauty and pleasure become a selfish indulgence? Why have the defense of the arts on the pleasure principle and the criticism that delights in artistic form been so strongly resisted through the centuries? Why has most Christian criticism of the arts been so oblivious to form and beauty, preferring a solemnly religious and philosophic approach?

The Fall and Human Sin

The Christian view of the world as fallen has far-reaching effects on how we should view the arts. Human evil and depravity are one of the leading subjects of art (and of the Bible). A great deal of literature and art is built on the bedrock of original sin.

Furthermore, the fallen nature of people makes it possible for the arts to express falsehood and to have an immoral effect on an audience. The whole need to discern truth from error as we assimilate works of art stems from the Fall. The abuse of the arts, which will occupy us at many points in this book, would not even be an issue in a perfect world.

The big question that results is, Exactly how negatively has the Fall affected human creativity, the attitudes embodied in works of art, and the ways in which people assimilate art? How often, and in what ways, do the arts perpetuate the depravity of the fallen world?

Stewardship and Calling

The Bible implies there is a duty attached to every talent or capacity that people possess. The capacity for art, beauty, creativity, and artistic experience is something people should cultivate. Related to this is the Christian concept of calling, which encourages a person to whom God has given a talent (such as writing poems or composing songs or painting pictures or analyzing works of art) to exercise that talent. In addition to stewardship of ability, there is stewardship of time, which prescribes that people use their time wisely and constructively.

The corresponding questions include these: Exactly how much energy or time should a person devote to the pursuit of the arts? How do people balance the claims that various opportunities place upon them? What place do the arts have in the life of a Christian who is also called to serve the needs of others and live sacrificially?

Transcendence, or Belief in the Other World

Christianity is the religion of the two worlds, both equally real. In addition to physical, earthly reality, there exists a world of spiritual reality (including God and heaven). Christians live simultaneously in both worlds. The earthly sphere can never, by itself, constitute "reality" for a Christian artist or critic. Sheer immersion in physical sensation can never by itself be a touchstone for determining whether a work of art is Christian in orientation.

It is curious that hosts of Christian critics emphasize that the Incarnation of Christ provides a model for the artist's absorption in earthly reality, but that none of them tells us the Ascension of Jesus into heaven provides a model for transcending the earthly sphere. The perplexing question is why so much "religious criticism" of the arts in recent decades has been unable to come to grips with the ideas of heaven, eternal life, spiritual reality, and a transcendent God as necessary ingredients in a Christian world view.

The transcendental strain in the Christian faith has produced some significant questions through the ages. How does the artist express in an earthly medium—a medium that depends at some level on the senses—the reality that transcends the physical world? What is the best method of portraying the spiritual reality that pervades the physical and human worlds? How can words express the inexpressible, or the human imagination capture a grace beyond the earthly?

The Incarnation

The doctrine of the Incarnation has been the cornerstone of most attempts at a Christian aesthetic. The Incarnation of Jesus in human, earthly form affirms forever that human, earthly reality is worthy of study and love. It lends sanction to the artist's immersion in human experience. It sanctions the critic's absorption in the products of human imagination. Furthermore, the example of Christ's patience in understanding the unregenerate mind and his willingness to embrace the human predicament gives a reason and methodology for a Christian's approach to the works of non-Christian artists.

The Incarnation of Christ provides a superb model for what a work of art is. Art, too, is a little incarnation—an embodiment of meaning in the concrete form of images, sounds, and stories.

There has been a one-sided emphasis on the Incarnation in Christian aesthetic theory to the neglect of other doctrines. One often gets the impression that to affirm every facet of earthly life, including its sin, is to follow the pattern of Christ. Yet Christ rejected as well as affirmed earthly life. He said some thoroughly uncomplimentary things about physical reality and earthly endeavor.

The questions that require scrutiny, therefore, include these: What are the exact links between Christ's Incarnation and a work of art? What was the precise nature of Christ's involvement in the world, and what were the limits to his endorsement of earthly reality and human experience? How, in turn, does that involvement and limiting affect the artistic portrayal of human experience? Does the doctrine of the Incarnation establish anything about the arts that the doctrine of creation does not?

Redemption and Sanctification

The doctrine of redemption shows that it is not sufficient to leave human experience where it is. Contrary to the statements of artistic theorists who are obsessed with the Incarnation, Christ came to redeem and transform human life, not simply to affirm what he saw. If redemption is the goal and central reality of human life, no artist's work has fulfilled its highest purpose if it only records the misery and evil of life. As with Christian artists, so with Christian critics: their calling is to wrest beauty and meaning from a fallen world, and to help others to do so.

Sanctification means becoming like God, responding to good and evil as God does. The Christian doctrine of sanctification or holiness defines the kinds of activity, behavior, and morality that are proper and improper for people. The Christian stands with Plato, and against modern trends, in attaching moral significance and earnestness to the artistic enterprise. The desire to see holiness prevail also helps to define the materials and methods of the Christian artist.

There are some related questions. Exactly how does the artist remain true to the fallen nature of reality and human nature while also suggesting the redemptive potential in that experience? How does one balance the fallen and redeemed aspects of life in the artistic portrayal of human experience in the world? Exactly how does the artist portray evil without violating norms of sanctification and holiness?

The Christian Sacraments

The Christian sacraments assert that earthly reality can point to spiritual reality. In the Christian sacraments, the things of earth become a vehicle for the things of heaven. The sacraments show that tangible images and symbols can express truth; they implicitly confirm the "sign-making" tendency of the arts.

This does not mean that the Christian sacraments lend sanction to every artistic expression, but they are an excellent analogy to illustrate how the arts can communicate truth. Just as the sacraments use water, bread, and wine to express spiritual realities, works of art can use concrete images and symbols to embody truth to the glory of God and the edification of people. Like the Incarnation, the sacraments provide a convenient model for what works of art are like.

As with the doctrine of the Incarnation, Christian sacramentalism has sometimes been taken to untenable extremes in aesthetic theory. The label "sacramental" has been pinned on every conceivable artist's work, leading to the how-to-be-religious-without-really-trying syndrome. We must remember how few physical elements are used in the Christian sacraments, and under what special circumstances they become sacramental. There is a decisive difference between the bread of the communion served in church and the bread we eat for lunch. On the other hand, the way in which the Christian sacraments express spiritual truth in earthly images certainly provides a model toward which Christian artists and their audiences can aim in their artistic experiences.

Questions that require our best thinking include the following: How can we preserve the usefulness of the analogy between the sacraments and the means by which art expresses truth, without trivializing the idea by using the sacraments to defend everything that artists produce? Exactly what do the Christian sacraments and works of art have in common? How are they different? In short, how can we differentiate between the legitimate and the superficial and sacrilegious applications of Christian sacramentalism to artistic theory and practice?

The Creativity and Inspiration of Artists

The Bible contains an abundance of data about the inspiration or endowment of artists and writers by God. Biblical writers, for example, picture themselves as receiving their message from God. The classic text is 2 Peter 1:21: "men moved [carried along] by the Holy Spirit spoke from God." God also inspired the artists who embellished the tabernacle. What this establishes is that the Holy Spirit can endow artists with the creative gift and equip them to create specific works.

How widely does this inspiration apply to artists in general? What is the nature of such inspiration for Christian artists? What is its nature for non-Christian ones? Does the Holy Spirit equip artists to produce the beauty of artistic form? Does the Holy Spirit guide artists in the content of their works? If so, how can we account for the untruthful content of much art? Does the Holy Spirit inspire mediocre as well as great works of art?

Worship and Witness

Worship and witness are central to Christian experience. Worship is adoration and devotion offered to God because of his worthiness and works. The content of Christian witness is the same, this time directed horizontally to people.

The worship described in the Bible is a gold mine of information about the religious use of art. Literature, visual art, and music are prominent in that worship, especially in the Old Testament. We find in these biblical passages that art has integrity on its own merits as art, although the religious context in which it appears transforms the beauty of art into a mode of religious experience. Art in religious worship suggests a principle of far-reaching importance: Anything offered to God can become an act of worship.

Christian witness consists of telling others about the Christian faith. We learn from biblical example that a Christian's witness is necessarily expressed in one cultural form or another. It is best expressed in the cultural forms that are most natural to the teller and the audience. Christian witness, moreover, needs to use the best cultural forms available, and to use all such forms in order to appeal to the whole range of society. The appropriate vehicle for Christian artists and critics is works of art and criticism.

The relationship of the arts to worship and witness has produced some vexing problems. How can artistic integrity be preserved when art is used for worship and witness? (Even the word *use* points up the problem, but in fact we always use art for something, even if for artistic enjoyment and admiration.) Why does art used for religious purposes so overwhelmingly favor unsophisticated or mediocre or overly transparent works of art? Why do religious artists so often produce propaganda instead of art? Why do most Christian churches feel uncomfortable about the presence of art, music, and literature in the church?

The Christian Telos (Purpose or End) of Glorifying God

The classic statement that the purpose of human life is to glorify God is 1 Corinthians 10:31: "So, whether you eat or drink or whatever you do, do all to the glory of God." This is a principle of far-reaching implications. It means that every dimension of the artistic enterprise—creativity, excellence of technique, artistic content, the enjoyment of works of art—can become a way of glorifying God.

If the ultimate aim of life is to glorify God, it is a betrayal of that ideal and a form of idolatry to substitute anything in the place of God. The goal of glorifying God spares Christian artists and audiences from making an idol out of art. It keeps them from either overvaluing or undervaluing their artistic experiences.

The questions we can pose include these: Exactly when is the production or enjoyment of art glorifying to God, and when is it not? How can we avoid turning the Christian telos of God's glory into a cliché by which we cloak our artistic experiences with a facade of piety? When does the artistic pursuit become an idol?

Summary

To think Christianly about the arts must begin with an awareness of the Christian doctrines that apply most directly to the production and study of the arts. These doctrines are those of special revelation, general revelation and common grace, creation, beauty and pleasure, sin, stewardship and calling, belief in transcendence, the Incarnation, redemption and sanctification, the sacraments, inspiration, worship and witness, and the telos of glorifying God in every activity.

These doctrines are the framework within which I propose to look at the arts—a lens or window through which we can see the truth about the production and study of works of art.

FURTHER READING

Dorothy L. Sayers, *The Mind of the Maker* (1941).

H. Richard Niebuhr, *Christ and Culture* (1951).

Henry R. Van Til, *The Calvinistic Concept of Culture* (1959).

Norman Reed Cary, *Christian Criticism in the Twentieth Century* (1975).

Leland Ryken, ed., *The Christian Imagination: Essays on Literature and the Arts* (1981).

Arthur Holmes, ed., *The Making of a Christian Mind* (1985). Includes an essay on "The Creative Arts" by Leland Ryken.

Frank E. Gaebelein, *The Christian, The Arts, and Truth,* ed. D. Bruce Lockerbie (1985).

Chapter 1

The Nature and Purpose of the Arts

This book is concerned with the integration of faith and art. The introduction brought into focus those aspects of a Christian world view that are particularly relevant to the arts; this chapter describes the arts themselves. For purposes of that description, I have decided to concentrate on what the arts aim to do, and will explore how they achieve those ends in subsequent chapters. In the present chapter I will look at the arts by themselves; later chapters will relate the arts to a Christian framework.

TWO EXAMPLES OF ART

> Art [is] the embodiment of man's response to reality and his attempt to order his experience of that reality.
>
> John W. Dixon Jr., *Nature and Grace in Art*

As a way into the topic of the nature and purpose of art, I wish to look briefly at two examples of art, a painting and a poem. As Exhibit A, consider a painting by the nineteenth-century British painter John Constable. It is entitled *The Cornfield*.

The Cornfield by John Constable
Reproduced by courtesy of the Trustees, The National Gallery, London

If we were standing before the original of the painting in the National Gallery in London, the first thing we would notice is the artistic skill evident in the painting. The colors themselves—the vivid green of the trees and foreground grass, the brilliant yellow of the grainfield in the middle, the blue and white of the sky—draw us into the picture. Then we are awed by the sheer quantity of detail, along with the careful planning and days of work that went into the composition. The artist's creativity and technical mastery tell us that we are in the presence of a masterpiece.

A Picture of Reality

As we continue to absorb the painting we become aware of the content. The picture covers an enormous range of human experience in the world. It is obviously a picture of both the beauty and the bounty of nature. It is also about the varied activities of life, from the work of the sheep boy drinking from the pool and the harvesters nearly hidden by the grain, to the leisure activity of the hunter near the gate. The village and church tower in the distance suggest civilization and religion. All in all, this is a memorable record of human well-being in God's world.

The painting is also about time. We are aware of the natural cycles with the dead tree at the left and the ripe grain being harvested. We also see the development of human life from childhood through adulthood to the hope of life beyond the physical world. In short, the painting puts us in touch with a broad range of human experiences.

The Imaginary Element

Although the picture reminds us of human life in the world, we are also aware of its imaginary and unlifelike qualities. When we look at the original we see at once that the painted surfaces are not solidly filled in as they are in life or a photograph. The very arrangement of the scene and positioning of figures in it have all the earmarks of a posed scene. Constable followed the conventions of Claude Lorraine by framing nature with trees on both sides. Furthermore, the church tower toward which the arrangement and lines of the picture move our gaze was something Constable added to the real-life landscape that served as his model.[1]

Art does not try to give a photographic copy of life; it rearranges the materials of life in order to give us a heightened perception of its qualities. Art is life at the remove of imaginative form.

The Interpretation of Reality

Constable's painting does more than picture a scene; it also interprets the scene. The painting is about the beauty and bounty of nature and the harmony of human and natural life. Everything in the picture contributes to this sense of harmony. The plants and animals in the landscape are domesticated; the harvest pictured in the middle is at the very heart of human relationship to nature; the structures built by people (the fence, the dam in the stream, the village) merge into the natural landscape. We do not need Constable's letter to his wife to know that he sensed God's providence in nature. The painting shows that awareness and makes us feel it.

Art aims to convey not primarily the facts of life but the truth and meaning of those facts. Art is not about things as they are, but about things as they matter. The arts are concerned with what the English poet Shelley called "the spirit of events." This is their contribution to human knowledge—a knowledge about human values. As we look at Constable's painting, we become aware of much that we value in life—the sustaining beauty of nature; work and leisure; community and church; human life itself.

Does art such as this communicate ideas? Not abstractly or propositionally. Instead, art creates an imaginary world into which we enter. We do not encounter ideas but a world of human experience. The meanings that art communicates are meanings that take hold of us both consciously and unconsciously as we enter into the imagined world of the work.

John Milton's Sonnet on His Blindness

For a second example of how art works, let's consider a poem written in the middle of the seventeenth century by the English poet John Milton. Milton wrote the poem after going totally blind at the age of forty-three or forty-four:

When I consider how my light is spent,
Ere half my days, in this dark world and wide,
And that one talent which is death to hide
Lodged with me useless, though my soul more bent
To serve therewith my Maker, and present
My true account, lest he returning chide,
"Doth God exact day-labor, light denied?"
I fondly ask. But Patience, to prevent
That murmur, soon replies: "God doth not need
Either man's work or his own gifts; who best
Bear his mild yoke, they serve him best. His state
Is kingly: thousands at his bidding speed,
And post o'er land and ocean without rest;
They also serve who only stand and wait."

This, too, is an expression of a recognizable human experience. As we absorb the poem, we listen to the voice of suffering humanity. For all its particularity, the poem arouses our awareness of something that is close to the experience of everyone—the tragedy of human life, the debilitating catastrophe that changes a person's whole life, the psychic pain that cannot be brushed aside because it is a daily reality. The poem does what art often does: it faces the facts of life at their worst. One function of art, therefore, is to allow us to grapple with our own problems from a safe distance.

The Role of Perspective

The perspective from which we view human suffering is a Christian one. Milton here contemplates his handicap under the aspect of God's providence. Even the anguish of the first eight lines is defined in Christian terms as the speaker fears God's condemnation of him for his inactivity now that he is blind. Having wrestled with the problem, the speaker's quest for satisfaction is also achieved in Christian terms: "they also serve who only stand and wait." That is, the speaker can stand justified before his God because of such avenues of service as submission, worship, and expectation of what God will yet send. The poem thus gives us a new slant on the timeless truth that all things work together for good to those who love God, and a new example of Paul's insight about learning to be content in any circumstance of life.

Milton does not say all this abstractly. He embodies his meanings in poetic form, which means that he speaks in images, metaphors, and allusions. The method of art is to incarnate meaning in concrete form. The artist *shows,* and is never content only to *tell* in the form of propositions. The strategy of art is to enact rather than summarize. In this poem, Milton embodies his message in the concrete form of a person meditating on a problem and searching for a solution. The result is that as readers we recreate in our imaginations the experience of the speaker in the poem, from the moment he embarks on his process of meditation ("When I consider . . .") to the final resolution in the famous aphorism with which the poem ends. The poem does not only ask us to grasp an idea with our minds; it also puts us through an experience.

The Need to Interpret

In achieving this experiential concreteness and immediacy, the poem works by a certain indirectness. Because of this indirection, art always puts a burden of interpretation on its audience. In the present instance, we have to know how to interpret figurative language. The vocabulary of the poem makes little sense unless we are familiar with three gospel statements by Jesus—the incident of the blind man whom Jesus healed (John 9:1-4), the parables of the workers in the vineyard (Matthew 20:1-16) and the talents (Matthew 25:14-30). As in those biblical passages, the images of the poem are heavily metaphoric.

"When I consider how my light is spent," the speaker begins. The poet has not literally lost any "light." He has lost his eyesight and the ability to perform active service. And besides, light cannot be "spent." The poet is already drawing upon the financial metaphor from the parable of the talents. As for the indirectness of literature, the poet conveys his deepest despair not by telling us about it but by linking himself with the one-talent servant of Christ's parable—the slothful servant who was punished by God by being cast into outer darkness.

Beauty of Form

Once we have assimilated the impact of what the poem says, our attention begins to focus on how the poem is put together. There is an abundance of artistry and technique here. For one thing, the poem is an Italian sonnet. This means that it is a 14-line poem with regular meter and an intricate rhyme scheme—*abba abba* in the first eight lines, followed by three new rhyming sounds in the last six lines *(cde cde).*

An Italian sonnet is built on a principle of artistic balance and contrast. The octave, or first eight lines, states a problem, raises a doubt, establishes a conflict, or asks a question. The sestet, or last six lines, solves the problem, resolves the doubt, or answers the question. Milton's sonnet is built on this principle of balance. In the first seven and a half lines the poet struggles with his despair over the fact that his blindness prevents him from serving God actively. The last six and a half lines resolve the problem and alleviate the despair by discovering an alternate way of service to God, the passive way of submission and worship.

The poem is built on an elaborate system of contrasts that correspond to the twofold division I have noted. There is a contrast of mood between the increasing despair of the octave and the peaceful submission of the sestet. There is a contrast of theme between the active service discussed in the first part and the passive service of submission of the second part. A contrast in focus is evident in the self-centeredness of the octave and the emphasis on God in the sestet. The best index to this is the shift in pronouns—in the octave "I" and "my" (line 1), "my" (2), "me" and "my" (4), "my" (5), "my" (6), and "I" (8), and in the sestet "his" (10), "his," "him," "his" (11), and "his" (12). The poem, in other words, contrasts despairing introspection on the one hand and self-abnegation and self-transcendence on the other.

A final bit of artistry is the contrasting syntax or sentence structure in the poem. The syntax of the octave collapses under its own weight as the poet piles one subordinate clause on another. This mirrors the disordered rebellion of the speaker. By contrast, the reply of "Patience" is direct, easily grasped, and simple in structure.

Heightened Awareness of Life

> When we are at a play, or looking at a painting or a statue, or reading a story, the imaginary work must have such an effect on us that it enlarges our own sense of reality.
>
> Madeleine L'Engle, *Walking on Water*

Having considered two examples of art, we are in a position to proceed to a more systematic anatomy of the nature and purpose of art. What are the arts designed to do for people and societies?

We can begin with the generalization that the subject of art is human experience. Perhaps we should make an exception right at the outset. A great deal of music and some visual art is nonrepresentational; that is, it depicts nothing from the external world but is merely an artistic pattern. Obviously such forms of art do not aim to depict recognizable human experience.

The overwhelming majority of visual art and virtually all literature aim to present some aspect of human life for our contemplation. The vocation of the artist is to observe life and then transmute it into the "language" of a given art form. "The poet," writes C. S. Lewis, "is someone who says 'look at that' and points."[2] Someone else has said that the task of the artist "is to *stare,* to *look* at the created world, and to lure the rest of us into a similar act of contemplation."[3] The function of the arts is to heighten our awareness and perception of life by making us vicariously live it.

Truthfulness to reality is one of the goals of art. American painter Andrew Wyeth once said in an interview, "I love to study the many things that grow below the corn stalks and bring them back into the studio to study the color. If one could only catch that true color of nature—the very thought of it drives me mad."[4]

Understanding of Human Experience

What are the benefits of looking closely at some aspect of reality or human experience? By looking at anything closely, we come to understand it better. There can be no doubt that the arts are one of the chief means by which the human race grapples with and interprets reality.

This is not to say that the arts regularly give us new information that we would otherwise lack. We do, to be sure, discover much about ourselves and our world as we read literature and look at paintings; more often, we recover insights we theoretically know but have forgotten. The wisdom that the arts convey is often a bringing to consciousness what people already know. In short, the reward of contact with the arts is heightened awareness—awareness of ourselves, of people, of the world, of God. The function of artists is partly that of revelation.

Artists often do this by "defamiliarizing" experience—by portraying it in a new way so we will take note of it. This is where the very artificialities of art become a positive advantage. How many narrative paintings have we not seen that cram far more people and objects into a confined space than we ever find in real life? Still life paintings are not photographically lifelike (nor, for that matter, is a photograph exactly what we see when we view a bowl of fruit with our own eyes). In works of art we look at the materials of life as they have been rearranged and heightened by the artistic imagination. If we are alert, we take note of things that escape us in the pressures of daily living.

The heightened awareness that we experience as we read stories and poems or listen to music or look at visual art is something that we can, in turn, carry with us into real life. The connections between life and art are vital. Art aims to help us cope with life by temporarily removing us from it and then sending us back to it with renewed understanding and zest.

Giving Form to Common Human Experience

One of the functions of art is to give shape to our own experiences, insights, and feelings. The Greek philosopher Socrates said that the unexamined life is not worth living. The artistic impulse is based on the premise that the unexpressed life is also incomplete. All people "live by truth and stand in need of expression," said Ralph Waldo Emerson; "notwithstanding this necessity . . . , adequate expression is rare."[5] Artists are people with the gift of expression. They express life with patterns of sound, with paint on a canvas, with stories and poems.

A rich confusion of awareness lies below the level of our consciousness. Artists reach into that confusion and give it an order. As we stand before a painting or listen to music or read a poem, we suddenly see our own experiences and insights projected onto the details of the work before us. Artists turn our pain into art so we can bear it. They turn our joys into art so we can prolong them. In song and statue, poem and painting, artists give shape to the affirmations and denials of the human race. By nature we long to express and confirm what we know.

The arts help us to understand and possess life. Matthew Arnold expresses it thus:

> The grand power of poetry [and by extension the other arts] is its power of so dealing with things as to awaken in us a wonderfully full, new, and intimate sense of them, and of our relations with them. When this sense is awakened in us, . . . we feel ourselves to be in contact with the essential nature of those objects, to be no longer bewildered and oppressed by

> them, but to have their secret, and to be in harmony with them; and this feeling calms and satisfies us.[6]

As the foregoing analysis suggests, the arts function in the following way:

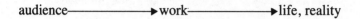

audience ———————→ work ———————→ life, reality

Experiencing a work of art is a bifocal experience. First we look at the work itself—its details and patterns and the meanings that these embody. But in addition to looking at the work, we look through it to our own experience in life. A work of art is a lens or window or lattice through which we see ourselves and our world.

Universal, Enduring Human Experience

Other branches of knowledge also tell us about human experience. It is not the subject matter of the arts that sets them apart. What, then, makes a novel different from *Time Magazine*, or a painting of a landscape different from a science textbook?

The news and the textbook go out of date. They give us localized facts that are true when written but that do not capture timeless truth. By contrast, the arts capture universal and enduring human experience. What Milton's sonnet on his blindness says about serving God is as true today as it was when Milton wrote the poem. Northrop Frye, the most influential critic of our century, has said that the role of the artist "is not to tell you what happened, but what happens: not what did take place, but the kind of thing that always does take place."[7] The test of whether a work of art has this quality is very simple: Whenever we can see our own experience in a work, it has expressed truth that is timeless.

Art is a mirror in which we see ourselves. At a commemorative ceremony at the tomb of Flemish painter Pieter Brueghel in 1924, Felix Timmermans said something that is true of the arts in general:

> In your work are reflected . . . our joys and our sorrows, our strengths and our weaknesses. . . . You are our mirror; in order to know how we are, we need only walk down the avenue of your work. . . . To know what we are, we have only to thumb through the book of your art, and we can know ourselves.[8]

What kind of knowledge is most worth having? Surely the truth and wisdom that endure represent a kind of knowledge at least as important as the factual data that is here today and gone tomorrow.

Exactly what is it that enables the arts to express enduring truth? What do they add to the facts that the news does not? They give us the event plus the meaning. A science textbook tells us the physical facts about nature; a Constable landscape painting or a nature lyric by Wordsworth gives us a sense of the moral meaning of a landscape. A newspaper obituary gives us the facts about someone's death; a poem on the same event tells us what the event means in human terms.

The arts are interested in capturing the spirit of life. They are full of imaginary details that violate known reality. But while they may disregard the literal facts, they picture the truth of life. Contemporary author Madeleine L'Engle once told a student that "you . . . look up facts in the encyclopedia. When you're looking for truth, then look in art, in stories, songs, sculpture."[9]

The arts are founded on a great paradox. They begin with the concrete realities of life. They constantly appeal to our senses—to what we can see and touch and taste and hear and smell. But they add an interpretive element to the experiences they record. In its highest reaches, art attains wisdom in a way that a mere record of facts does not. The daily news can give us the facts about the latest murders, but we turn to Shakespeare's *Macbeth* to understand the human horror and moral evil of murder. "The only knowledge that is worthwhile," writes Northrop Frye, "is the knowledge that leads to wisdom, for knowledge without wisdom is a body without life."[10]

Organizing Our Experiences of Life

The knowledge the arts convey to us depends partly on their ability to organize reality in our minds. Our impulse to organize reality is innate and occurs at both the conscious and subconscious levels. We automatically put our daily experiences into certain patterns so we can both understand and remember them. When we speak of having had a "bad day," we have condensed our experiences into a pattern of things that went wrong. When we recall the events of our lives as a whole, we do not relive them as they happened. Instead, we perceive them in more condensed versions categorized as good, bad, major, minor, and so forth.

The artistic imagination, too, organizes life for us. If our individual memories are the selective and organizing agents in our lives, artists serve the function of remembering for the human race. In their paintings and songs and stories and poems, they organize the experience of the entire race. Works of art are the collective memories of what human experience is like, arranged into the patterns of the imagination.

Enlarging Our Range of Experiences

Thus far I have focused on how the arts aim to put us in touch with familiar human experience. Equally important is the ability of art to enlarge our own fund of experiences. C. S. Lewis made this his final defense for literature:

> We seek an enlargement of our being. We want to be more than ourselves. Each of us by nature sees the whole world from one point of view with a perspective and a selectiveness peculiar to himself. . . . We want to see with other eyes, to imagine with other imaginations, to feel with other hearts, as well as with our own. . . . We demand windows. . . . This, so far as I can see, is the specific value or good of literature. . . ; it admits us to experiences other than our own.[11]

To use a current phrase, the arts raise our consciousness. They alert us to human needs and longings. They put us in touch with the experiences of people from other times and places, as well as people whose outlooks differ from ours. The arts have the potential to enlarge our sense of compassion because they lead us to encounter experiences that we would otherwise avoid.

The Social Function of the Arts

What I have said about the place of the arts in our individual lives applies equally to societies. The arts are perhaps the chief means by which a society focuses attention on its own values. This is, in fact, one of the expectations that a society places on its artists.

Such a focus on values arises not only from the works of art that a culture produces, but can be seen in the works from the past to which a given society gravitates. If left to ourselves, we turn to works of art that express experiences and values that are important to us. There is, in addition, the phenomenon of a generation reinterpreting works of art from the past. How a society sees and interprets the art and music and literature from the past tells us a lot about that culture.

The arts are a great humanizing force in society. The masterpieces of any nation become a social bond. The arts form an indispensable ingredient in our education and because the subject of art is so consistently the human response to life, the arts have a strange power to put people in touch with each other.

The Arts as Celebration and Refreshment

That is how it is with poetry: created and developed to give joy to human hearts.

Horace, *The Art of Poetry*

My description of the purpose of the arts thus far has focused on what might be called the utilitarian principle, that is, the practical usefulness of the arts as a contribution to human knowledge. But there is another dimension to the arts, a dimension that falls under the pleasure principle. "One of the prime achievements in every good fiction," writes C. S. Lewis, "has nothing to do with truth or philosophy . . . at all. . . . Every episode, explanation, description, dialogue—ideally every sentence—must be pleasurable for its own sake."[12]

The arts tell us a lot about human experience, but they also exist to be delightful in themselves. For one thing, artistic technique is a type of beauty and skill that calls attention to itself. When storytellers and composers and painters create their works, they follow principles of aesthetic form. They want their works to have unity and coherence and balance. Painters aim to dazzle us with their mastery of colors, writers with their mastery of words, musicians with their mastery of sound. All of them flaunt their mastery of form and expect us to admire what they have created.

The Arts as Entertainment

The arts are a form of entertainment. We pursue them in our leisure time. As a form of refreshment and artistic enrichment they carry their own reward. We do not attend a concert or play with the same utilitarian goals with which we go to a grocery store. Why do people hang paintings on walls? Because they enjoy the beauty these add to a room.

Even at the level of subject matter, the arts are meant to be enjoyed, not simply valued for the understanding of human experience they impart. The arts celebrate life. The sounds of the musician, the colors of the painter, the images of the poet all celebrate and affirm life as we know it. In fact, we often make the arts a part of our celebrations, even if it is only to add visual decoration to a room or put on a pageant at a program.

Creativity as a Purpose of Art

For artists themselves, creativity is part of the joy of art. It is the appointed consummation of their vocation. Mozart exclaimed about the creative experience, "What a delight this is

I cannot tell!"[13] The poet Shelley found his moments of inspired creativity "elevating and inspiring beyond all expression."[14] "The excitement in artistic creativity," writes musician Harold Best, "is excitement about the mystery of existence itself."[15]

What do people mean when they call great works of art "one of mankind's better moments"?[16] They mean that here we can find an inspiring example of human achievement. Great works of art make us feel small by comparison with the artist, but they paradoxically also invigorate us as we enter into the perfection of the work.

Summary

At their best, the arts serve many essential functions. By silhouetting the human experiences that they portray with striking clarity, art, music and literature heighten our awareness of reality. They give expression to the feelings, experiences, and beliefs of the human race and of ourselves. They intensify our involvement with life.

The arts are delightful as well as useful. They are a form of enjoyment and refreshment. And they enrich human life by adding to its beauty.

Further Reading

Walter Allen, ed., *Writers on Writing* (1948).

C. S. Lewis, *An Experiment in Criticism* (1961).

The Arts and Man [no editor] (1969).

Leland Ryken, *Windows to the World: Literature in Christian Perspective* (1985).

Chapter 1, Notes

1. Charles Constable is my source for the observation that the painter invented the church in the distance. See John Walker, *John Constable* (New York: Harry N. Abrams, 1978), p. 122.

2. C. S. Lewis and E. M. W. Tillyard, *The Personal Heresy* (London: Oxford University Press, 1939, 1965), p. 11.

3. Nathan A. Scott, Jr., *Modern Literature and the Religious Frontier* (New York: Harper and Brothers, 1958), p. 52.

4. Andrew Wyeth, quoted by Virginia Stem Owens, "On Praising God with Our Senses," in *The Christian Imagination: Essays on Literature and the Arts*, ed. Leland Ryken (Grand Rapids: Baker, 1981), p. 380.

5. Ralph Waldo Emerson, "The Poet," in *Major Writers of America*, ed. Perry Miller (New York: Harcourt, Brace and World, 1962), 1:531.

6. Matthew Arnold, *Essays in Criticism*, as excerpted in *The Norton Anthology of English Literature*, fourth edition, ed. M. H. Abrams et al. (New York: W. W. Norton, 1979), 2:1423.

7. Northrop Frye, *The Educated Imagination* (Bloomington: Indiana University Press, 1964), p. 63.

8. Felix Timmermans, as quoted in Bob Claessens, *Brueghel* (New York: Alpine, n.d.), preface.

9. Madeleine L'Engle, "The Mysterious Appearance of Canon Tallis," in *Spirit and Light: Essays in Historical Theology*, ed. L'Engle and William B. Green (New York: Seabury, 1976), p. 26.

10. Northrop Frye, *The Stubborn Structure: Essays on Criticism and Society* (Ithaca: Cornell University Press, 1970), p. 15.

11. C. S. Lewis, *An Experiment in Criticism* (Cambridge: Cambridge University Press, 1961), pp. 137-139.

12. Ibid., pp. 83-84.

13. Wolfgang Mozart, "A Letter," in *The Creative Process*, ed. Brewster Ghiselin (New York: Mentor, 1952), p. 45.

14. Percy B. Shelley, "A Defence of Poetry," in *Criticism: the Major Statements*, ed. Charles Kaplan (New York: St. Martin's, 1964), p. 376.

15. Harold Best, "Christian Responsibility in Music," in *The Christian Imagination: Essays on Literature and the Arts*, ed. Leland Ryken (Grand Rapids: Baker, 1981), p. 405.

16. I borrow the phrase "mankind's better moments" from Barbara W. Tuchman's essay by that title in *The American Scholar*, Autumn 1980, pp. 449-463. Tuchman calls art "man's most enduring achievement. . . . At its best, it reveals the nobility that coexists in human nature, along with flaws and evils, and the beauty and truth it can perceive. Whether in music or architecture, literature, painting or sculpture, art opens our eyes, ears, and feelings to something beyond ourselves, something we cannot experience without the artist's vision and the genius of his craft."

Chapter 2

What the Bible Says about the Arts

Literature in the Bible

> Christianity is the most literary religion in the world: it is crammed with characters and stories; much of its doctrine was enshrined in poetry. . . . It is a religion in which the word has a special sanctity.
>
> J. B. Broadbent, *Paradise Lost: Introduction*

The chief biblical commentary on literature is to be found in the literary nature of the Bible itself. The Bible is overwhelmingly (though not exclusively) a work of literature. The one thing that the Bible is not is what Christians so often picture it as being—a theological outline with proof texts attached.

The characteristic way of expressing religious truth in the Bible is through story, poem, vision, and letter. By comparison, expository essays, theological discourses and sermons are a relative rarity.

The Literary Bent of Biblical Authors

One way to sense the high proportion of literary material in the Bible, as well as the literary sophistication of its writers, is to list the literary genres found there. The biggest category is narrative or story. Under that heading we find examples of hero stories, epic, tragedy, parable, and gospel. The list of poetic types is even longer: lyric, proverb, epithalamion (wedding poem), pastoral, encomium (a poem that praises a character type or an abstract quality), hymn, prophetic oracle, and elegy (funeral poem). Some additional forms include oratory, visionary literature (including apocalyptic), satire, and the street theater of some of the prophets.

The example of Jesus is particularly important in establishing the biblical endorsement of literature. Jesus is one of the greatest storytellers and poets the world has ever known.[1] His typical discourse was concrete, anecdotal, fictional (parabolic), metaphoric, poetic. Oliver Cromwell said about the experiential concreteness of Jesus' discourses that Jesus "spoke things." When asked to define neighbor, Jesus told a story (the parable of the good Samaritan). He constantly spoke with metaphors and symbols: "I am the light of the world"; "you are the salt of the earth"; "my sheep hear my voice."

Imagination As a Vehicle for Truth in the Bible

It is apparent that Jesus and the writers of the Bible trusted literary forms to express religious truth. In particular, they operated on the literary premise that the imagination ("image-making") serves as a powerful vehicle for expressing truth.[2] They were not afraid of the indirection of metaphor or symbol, even though these literary forms require the interpretation of a reader to complete their meaning. In comparing God to a shepherd, for example, the Psalmist trusted his readers to draw the right conclusions about what God is like.

The Bible repeatedly appeals to the intelligence through the imagination. When Jesus was asked why he relied on parables to express religious truth, he outlined a theory of communication in which the message is not immediately apparent (Matthew 13:10-17). Most people in our culture equate reason with the abstract intellect, with concepts and propositions, but when God reasons with his people, he speaks in image, metaphor, and paradox (Isaiah 1:18):

> "Come now, let us reason together,
> says the LORD:
> though your sins are like scarlet,
> they shall be as white as snow;
> though they are red like crimson,
> they shall become like wool."

Even the most overtly theological parts of the Bible do not use only theological abstraction. They rely equally on metaphor and symbol. Consider this specimen passage from the most theological book in the whole Bible:

> But now that you have been set free from sin and have become slaves of God, the return you get is sanctification and its end, eternal life. For the wages of sin is death, but the free gift of God is eternal life in Christ Jesus our Lord. . . . Likewise, my brethren, you have died to the law through the body of Christ, . . . who has been raised from the dead in order that we may bear fruit for God (Romans 6:22-23; 7:4).

This passage is thoroughly theological, but it is not predominantly abstract and conceptual. It relies on the metaphors of the imagination in which one area of experience is used to illuminate another area. Salvation is like the freedom granted to a slave (yet paradoxically it is itself a form of slavery to God). It is death (to the condemnation of the law), yet paradoxically like a tree that is very much alive and bearing fruit. The effects of sin are like wages that a worker earns, while salvation is a gift that God gives.

The point is not simply that the Bible allows literary forms of communication. It is rather that the biblical writers and Jesus found it impossible to communicate the truth of God without using literary discourse. The Bible does more than sanction literature. It shows how indispensable literature is. In the words of C. S. Lewis, "There is a . . . sense in which the Bible, since it is after all literature, cannot properly be read except as literature; and the different parts of it as the different sorts of literature they are."[3]

"Secular" Literature in the Bible

Although the Bible is a predominantly religious book, it includes plenty of literature that is not specifically religious. The Song of Solomon is a collection of love lyrics that keeps the focus on human love and does not explicitly bring God or spiritual values into the picture. The Bible records a patriotic elegy by David about national heroes that does not mention God (2 Samuel 1:17-27). Many of the stories in the historical narratives of the Bible have no obvious religious purpose (for example, the burial of Sarah in Genesis 23, Isaac's run-in with Abimelech over a well in Genesis 26, and the attempts of Jacob and Laban to out-trick each other in Genesis 29-30).

While many of the proverbs of the Bible are deeply spiritual and moral in nature, others simply represent the wisdom of the human race on prudential matters of everyday living: "Like cold water to a thirsty soul, so is good news from a far country" (Proverbs 25:25); "He who meddles in a quarrel not his own is like one who takes a passing dog by the ears" (Proverbs 26:17). The lesson to be learned from the "secular" literature in the Bible has been well stated by Francis Schaeffer:

> Christian art is by no means always religious art, that is, art which deals with religious themes. . . . Man as man—with his emotions, his feelings, his body, his life—this is important subject matter for poetry and novels. . . . What a Christian portrays in his art is the totality of life.[4]

This is reinforced by the readiness with which some biblical writers used the existing literary forms from their surrounding (pagan) culture. It is now a commonplace of evangelical biblical scholarship that the book of Deuteronomy in general and the Ten Commandments in particular are cast in the same form as the suzerainty treaties that ancient Near Eastern kings imposed on their subjects.[5] The wisdom literature of the Bible was not produced in a vacuum. Such proverbs were an international phenomenon (see references in 1 Kings 4:30 and Acts 7:22), and there are plenty of parallels between proverbs in the Bible and those of other ancient cultures.[6] Some of the love lyrics in the Song of Solomon have parallels in Egyptian love poetry.[7] The New Testament epistles, despite their unique features, have many affinities to the letters of other ancient cultures.[8]

What do we make of this pattern of biblical writers using the literary forms of their culture? Simply that Christian writers are free to model their own writing on human literature wherever they find it. There is no "sacred" form of literature. Literature belongs to the human race.

Realism and Fantasy in the Bible

As a literary model, the Bible shows a liberating scope in yet another way: it affirms the twin literary impulses toward realism and fantasy. Literary realism aims to give us a "slice of life." Its impulse is to copy or "imitate" characters and events and settings as we find them in real life. Biblical storytellers tell about real, historical people. They tend to be utterly realistic:

> And Ehud reached with his left hand, took the sword from his right thigh, and thrust it into his [Eglon's] belly; and the hilt also went in after the blade, and the fat closed over the blade, for he did not draw the sword out of his belly; and the dirt came out (Judges 3:21-22).

But the writers of the Bible are equally at ease with fantasy—literature that takes us to an alternate world that is remote from lifelike reality. In a single short chapter of Zechariah, for example, we read about a flying scroll that destroys the wood and stones of houses, a woman named Wickedness sitting inside a cereal container, and two women with wings like those of a stork who lift the container "between earth and heaven" (Zechariah 5).

In predicting Assyria's invasion of Judah, Isaiah resorted to fantasy and pictured, not armies, but a dread river that would overflow the nation (Isaiah 8:5-8). In Daniel's preview of subsequent history, he pictured a ram's horn that grew to the sky and knocked stars to the ground (Daniel 8:9-10). As Francis Schaeffer notes, "Christian artists do not need to be threatened by fantasy and imagination. . . . The Christian is the really free person . . . whose imagination should fly beyond the stars."[9]

Literary Artistry in the Bible

Thus far I have explored the way in which the Bible uses literary forms to express truth. But biblical example also shows the value that its writers placed on the artistic beauty of their writing. Passage after passage in the Bible shows a perfection of artistry that can scarcely be accidental.

Let me cite just two famous examples. Biblical narrative has been much praised in recent scholarship for its highly economical, carefully crafted artistry in which everything superfluous has been omitted and every remaining detail counts significantly. Secondly, biblical poetry is written in the verse form known as parallelism. Two or more lines are carefully constructed on a similar grammatical pattern and fit together with obvious symmetry.

People do not just happen to tell well-made stories, nor do they unconsciously speak in parallel lines. They do so by artistic design and inspiration. The result is artistic beauty and technical excellence that are delightful in themselves and that intensify the impact of an utterance.

Biblical References to Extrabiblical Literature

Although biblical example is the chief way in which the Bible contributes to our understanding of literature, that example is supplemented by some key references to extrabiblical literature. The most crucial of these references are made by Paul in the New Testament.

Several times Paul quotes from pagan poets, just as he quotes from the Old Testament to prove a theological point. In his speech in Athens to the Areopagus, for example, Paul quotes from the Greek Stoic poets Cleanthes, Aratus, and Epimenides, drawing attention to his quotations by saying, "As even some of your poets have said" (Acts 17:28). In the same speech, Paul's comment that God intends people to "feel after him and find him" may allude to Homer, where the verb "feel after" is used to describe the groping of the blinded cyclops Polyphemus as he sought the entrance of his cave, and to Plato, who uses the word in the *Phaedo* to describe man's guesses at the truth.[10]

Paul makes other allusions to classical literature. First Corinthians 15:33 ("Bad company ruins good morals") is a quotation from the play *Thais* by the Greek dramatist Menander. Titus 1:12 is a quotation from Epimenides, a native of Crete: "One of themselves, a prophet of their own, said, 'Cretans are always liars, evil beasts, lazy gluttons.'" Paul follows the quotation with the statement, "This testimony is true" (Titus 1:13).

Since Paul did not have a *Bartlett's Familiar Quotations* to aid him, we would have to conclude that he had a firsthand acquaintance with Greek literature, including its fiction, and knew parts of it by heart. The principle that emerges is that the Bible affirms, in a variety of ways, the value of reading literature, since it tells us things that are true and worth knowing.

Music in the Bible

> It is in the nature of things that people should want to "sing to the Lord.". . . The injunction "Sing to the Lord," so characteristic of the Psalmists and other singers . . . is less a demand for specific action than a signal that what has been waiting for expression may now be given it.
>
> Eric Routley, *Church Music and Theology*

References to music in the Bible are more numerous than references to art and literature. They are impressive for their range and for their tendency to embrace both poles of what we so often regard (perhaps wrongly) as opposites. We read about music that is formal and about music that is spontaneous or ecstatic. Music in biblical cultures was both amateur and professional. It appears in the contexts of both daily life and worship. And it is both instrumental and vocal.

Music in Everyday Life

Since the biblical references to music in worship are so well known, I wish to begin my survey with the less familiar part of the picture. It is important for us to realize the variety of "secular," everyday contexts in which the Old Testament Israelites practiced music. The first recorded instance is the spontaneous musical celebration that erupted after the Red Sea deliverance (Exodus 15). We read here about the song that "Moses and the people of Israel sang . . . to the Lord" (vs. 1). The text of the song is followed by this further bit of narrative:

> Then Miriam . . . took a timbrel in her hand; and all the women went out after her with timbrels and dancing. And Miriam sang to them . . . (vv. 20-21).

Is this a worship experience? Not in any formal sense, but when all of life is perceived as being under the guidance of God, the old sacred-secular dichotomy becomes virtually meaningless. Other categories also break down as we ponder the passage: the music involves both instrumental and vocal music, both men and women, both music and dance.

Music permeated all of life in the believing community of the Old Testament. We read, for example, about working songs. Numbers 21:16-18 contains the song of the well, sung while people dug a well. Isaiah 16:10 gives a glimpse of songs sung in the vineyards during harvest time. Elsewhere we read about watchmen's songs (Isaiah 52:8-9).

Music also appears regularly in military situations among the Israelites. In Numbers 10:9 we read of God's promise to help Israel in battle when the silver trumpets were played. Trumpets summoned God's help at Jericho (Joshua 6:20) and played a part in Gideon's conquest of the Midianites (Judges 7:20-21). In Numbers 21:27-30 we read about (professional?) ballad singers who celebrated a military victory.

The power of music to influence human behavior has been a common theme throughout the history of music. The Bible perpetuates the theme. Elisha, for example, asked for a minstrel to play as a preparation to prophesying (2 Kings 3:15). Music for therapy appears in the famous story of David playing his lyre to exorcise the evil spirits that troubled Saul (1 Samuel 16:14-23).

Music in Worship

The most frequent context for music in the Bible is religious worship. The supreme example is the book of Psalms, which was originally a Temple hymnbook. But there are many other examples of music in worship, where it was often associated with the presence of God. When Solomon's Temple was dedicated, a huge ensemble of singers and instrumentalists participated in the ceremony. As they raised the sound of music, the cloud of God's presence filled the building (2 Chronicles 5:11-14). On the occasion that King Saul became numbered among the prophets, the sound of "harp, tambourine, flute and lyre" accompanied his prophesying (1 Samuel 10:5-6).

Temple Music

The most formal and highly organized music about which we read in the Bible is the music of the Temple. It was performed by professionals. Initiated by David, the music program included "singers who should play loudly on musical instruments, on harps and lyres and cymbals, to raise sounds of joy" (1 Chronicles 15:16). Control of the music was based on talent (1 Chronicles 15:22). Under David's plan, the number of professional musicians at the Temple was 288 (1 Chronicles 25:7).

Is instrumental music without accompanying words a legitimate form of worship? This question is sometimes troublesome in our day, but we should note the large role played by instrumental music in Temple worship. Psalm 150 contains the most complete list of such instruments:

Praise the LORD! . . .
Praise him with trumpet sound;
praise him with lute and harp!
Praise him with timbrel and dance;
praise him with strings and pipe!
Praise him with sounding cymbals;
praise him with loud clashing cymbals!

The most prevalent interpretation of the notation "Selah" in some of the psalms is that it indicates places where instrumental music took over while the singing ceased temporarily.

Can musical sound by itself be a form of worship? The Psalms provide plenty of evidence that it can. The lesson to be learned from the worship practices at the Temple is that it is possible to be overly word-conscious about the music of worship.

Two further aspects of music in Temple worship may help to explain why instrumental music was as appropriate as music with words. The function of Temple music was partly to express the emotional side of religious experience. Moods can be expressed by musical sound without accompanying words. The prime emotion associated with music in the Psalms is joyful praise, though we can infer from the content of the Psalms that the feelings of serenity, peace, depression, and anguish could also receive musical expression. Still, "more than one hundred references command the use of music for praising God."[11]

The other context that helps us to understand how musical sound can be worshipful is the Bible's continual and repeated assumption that God is the chief listener of the believer's music. The Song of Moses was sung by Moses and the people "to the Lord" (Exodus 15:1). The command to "sing to the Lord" is repeated throughout the Bible (e.g., Exodus 15:21; 1 Chronicles 16:9; Psalm 96:1; Isaiah 42:10; Jeremiah 20:13). Someone who made a tabulation of references to music in the Psalms found that 91 out of 107 references specify God as the audience of music.[12] The principle that emerges from this is significant for the arts: Anything offered to God can become an act of worship.

Music in the New Testament

References to music are also common in the New Testament, where the focus is on the hymns of the early church. First Corinthians 14:26 asserts regarding worship, "When you come together, each one has a hymn. . . ." Ephesians 5:19 delineates three distinct genres of church songs: "addressing one another in psalms and hymns and spiritual songs, singing and making melody to the Lord with all your heart." Colossians 3:16 names the same three types in a command to "sing psalms and hymns and spiritual songs." Music in the New Testament, we should note, is no longer priestly and professional. It is solidly social, congregational, and "amateur."

These references to hymns are fleshed out with some rich specimens of actual hymn texts. From the accounts of the nativity come the Magnificat (Luke 1:46-55), the song of Zechariah (Luke 1:67-79), and the song of the angels (Luke 2:14). Modern scholarship generally believes that scattered passages of poetry in the epistles are hymn texts. The list includes 1 Timothy 3:16; Ephesians 5:14; Philippians 2:6-11; and Colossians 1:15-20. To these must be added the magnificent hymns of worship in the book of Revelation: 4:8, 11; 5:9-10; 11:17-18; 15:3-4; 19:1-8.

The Abuse of Music

The biblical references to music are overwhelmingly positive, but there is a negative note as well. The Bible makes it clear that music can never be an adequate substitute for piety and morality. The prophet Amos sounds the keynote (Amos 5:23- 24):

> "Take away from me the noise of your songs;
> to the melody of your harps I will not listen.
> But let justice roll down like waters,
> and righteousness like an everflowing stream."

Elsewhere, Amos seizes upon music "as a symbol of secular triviality":[13]

"Woe to those who lie upon beds of ivory, . . .
who sing idle songs to the sound of the harp"
(Amos 6:4-5).

A parallel passage in Isaiah 5:11-12 condemns an indulgent lifestyle in which wine and music have replaced the fear of the Lord. In the biblical view, music and the whole aesthetic life can clearly become degraded.

The Visual Arts in the Bible

> On Mount Sinai God simultaneously gave the Ten Commandments and commanded Moses to fashion a tabernacle in a way which would involve almost every form of representational art that men have ever known.
>
> Francis A. Schaeffer, *Art and the Bible*

Biblical references to the visual arts cluster in the passages describing the Old Testament tabernacle and Temple. To get a "feel" for what the Bible says about art, therefore, a person can do no better than to read the three key passages: Exodus 25-28 and 35-40, 1 Kings 5-7, and 2 Chronicles 3-4. The cumulative effect of these passages is quite overpowering.

Although the context of art in the Bible is solidly religious, the passages describing it are filled with surprises and challenges to modern stereotypes about what constitutes appropriate art in a place of worship. For a thorough treatment of the subject, I heartily commend a book to which my own discussion is indebted at every turn, Gene Edward Veith's *The Gift of Art: The Place of the Arts in Scripture*.

God's Gifts to the Artist

The description of the tabernacle in Exodus is preceded by two remarkable passages dealing with the artists who performed the work (Exodus 31:1-11; 35:30-36:2). They are a treasure of biblical principles about the vocation of the artist and will repay our close attention. The text of the second passage is this:

> And Moses said to the people of Israel, "See, the Lord has called by name Bezalel the son of Uri, son of Hur, of the tribe of Judah; and he has filled him with the Spirit of God, with ability, with intelligence, with knowledge, and with all craftsmanship, to devise artistic designs, to work in gold and silver and bronze, in cutting stones for setting, and in carving wood, for work in every skilled craft. And he has inspired him to teach, both him and Oholiab the son of Ahisamach of the tribe of Dan. He has filled them with ability to do every sort of work done by a craftsman or by a designer or by an embroiderer in blue and purple and scarlet stuff and fine twined linen, or by a weaver—by any sort of workman or skilled designer. Bezalel and Oholiab and every able man in whom the Lord has put ability and intelligence to know how to do any work in the construction of the sanctuary shall work in accordance with all that the Lord has commanded."

Although this passage tells what happened on a specific occasion, there are good reasons to believe that it describes universal principles.[14] What, then, do we learn about the artist from this marvelous passage?

The first principle is that artistic ability is a gift from God. Just look at the terminology used in the passage: God filled the artists with his Spirit, inspired Bezalel to teach artistic methods, put artistic ability into the artists, and stirred up the artisans to do the work. This is the opposite of the humanistic theory of art as a strictly human talent and the romantic view of artists as a race of geniuses far superior to ordinary people. The Bible puts the artist (like everyone else) into a circle of grace. God is the source of artistic ability. Art is his gift.

The second thing we learn is that art can be a vocation. God called Bezalel to his role as artistic director of the project. That calling was special, addressed specifically to Bezalel: "the

Lord has called by name Bezalel the son of Uri, the son of Hur, of the tribe of Judah." Having called Bezalel and the other artists, God then filled them with the ability to perform that calling. The work of the artists also met the criterion of service to God and others that we associate with the idea of calling or vocation. Unlike what often happens in Christian circles today, the artist's vocation was not regarded as suspect or second best. It was exalted, a sacred trust from God.

The third principle that emerges is that God endows artists with the specific talents that art requires. The list of the artist's gifts in Exodus 35:31 is carefully chosen: "he has filled him with the Spirit of God, with ability, with intelligence, with knowledge, and with all craftsmanship." In the case of Bezalel, the gift of the Spirit was a personal experience with God that went beyond the common grace that God bestows on unbelievers and believers alike. The fact that God gave Bezalel ability confirms what we all know from grade school days on—that some people have talent for art that most people simply lack.

That God gave Bezalel intelligence disproves a popular stereotype of the artist as an irrational, completely intuitive person lacking analytic and practical skill. The knowledge that God gave Bezalel perhaps refers to the knowledge of life and the world that form the content of art, and a grasp of the properties of the physical materials with which the artist works. Finally, God endows the artist with the gift of craftsmanship—the mastery of material and artistic technique.

So much for the scriptural teaching about the artist. When we proceed to the descriptions of the actual art of the tabernacle and Temple, it so happens that we can find examples of the three big kinds of artistic style—abstract (nonrepresentational), representational, and symbolic.

Symbolic Art

The type of art we most readily expect to be sanctioned in the Bible is symbolic art. In this context, symbolic art can be defined as the use of physical images to stand for a corresponding spiritual reality. Such symbolic art is a familiar part of everyone's religious experiences, and it appears in verbal form all through the Bible. We think at once of the cross, water, bread, wine, shepherd, and light.

Symbolic art was prominent in the tabernacle and Temple. A golden altar symbolized atonement. A golden table with sacred bread on it pictured God's provision for human life. Various types of vessels with water in them made a worshiper aware of spiritual cleansing. Lampstands of pure gold were a picture of the illumination that God's revelation affords.

We can profitably link the Christian sacraments of baptism and communion with the symbolic art of the tabernacle and Temple. We do not ordinarily think of the sacraments as art, but they are based on the same principle on which symbolic art is based. The sacraments use the physical elements of water, bread, and wine to express spiritual realities.

What do the sacraments and the symbolic art of the Old Testament places of worship tell us? They confirm that visual images can symbolically picture spiritual reality to the glory of God and the edification of people.

Representational Art

Representational art portrays the objects of the physical world in a recognizable form. In the terms of the classical theory of art, representative art imitates the forms of life as they pass before our gaze.

There was an abundance of representative art in the decorations of the tabernacle and Temple. Consider, for example, the golden lampstand of the tabernacle:

> The base and the shaft of the lampstand shall be made of hammered work . . . ; and there shall be six branches going out of its sides . . . ; three cups made like almonds, each with capital and flower, on [each] branch . . . (Exodus 25:31-33).

Given the stereotyped notions of "sacred art" that often prevail in Christian circles, the decoration on the lampstand might seem frivolous and out of place. As the Old Testament worshipers stared at the lampstand with its symbolic as well as literal illumination they saw, not angels and cherubim, but things of natural beauty—flowers and blossoms.

The Temple flaunted representational art even more than this. The pillars were decorated with pomegranates and lilies (1 Kings 7:15-22). The stands for the brass lavers were adorned with lions, oxen, and palm trees (1 Kings 7:29, 36). The doors to the inner sanctuary were covered with carvings of "palm trees and open flowers" (1 Kings 6:32).

What are we to make of this exuberance over the forms of nature in the most holy places of Old Testament worship? Above all it completely undercuts any sacred-secular dichotomy for art. Whatever God created is a suitable subject for the artist. If God made the flowers and ocean and sky, they are worth painting or carving.

Abstract Art

Our surprise at the representational art of the tabernacle and Temple expands into mild shock, perhaps, when we see how much abstract or nonrepresentational art was present. Abstract art is art that represents nothing beyond itself. It is simply a pattern or design that is complete in itself.

Abstract art has received bad press among contemporary Christians because modern abstract art has usually expressed the confusion, despair, and meaninglessness of an unbelieving culture. But this is not the only type of abstract art. Think of a Persian tapestry or a wrought-iron fence. They, too, are abstract art, and they express a belief in order and design.

As the Old Testament worshipers approached the Temple, they saw two gigantic freestanding bronze pillars over twenty-five feet high (1 Kings 7:15-22). These monoliths had no architectural weightbearing function. They did not resemble anything in created nature. They were simply beautiful and suggested by their very size and form the grandeur, stability, and power of God. They also made the worshipers feel small as they stood beside them, and this, too, made a religious statement in a purely artistic, nonverbal way.

We need to remind ourselves that God himself is the great abstract artist. When God created the rose and the hippopotamus and lizard and elm tree, he was not imitating anything. He simply imagined them. Nature continues to be one of our richest sources of nonrepresentational art. If you doubt this, simply photograph a sunset or leafless tree, cut off the horizon or tree trunk, and frame the result. You will have created a piece of abstract art!

If pattern and design have value in themselves, so do colors. Worship at the tabernacle and Temple occurred amid a riot of color. The splendor of gold and bronze glittered everywhere. The veils of both the tabernacle and Temple were made of blue, purple, and scarlet cloth (Exodus 26:1; 2 Chronicles 3:14). The robe of Aaron was "all of blue," ornamented with blue, purple, and scarlet pomegranates and bells of gold (Exodus 28:31-35).

The Role of Imagination

Some of the art in the Old Testament was realistic, but there was no requirement that it had to be so. At the tabernacle there were carved flowers, but there were also blue pomegranates on the robe of Aaron. What's so unusual about that? In nature there are no blue pomegranates.

The artifact at the Temple that most intrigues me is the molten sea (1 Kings 7:23-26). It was a huge circular basin forty-five feet in circumference and holding up to 10,000 gallons of water. Under the brim were engravings of gourds. The whole grand design rested on the backs of twelve statuesque oxen. Now where in the real world can we find a sea held up on the backs of oxen? It is an utterly fantastic conception, all the more delightful for its imaginary qualities. Who could have thought that up? we ask.

The Perversion of Art

In the Bible, as in life, art can be perverted from its God-given purposes. It was as an artist that Aaron fashioned a golden calf "with a graving tool" (Exodus 32:4). Art can become an idol that leads people away from God, regardless of how good it might be as art. Romans 1:21-23 describes how pagans "exchanged the glory of the immortal God for images resembling mortal man or birds or animals or reptiles." We can see this art in any gallery containing art of pagan or classical origin. Some of it is beautiful art, but in its original setting it was used for idolatrous purposes. This should lead us to reject an argument that is surprisingly prevalent among enthusiasts for the arts—that any excellent piece of art honors God and is "Christian art."

Out of the numerous ways in which art can be perverted, the Bible denounces two abuses. One is idolatry. Throughout the Bible we read about the ease with which ancient cultures worshiped objects of visual art. The prohibition in the Second Commandment against making a graven image and then worshiping it is not a comment against art per se. It is a condemnation of idolatry, with art simply serving as the agency by which the idol is formed.

The modern version of such idolatry is the tendency of some to worship art and set it up as a substitute for the Christian faith. This is admittedly not an overwhelming temptation for the masses in our culture, who are far more likely to worship other things. But during the last two centuries, religious veneration of art has been one of the commonest practices of non-Christians who have cared greatly about the arts.

The incident of Aaron's golden calf (Exodus 32:1-29) combines idolatry with another perversion of the artist's gift. Where did Aaron the artist go wrong? Did he have a latent propensity to worship physical idols? Not at all. His problem was the ever- present temptation that all artists face (including musicians and writers): Aaron catered to the demands of an ignoble audience.

Aaron admitted this when his brother Moses cornered him. "What did this people do to you. . . ?" asked Moses (Exodus 32:21). Aaron's reply confirms that the pressure to please his audience was his problem: "They said to me, 'Make us gods. . .'" (Exodus 32:23). The pressure to gain an audience by pandering to its godless tastes has been a curse to artists of every kind, from the idolatry at Sinai to "the compulsory sex scene" of contemporary art forms.

The Arts in Biblical Perspective

> Our excuse for our esthetic failure has often been that we must be about the Lord's business, the assumption being that the Lord's business is never esthetic.
>
> Clyde S. Kilby, "Christian Imagination"

Having looked at the arts individually, it is essential that we synthesize what the Bible says about the arts in general. This is appropriate because the arts are so closely related. Are hymns the domain of literature or music? Do the symbolic images that we read about in the Bible belong to literature or visual art? In the worship of the Temple, art, music, and literature were all fused into a unified whole. What the Bible says about a specific art form is almost always true in principle of the parallel arts as well. To bring this chapter into focus, therefore, let us summarize what the Bible says about the arts.

The overriding principle is that God himself regards the arts as essential. God gave Moses the instructions for the art of the tabernacle. He endowed the artists with their ability. He revealed his presence with music on various Old Testament occasions. The book that reveals God to people is in large part a literary work, replete with artistic beauty.

Secondly, we learn that the arts are essential to human civilization. The most explicit statement of that theme occurs in the genealogy of the line of Cain in Genesis 4:20-22. In this outline of the early progress of human civilization, we read about the invention of farming, music (and by extension the arts in general), and technology. This scheme stands as a corrective to a common bias among historians, who tend to trace the development of the human race in terms of tools and weapons. The genealogy in Genesis provides support for one scholar's claim that the "overweighting of tools, weapons, physical apparatus, and machines has obscured the actual path of human development. . . . Esthetic invention played fully as large a part as practical needs in man's effort to build a meaningful world."[15]

The arts are essential to personal wellbeing as well as to the progress of civilization. People were created by God as aesthetic creatures possessed of a capacity for beauty, craving the expression of their experiences and insights. What Eric Routley says about music in the Bible has its counterpart in art and literature as well:

> It is in the nature of things that people should want to 'sing to the Lord.'. . . The biblical command to 'sing to the Lord' is less a demand for specific action than a signal that what has been waiting for expression may now be given it.[16]

Everyone in our culture indulges his or her artistic sense, even if it consists simply of painting the walls of a room or listening to popular music or singing hymns. The question is not whether we need the arts but rather what the quality of our artistic experiences will be.

Another principle that emerges from the biblical data is that artistic form has value in itself. A piece of music does not require words before it becomes worthwhile. A statue or visual design need not be a picture of anything in the real world in order to have value. The artistry of a poem or story does not exist solely as a vehicle or decoration for the ideas. These things have value in themselves. The embellished garments of Aaron and his sons were "for glory and for beauty" (Exodus 28:2, 40).

Obviously, the Bible respects the ability of the arts to express the truth with power. The literature of the Bible is the great proof of that statement. But the prominence of visual art and music in worship and everyday life in biblical cultures confirms the same principle. The arts not only make life more beautiful and pleasurable—they are also capable of telling us the truth in their own unique ways.

We can also infer that to be an artist can be a calling or vocation from God. God "called by name Bezalel" to be the chief artist for the tabernacle (Exodus 35:30). Moses "called . . . every able man in whose mind the LORD had put ability" to help Bezalel (Exodus 36:2). For the making of priestly garments, God told Moses to enlist "all who have ability, whom I have endowed with an able mind" (Exodus 28:3). Music was the full-time vocation of the musicians who presided at the Temple. The writers of the Bible repeatedly convey to us the impression of having been called and inspired by God to their task.

In the Bible, furthermore, the arts have a central place in the worship of God. Music, visual art, and poetry converged in Temple worship to form a unified artistic and spiritual experience. Such a picture leads to some perplexing questions about evangelical worship in our time. Why do the visual arts get so little attention in public and personal worship? Why don't we have more devotional poetry in church bulletins and church services and midweek services? Why is great music, especially instrumental music, considered out of place in church?

Although worship is a frequent context for the arts in the Bible, it is equally obvious that in the Bible the arts take all of life as their province. A work of art does not have to be about a "religious" subject in order to be legitimate. Poetry can be about romantic love and nature as well as about God. Songs can be about harvest or can be purely instrumental. Artists can carve flowers or cherubim or oxen with equal sanction from God.

Corresponding to this breadth of subject matter is the biblical teaching that there is no prescribed style for the artist. Visual art can be representative, symbolic, or abstract. Music can be spontaneous folk music as well as formal and liturgical. Literature can range all the way from simple, unembellished stories to the highly sensuous and figurative poetry of the Song of Solomon.

Finally, the Bible suggests some of the ways in which art can be corrupted. Art can become an idol. It can become an expression of the triviality of life in a secular society (witness the cynical comments about music by Amos). And it can debase artists who pander to the depraved demands of their audience.

SUMMARY

The Bible endorses the arts in principle. The Bible is itself literary in nature. From the pages of the Bible we learn that music, literature, and visual art are meant to be a central ingredient in the worship of God. But they also permeate all of life. Corresponding to this breadth is the fact that in the Bible there is no prescribed style or content for art. God-glorifying art can be realistic or fantastic, representational or symbolic or abstract.

The arts are the gift of God. Like other gifts, they can be abused and perverted from their God-given purpose. The arts can become an idol and a channel for leading people away from God. The Bible's attitude toward the arts, therefore, steers a middle course between overvaluing and undervaluing artistic creativity.

FURTHER READING

Egon Wellesz, ed., *The New Oxford History of Music* (1957), 1:283- 312.

Francis A. Schaeffer, *Art and the Bible* (1973).

Dale Topp, *Music in the Christian Community* (1976).

Donald P. Hustad, *Jubilate! Church Music in the Evangelical Tradition* (1981).

Gene Edward Veith, Jr., *The Gift of Art: The Place of the Arts in Scripture* (1983).

Leland Ryken, *The Literature of the Bible* (1974), and *How to Read the Bible as Literature* (1984).

Chapter 2, Notes

1. For some good comments, see the excerpts under the headings "Jesus as Poet" and "Parable" in *The New Testament in Literary Criticism*, ed. Leland Ryken (New York: Frederick Ungar, 1984).

2. For a good brief treatment of the importance of images in Scripture, see Luci Shaw, "Imagination: That Other Avenue to Truth," *Christianity Today*, January 1981, pp. 32-33.

3. C. S. Lewis, *Reflections on the Psalms* (New York: Harcourt, Brace and World, 1958), p. 3.

4. Francis A. Schaeffer, "Some Perspectives on Art," in *The Christian Imagination: Essays on Literature and the Arts,* ed. Leland Ryken (Grand Rapids: Baker, 1981), pp. 95-96.

5. For details, see Meredith G. Kline, *Treaty of the Great King: The Covenant Structure of Deuteronomy* (Grand Rapids: William B. Eerdmans, 1963).

6. See the sources and examples cited in Carole R. Fontaine, *Traditional Sayings in the Old Testament: A Contextual Study* (Sheffield: Almond Press, 1982); and William McKane, *Proverbs: A New Approach* (Philadelphia: Westminster, 1970).

7. See John Bradley White, *A Study of the Language of Love in the Song of Songs and Ancient Egyptian Poetry* (Missoula: Scholars Press, 1978); and Hugh J. Schonfield, *The Song of Songs* (New York: Mentor, 1959), pp. 40-44.

8. For a good overview of past and current scholarship on the New Testament Epistles as ancient letters, see William G. Doty, *Letters in Primitive Christianity* (Philadelphia: Fortress Press, 1973).

9. Schaeffer, p. 96.

10. My comments on the classical allusions in Paul's speech are indebted to E. M. Blaiklock, *The Acts of the Apostles: An Historical Commentary* (Grand Rapids: William B. Eerdmans, 1959), pp. 144-145.

11. Dale Topp, *Music in the Christian Community* (Grand Rapids: William B. Eerdmans, 1976), p. 16.

12. Topp, p. 13.

13. Eric Routley, *Church Music and the Christian Faith* (Carol Stream, IL: Agape, 1978), p. 8.

14. Does the passage in Exodus that describes God's endowment of the artists who built the tabernacle describe universal principles or something that happened only once? There are several good reasons for concluding that this passage states what is true of artists generally. For one thing, the many-sided description of the artist's abilities that emerges from the passage accords with what we can prove from observation. In the Exodus account we find the theological explanation of artistic ability. Then, too, it is in keeping with the whole tenor of biblical teaching that God is the ultimate source of all human talent. James 1:17 states the principle in kernel form: "Every good endowment and every perfect gift is from above, coming down from the Father of lights. . . ." The passage from Exodus shows how this principle applies specifically to artistic ability. Finally, it is a rule of biblical interpretation that we can draw universal principles from the historical events that are recorded unless there is a compelling reason to regard them as unique. When Jacob wrestles with God, there are principles that apply to us. The fall of Adam and Eve happened only once, but the principles involved in the Fall happen repeatedly in our lives.

15. Lewis Mumford, *The Myth of the Machine: Technics and Human Development* (New York: Harcourt, Brace and World, 1966), pp. 5, 153.

16. Routley, p. 6.

Chapter 3

Creativity, Beauty, and Recreation

Creativity In Christian Perspective

> This word—this idea of Art as creation is, I believe, the one important contribution that Christianity has made to aesthetics.
>
> Dorothy L. Sayers, "Towards a Christian Aesthetic."

Creativity pervades many human pursuits, but nowhere is it more central than in the process of artistic composition. Art is synonymous with creativity. The creative element in art begins with the artist's choice of a subject and medium. It is then the presiding spirit at every stage of composition.

We cannot remind ourselves too often that the arts belong to the human imagination, and that the imagination is essentially creative. Imagination implies the ability to imagine—to make things up. The imagination is not limited to observable reality. In the words of one writer, art "has flowers that no forests know of, birds that no woodland possesses."[1] Works of art can never be fully explained by a previously existing model.

God as Creative Artist

Human creativity is rooted in divine creativity. Artists create because God created first. Genesis 1 is the starting point for thinking Christianly about artistic creativity.

The first thing the Bible does is introduce us to the God of the universe. He is introduced as a creative artist. Before we know anything else about him, we know that "In the beginning God created the heavens and the earth" (Gen. 1:1). This divine artist began, as all artists do, with something formless: "The earth was without form and void" (Gen. 1:2). God then proceeded to create the forms that comprise our universe. Like a painter working on a canvas, God assembled one detail after another until the picture was complete. He then pronounced his creation "very good" (Genesis 1:31).

The Image of God in People

But God's creation of the world was only the start of his creative activity. He delegated the ongoing work of creation to his human creatures. We read in Genesis 1:27 that "God created man in his own image."

Exactly what does this mean? When we first read about the image of God in people in Genesis 1, we have as yet heard nothing about God as redeemer or the God of providence or the covenant God or the God of moral truth. The one thing that we know about God is that he created the world. In its immediate narrative context, then, the doctrine of the image of God in people emphasizes that people are, like God, creators.

The classic study of what the image of God in people means to aesthetic theory is Dorothy L. Sayers's book *The Mind of the Maker*. Sayers writes:

> How then can [man] be said to resemble God? Is it his immortal soul, his rationality, his self-consciousness, his free will, or what, that gives him a claim to this rather startling distinction? A case may be argued for all these elements in the complex nature of man. But had the author of Genesis anything particular in his mind when he wrote? It is observable that in the passage leading up to the statement about man, he has given no detailed information

> about God. Looking at man, he sees in him something essentially divine, but when we turn back to see what he says about the original upon which the "image" of God was modeled, we find only the single assertion, "God created." The characteristic common to God and man is apparently that: the desire and the ability to make things.[2]

Why People Create

What does the image of God in people say about the artistic enterprise? It affirms human creativity as something good since it is an imitation of one of God's own acts and perfections. Abraham Kuyper wrote, "As image-bearer of God, man possesses the possibility both to create something beautiful, and to delight in it."[3] The creative impulse of the artist is an expression of human likeness to God. Laurence Perrine has said that "the primal artistic act was God's creation of the universe out of chaos, shaping the formless into form; and every artist since, on a lesser scale, has sought to imitate him."[4]

The biblical doctrine of the image of God in people is thus the theological reason why people write literature and paint pictures and compose music. They create because they have been endowed with God's image. This, in turn, deflects the ultimate praise for artistic achievement from people to God, as Christian artists have acknowledged and as pagan artists have perhaps hinted when they invoked the muses to inspire them.

Toward a Definition of Art

The link between divine and human creativity helps to define art. Throughout the history of Western art there have been two main theories of what art is. The classical theory that art is an imitation of reality dominated aesthetic theory from the time of Aristotle through the eighteenth century. The other theory is that art is a created artifact, to be explained not so much as a copy of real life but as a new imaginative world that the artist creates.

Christians have championed both views. C. S. Lewis came to the conclusion,

> If I have read the New Testament aright, it leaves no room for "creativeness" even in a modified or metaphorical sense. . . . An author should never conceive himself as bringing into existence beauty or wisdom that did not exist before, but simply and solely as trying to embody in terms of his own art some reflection of eternal Beauty and Wisdom.[5]

But such a theory of art fails to do justice to the Christian doctrine of creation and the image of God in people. It is to the Old Testament that we should turn for our aesthetic theory on this point. The Renaissance poet Sir Philip Sidney points the way. He writes that we should "give right honor to the heavenly Maker of that maker [i.e., the human artist], who, having made man to his own likeness, set him beyond and over all the works of that second nature [i.e., the world of the artistic imagination]."[6]

Human Creativity as a Value

Can a student justify the time involved in taking a course in fiction writing or poetry writing? Can a person in good conscience spend hours painting a picture? Is it worthwhile to take two hours to attend something as non-utilitarian as a concert or art gallery? The Christian doctrine of creation answers "Yes." Chad Walsh, a contemporary Christian poet, writes that the creative artist "can honestly see himself as a kind of earthly assistant to God (so can the carpenter), carrying on the delegated work of creation, making the fullness of creation fuller."[7]

What I have said about the creative artist applies equally to those who are not themselves artists but instead constitute the audience of art. They are the ones who enter into the creativity of others. To do so is to acknowledge the worth of human creativity and to honor the God who gave the gift of creativity to the human race. To delight in the work of the human imagination is to value the image of God in people, just as producing creative works is. The Christian doctrine of creation does not allow for a disparagement of artistic creativity.

Christians have traditionally defended their immersion in art on the basis of its didacticism (teaching ability) or realism. I believe that the Christian doctrine of creativity suggests an additional defense: Works of art have value because they are imaginative and creative. They are the product of human creativity and ultimately of God's image implanted in artists.

Good and Bad Creativity

We must not overstate the case for the merits of artistic creativity. Human creativity did not escape the effects of the Fall. Artistic creativity, too, is subject to moral and intellectual criticism. We have no basis for approving of a painting or song or novel simply because it is the product of human creativity. We must differentiate between good and bad manifestations of the creative impulse. What are our criteria for such discrimination?

One is the purpose or telos that underlies an artist's creative effort. Art that is designed to serve humanity and glorify God has a nobler purpose than art designed to make an artist famous or wealthy. Sincerity has always been a criterion for artistic integrity; by it we mean that an artist has been true to himself and his or her conception of truth, as compared (for example) with the attempt to flatter a patron or please an audience.

Another criterion for judging the worthiness of human creativity is its effect on an audience. We rightly admire art, music, and literature whose effect is to make people more sensitive, more moral, or more humanly refined people. By contrast, art whose effect is to encourage people to behave selfishly, immorally, or coarsely does not merit our approval at this level, no matter how creative it is.

A third standard by which we can judge artistic creativity is aesthetic excellence. Poorly executed paintings or musical compositions or stories might be the products of someone's creativity, but they do not for that reason merit our admiration. Technical excellence, on the other hand, is one of the very aims of artistic creativity. We might note, therefore, that the Christian content of a work of art that is technically mediocre does not redeem the work as a piece of creativity. In fact, the lack of artistic excellence detracts from the impact of the Christian content.

Artistic creativity is a great gift, but it is not inherently sacred or good. For nearly two centuries now, non-Christian enthusiasts for the arts have tended to make art a substitute for the Christian religion. Many of them have virtually deified free creativity. The Romantic artists of the early nineteenth century regarded the imagination as the religious faculty by which people have contact with the supernatural.

Creativity and imagination can never hold such an esteemed place in a Christian world view. There is wisdom and beauty but not salvation in a work of art.

ARTISTIC BEAUTY

> For as God is infinitely the greatest Being, so he is allowed to be infinitely the most beautiful and excellent: and all the beauty to be found throughout the whole creation, is but the reflection of the diffused beams of that Being who hath an infinite fulness of brightness and glory; God . . . is the foundation and fountain of all being and all beauty.
>
> Jonathan Edwards, *The Nature of True Virtue*

> As image-bearer of God, man possesses the possibility both to create something beautiful, and to delight in it.
>
> Abraham Kuyper, "Calvinism and Art"

A Christian philosophy of the arts rests not only on the fact that God created the world but also on an awareness of the particular type of world that he created. We know that God created a world that is beautiful and orderly. The implications for art are many and crucial.

The Beauty of God's Creation

We need only use our senses to know that God created a world that is beautiful as well as functional. From a purely utilitarian point of view, God did not have to make a world filled with beautiful colors and symmetrical forms and varied textures and harmonious sounds.

What we find here is not only a functional mind at work but also an artistic imagination. The kind of world God made is a model of what artists should strive to make and what all people should delight in. The Christian doctrine of creation, therefore, affirms as good the artistic concern of both the creative artist and the audience with form, beauty, and artistry.

The beauty of God's created universe, even in its fallen condition, is regarded by biblical writers as a picture of God's beauty and craftsmanship. A biblical poet declared, "The heavens are telling the glory of God; and the firmament proclaims his handiwork" (Psalm 19:1). That God, in his role as creator, is a craftsman with an awesome regard for beauty is equally clear from the descriptions of the new heaven and the new earth (Revelation 21), just as all the biblical descriptions of heaven portray it as a place of transcending beauty.

The God of Beauty

The Bible ascribes beauty to God as one of his perfections. God himself is the source of beauty. We must conclude this, it seems to me, even though the word translated "beauty" in English versions of the Bible encompasses a variety of Hebrew terms and includes the idea of spiritual as well as physical or artistic beauty.

David "asked of the Lord . . . to behold the beauty of the Lord" (Psalm 27:4), suggesting not only that beauty is an attribute of God but that beholding it is the desire of the believer. In the prophecy of Ezekiel we read that God gave to his people the gift of his beauty, which was perfect until people in their sinfulness desecrated it:

> And your renown went forth among the nations because of your beauty, for it was perfect through the splendor which I had bestowed upon you, says the Lord God. But you trusted in your own beauty. . . . You also took your fair jewels of my gold and of my

> silver, which I had given you, and made for yourself images of men (Ezekiel 16:14-15, 17).

From such a passage we can infer that beauty is the possession of God, that he bestows it as a gift to people, and as with all of God's gifts, people can either use beauty to God's glory or defile it by making it the object of religious devotion.

The Bible gives reason to believe that God not only creates but also takes pleasure in contemplating the beauty of His creation. We can infer from the repeated phrase in Genesis 1, "God saw that it was good," that God experienced a delight and satisfaction in contemplating the perfection and beauty of what he had made. Abraham Kuyper has commented, "After the Creation, God saw that all things are good. Imagine that every human eye were closed and every human ear stopped up, even then the beautiful remains, and God sees it and hears it."[8]

Beauty is also joined with the worship of God in the Old Testament, and these passages, too, link God with beauty. God is pictured as having a concern for more than functional practicality when we read that it was God Himself "who put such a thing as this into the heart of the king, to beautify the house of the LORD . . ." (Ezra 7:27). The Hebrew worshiper could declare regarding his God that "strength and beauty are in his sanctuary" (Psalm 96:6). In prophesying the restoration of Israel, God, speaking through Isaiah, is recorded as saying, "The glory of Lebanon shall come to you, the cypress, the plane, and the pine, to beautify the place of my sanctuary; and I will make the place of my feet glorious" (Isaiah 60:13).

Beauty Needs No Excuse

The lesson to be learned from the Bible's portrait of God is that God values beauty as well as utility. He did not create a purely functional world. From a utilitarian point of view, God did not have to create a world filled with colors and symmetrical forms. He could have made everything a drab gray color, or he could have created people color-blind. Surely God could have made trees whose leaves do not turn to beautiful colors in the fall of the year, or a world in which all flowers are brown in color or grass that is gray instead of green.

The biblical view of creation encourages us to believe that artistic beauty needs no justification for its existence, any more than a happy marriage does, or a bird, or a flower, or a mountain, or a sunset. These things have meaning because God made them. Artistic beauty has meaning in itself because God thought it good to give beauty to people quite apart from any consideration of practical usefulness. Abraham Kuyper expressed it well when he wrote,

> The beautiful . . . has an objective existence, being itself the expression of a Divine perfection. . . . We know this from the creation around us . . . for how could all this beauty exist, except created by One Who preconceived the beautiful in His own Being, and produced it from His own Divine perfection?[9]

Artistic form and beauty have value in themselves. Their function is to be beautiful. The embellishment of Aaron's priestly garment was "for glory and for beauty" (Exodus 28:2).

God made provision for the quality of human life, not simply its survival. The key biblical verse in this regard is Genesis 2:9, which tells us that when God created Paradise he "made to grow every tree that is pleasant to the sight and good for food." The perfect human environment, in other words, satisfies a dual criterion, both aesthetic and utilitarian. The conditions for human well-being have never changed from that moment in Paradise. One of the good effects of artistic beauty is that by being essentially nonutilitarian it draws a boundary around the compulsion to make money. It clears a ground in which people can recover and celebrate human values for their own sake. It thus serves as an invaluable antidote to the materialism and acquisitiveness that are always threatening to overwhelm the human race and are especially prominent in our own technological society.

In view of the biblical emphasis on beauty, it is most unfortunate that an influential theorist in the Christian tradition should write that "beauty is not a biblical notion or term" and that "the Scriptures speak . . . very little or not at all of beauty."[10] Even worse is the statement of a Christian scholar who speaks of "the curse of beauty."[11]

Such viewpoints do not accurately reflect the Bible's comments, direct and indirect, about artistic beauty, and they represent the kind of thinking that has hampered the formation of a truly Christian aesthetic. Even a cursory glance at a concordance reveals that the Bible uses the words beauty, beautiful, and beautify frequently and in an overwhelmingly positive sense.

Life Is More than Utilitarian

What does all this discussion of the biblical affirmation of beauty have to do with thinking Christianly about the arts? I have laid a biblical foundation carefully because I think it refutes some common attitudes toward the arts.

One is the utilitarian or functional outlook that belittles anything that is not directly useful in mastering the physical side of life. The utilitarian disparagement of the arts has been a persistent Christian ailment through the centuries. The same attitude has taken a secular turn in our own technological culture. When applied to the arts, this mindset either disparages the arts altogether or values them only for their ideas or usable content.

A Christian world view stands opposed to such a reduction of life to the directly utilitarian. God did not create a purely functional world. Instead he planted a garden in which the trees were "pleasant to the sight" as well as "good for food" (Genesis 2:9). The writer of Psalm 19 valued nature, not because it was useful to him, but because it gave him the opportunity to contemplate the beauty and handiwork of God.

The capacity for beauty is God-implanted. Many of the most worthwhile things in life are of no practical use. Why do people paint the walls of rooms and wear colored clothing? What can a person do, in any utilitarian sense, with a sunset or a snowy mountain peak, or with mists on a summer morning or a beautifully shaped tree?

By the same token, the value of a piece of literature or music, or a painting or sculpture, does not depend on its ideational content alone. The Christian poet Gerard Manley Hopkins theorized that the purely artistic dimension of poetry exists "for its own sake and interest even over and above its interest of meaning."[12]

The Modern Disparagement of Artistic Beauty

The biblical attitude toward beauty also stands opposed to a movement within contemporary art and aesthetics (the philosophy of art) that disparages beauty and form in the arts. At its most extreme, this impulse results in the cult of the ugly and grotesque. In its milder version, it produces art that deliberately attempts to destroy form in art.

By means of this assault on beauty and form, artists are "making a statement." But what kind of statement is it? That the universe is ugly and meaningless and chaotic. This is not the Christian view of the universe. In a Christian world view, the universe has meaning. That the world is fallen and frequently ugly is something that Christians know even better than others. But at the heart of Christianity is the redemptive principle that it is not enough to leave the fallen world where it is.

What Is Artistic Beauty?

The term beauty covers a whole range of qualities that people enjoy in works of art. One theorist lists them as the ability of art to satisfy the soul, a harmony between the artistic object and the perceiver, effective technique or perfection of form, a work's quality of being the best of its kind, and purposeful creativity.[13]

The word *beauty* need not imply any specific artistic ideal from past eras. I use the term without any specific artistic style in mind. Modern abstract art, discordant music, or modern poetry can all possess elements of symmetry, balance, contrast, repetition, centrality, unity, and progression. Any work of music, art, or literature that possesses these qualities may fit my definition of artistic beauty.

No single work of art needs to possess all of the qualities named above. Some are more appropriately applied to one of the arts than the others. The elements of artistic form are what the arts share. They differ in the medium by which they incarnate them. Music presents these elements of form through the medium of sound. Literature embodies them by means of words. Painting uses color, line, and texture to present them.

Artistic beauty or excellence consists of the skillful composition and manipulation of the elements of aesthetic form. Such proficiency in the control of artistic technique is an important part of the value that we attach to the arts. Sometimes the creation of beauty is virtually the whole point of a work of art. In other cases, it reinforces the impact of the content of a work while being delightful in its own right.

Although *beauty* is currently out of vogue as the word to use when talking about the aspect of the arts that I have been discussing, there are several good reasons to retain the word. It is the word that through the centuries artists and critics have most often used. As one authority writes, "The aesthetic has always had some connection to the beautiful."[14] It is, moreover, the word with which ordinary people still resonate. Whatever word we might choose for the purpose, we obviously need some term by which to denote the technical excellence that we admire in an artistic work.

The Importance of Beauty in the Arts

How important is technique in the artistic enterprise? There are four ways to answer that question.

The practices of artists reveal how painstakingly they polish and refine the technical beauty of their compositions. Ernest Hemingway rewrote the conclusion of his novel *A Farewell to Arms* seventeen times in an effort to get it right. The Welsh poet Dylan Thomas made over 200 handwritten manuscript versions of his poem "Fern Hill." Beethoven sketched and resketched his compositions. Leonardo da Vinci drew a thousand hands.

We should listen, secondly, to the statements of artists. The poet Dylan Thomas said that he liked "to treat words as a craftsman does his wood or stone . . . , to hew, carve, mold, coil, polish, and plane them into patterns, sequences, sculptures, fugues of sound."[15] According to the modern German painter Wassily Kandinsky, the artist is the "guardian of beauty, beauty . . . measured only by the yardstick of internal greatness and necessity."[16] Seventeenth-century painter Nicolas Poussin called beauty "the mark and, as it were, the goal of all good painters."[17]

Statements by critics and aesthetic theorists point in the same direction. One of them writes that the audience of art "is interested, like the artist, in technique, . . . in structure, the esthetic properties of the thing made, its architectonic features such as unity, balance, emphasis, rhythm, and . . . shapely pattern. . . . When the whole work finally springs to life in his mind, the critic experiences a delight, a joy in the thing of beauty, akin to that of the artist when his vision at length fell into shape."[18]

We can look, finally, at the inherent nature of artistic works. Works of art inevitably possess elements of artistic form. Artists cannot avoid putting them into their works if they tried, for these are the things out of which art, music, and literature are made. I have had some interesting discussions in this regard with experts on modern art, where artists claim not to be creating artistic beauty. As we look together at a typical modern abstract painting, I point out elements of symmetry, centrality, balance, contrast, and unified impact. In response, I am told something to the effect, "Well, yes, you can see these things there if you want to, but for the artist this is simply an irrelevance." I regard that as the artist's problem, not mine. There are norms for art that artists cannot disregard, and in practice they do not disregard them.

A major share of our experience of artistic works is our admiration of the artist's control of technique. In the cases of abstract art like a Persian tapestry or music without words, the creation of beauty or technically excellent form is virtually the whole point of the work. And even in representational art, where part of our attention is focused on the depiction of some aspect of human experience or external reality, the beauty of technical excellence remains an important part of the total effect.

in Just-
spring   when the world is mud-
luscious the little
lame balloonman

whistles   far   and wee

and eddieandbill come
running from marbles and
piracies and it's
spring

when the world is puddle-wonderful

the queer
old balloonman whistles
far   and   wee
and bettyandisbel come dancing

from hop-scotch and jump-rope and

it's
spring
and
    the

        goat-footed

balloonMan   whistles
far
and
wee

I remember how formless and chaotic this poem struck me when I first encountered it. I now view it as one of the most highly patterned poems in the language. There is pattern or design in the three-part structure of the poem. Three successive times the poet describes a happy springtime setting, replete with the play of children, followed by the introduction of the balloonman into the scene. The cycle falls into sections, each of which begins with the naming of the spring season—"in Just-spring," "it's spring," "it's spring"—as follows: (1) lines 1-8a; (2) lines 8b-15; (3) lines 16-24.

Aptness or suitability or fittingness is an important part of artistry. In this poem it consists of the selection of colloquial words and children's constructions to capture the language actually used by children: "Just-spring," "mud- luscious," "puddle-wonderful." The effect of a child's consciousness is reinforced by the run-together "and" clauses and names ("eddieandbill," "bettyandisbel"), suggesting exactly how children talk when they are excited. The genius of the poem, in short, is that it allows us to see the springtime world through the eyes and consciousness of a child.

The poem also makes significant use of progression. The key to the poem's meaning, in fact, is the progressive characterization of the balloonman. In part one he is "little" and "lame." In part two he is "queer" and "old." In part three he is "goat-footed" and is identified as "Man," with a capital "M." This is an increasingly sinister portrait.

The "goat-footed" balloonman turns out to be a figure from classical mythology—the lustful satyr or faun, half animal and half man. In classical mythology, the satyrs and fauns are associated with sensuality, and some of the stories are about their seduction of nymphs in a forest setting. The cloven feet of the satyrs and fauns became a part of Christian iconography during the Middle Ages, when the devil was pictured as having goat's feet. We should also remember the biblical imagery of sheep and goats.

Form includes the idea of unity or central theme. As we stand back from this poem, its controlling motif is obvious. The poem is built around a literary theme of universal significance—the fall from innocence. The poem's topic is the same as that of

Genesis 3 and *Paradise Lost* and Hawthorne's short story "Young Goodman Brown."

Every part of Cummings's poem contributes to the theme of the "seduction" (figuratively speaking) of children from childhood into adulthood. The balloonman's call of the children from their play (the pied piper motif) is a symbolic act. This explains why Cummings capitalizes two words in the poem, "Just" and "Man." The balloonman is "just man," that is, universal adulthood, fallen and evil at heart. The poem does not end—it simply trails off into the distance, as if to suggest the way in which the innocent play of the children passes imperceptibly into adulthood.

It is evident, then, that an important part of the poem's strategy is based on contrast. There are contrasts throughout the poem between youthfulness and old age, child and adult, the natural springtime setting and the unnatural figure of the lame, goat-footed balloonman, the innocence of the children's games and the implied evil of the adult world to which the children are called, and between the contemporary urban setting and the old mythic world of satyrs and fauns and pied pipers.

Does Cummings's poem give the reader an experience of beauty? How can it, if at the level of subject matter the poem uncovers something morally ugly? The poem thus delineates something that has been true of art throughout the centuries but is especially prominent as a feature of modern art. Most modern artists disavow that their aim is to create beauty. They are much more likely to say that the artist's task is to get beneath the beautiful surface of life and expose the ugliness that is there.

But look at the skill with which a poet such as Cummings expresses himself. A scrutiny of the sheer proficiency and skill of verbal craftsmanship shows that modern poems are just as artistic—and artistic in the same ways—as poets who in earlier eras defined poetry partly as the creation of beauty. There is always a purely artistic dimension to poems and paintings and musical compositions, regardless of the subject. In fact, it is a principle of art that when the subject is something evil or terrifying, the artist finds ways to distance that subject so we can contemplate it with a measure of safety and even pleasure.

We are frequently left, then, with a paradox: works of art can simultaneously present ugliness (at the level of subject or content) and beauty (at the level of form). People who want things tidy and controlled will stumble at that paradox, but we will make far more sense of modern art if we are bold enough to accept the paradox. H. R. Rookmaaker has written, "Can there be a beautiful work of art which has as a subject-matter something horrible and ugly? The answer is yes, of course, for there are abundant examples."[19]

Distinguishing between Form and Content

To respond to artistry requires that we make a distinction between a work's content and its form. It is an established principle of artistic theory that the aesthetic response can, and sometimes should, be separated from the intellectual or moral response. It is true that the content of a work cannot be understood apart from the form through which that content is communicated. But it is quite possible to respond (though it is never one's total response) to the formal or artistic dimension of a work in isolation from the theme or message.

The advantage of this approach for Christians is that it allows them to affirm the value of artistic works whose content or world view they may dislike or abhor. If God is the source of all beauty and artistry, then the artistic dimension of art is the point at which Christians can be unreserved in their enthusiasm for the works of non-Christian artists.

The willingness to differentiate between the purely artistic dimension of a poem or song or painting and its subject matter may, in fact, have been something that Christianity contributed to aesthetics. John Milton, in a famous autobiographical passage in which he outlines the history of his own literary development, writes that the Roman elegiac poets exerted an early literary influence on him. Milton gradually came to deplore the ethical viewpoint of these pagan authors, but he notes that "their art I still applauded."[20]

Milton's experience is representative of a whole tradition. One scholar writes that "it was the Christians who finally taught men to appraise poetry by a purely aesthetic standard—a standard which enabled them to reject most of the moral and religious teaching of the classical poets as false and ungodly, while accepting the formal elements in their work as instructive and aesthetically delightful."[21]

Failure to distinguish between the levels of form and content has led to two significant errors. On the one hand, it has led Christians who want to avoid being provincial in their tastes to endorse, at the level of ideas or viewpoint, works that no one should claim to be consonant with Christianity. And, on the other side, Christians who have shown good judgment in measuring non-Christian world views by a Christian standard have unfortunately devalued or rejected works that can offer much to a Christian's artistic experience. The corrective to both errors is to distinguish the artistic from the moral/intellectual response and to be unreserved in affirming the value of non-Christian art at the level of craftsmanship and beauty.

Isn't Truth More Important than Beauty?

I can imagine many people protesting against my emphasis on the value of beauty. The most common protest runs something like this: Aren't truth and intellect more important than beauty and imagination? Aren't facts what we need? Isn't it trivial to speak of the arts in terms of beauty and pleasure? I am not, of course, building my entire case for the arts on their beauty and artistic competence.

Is truth more important than beauty? I think the answer is a very qualified "yes." Surely religious truth is more important than artistic beauty. People will be eternally saved or lost on the basis of their response to truth, not on the basis of their artistic experience. But once we get beyond the matter of religious truth, I would begin to quibble with the common assumption that truth is more important than beauty.

It is not at all true that the facts one learns in disciplines other than the arts are necessarily more important than the ability to enjoy the arts. Behind the usual assumption is the premise that facts are important because they are useful, while enjoying artistry and beauty is useless. But not all facts are as useful as is claimed in our computer age, and beyond that, I would appeal to human nature to support my claim that people have other important needs besides factual knowledge. The experience of beauty is one of them.

Matthew Arnold was right when he defended a literary education against the encroachment of science by appealing to human nature. "When we set ourselves to enumerate the powers which go to the building up of human life," wrote Arnold, we find that "they are the power of conduct, the power of intellect and knowledge, the power of beauty, and the power of social life and manners." Arnold then made the convincing point that "human nature is built up by these powers; we have the need for them all. . . . Such is human nature."[22]

Isn't Beauty Irrelevant?

Some will object to my emphasis on beauty by asking, Isn't artistic beauty irrelevant in an age of great social problems? Shouldn't people generally and Christians especially devote themselves to solving social problems instead of pursuing the arts? The attitude implied by such questions is of course partly right. The arts are something people cultivate after their basic needs for survival have been met. They are a form of enrichment and refreshment.

But more needs to be said. We are hardly ever faced with the absolute alternatives of combating social problems or pursuing the arts. Whenever we have to choose between enjoying artistic beauty and showing compassion to someone in need, we should of course do the compassionate act and forget about artistic beauty. But over the long haul, this is not the kind of situation people face. Nearly everyone's life gives an abundant opportunity to enjoy art as well as serve one's fellow humans. In fact, to encourage others in the wise use of leisure is increasingly an act of compassion.

Furthermore, I would dispute the common assumption

that the arts are irrelevant to the solution of social problems. Many social problems have arisen precisely because our society has not taken the time and expended the energy to be truly artistic and to value beauty. It may sound simplistic, but it is true that some inner-city problems will be solved only on an aesthetic basis. If our society would uphold beauty as a value not to be violated, our cities would not be concrete jungles, and our streams would not be polluted.

Our practical modern world has regarded beauty as an extraneous luxury, and we are left in horror at the kind of world this attitude has produced. If we look honestly and deeply within the human spirit as created by God, we will find a hunger for beauty as well as for truth and righteousness. Have you ever seen some of the drawings done in the concentration camps of the Second World War? And if we look beyond the human spirit to the God of the Bible and the God of creation, we will conclude that God does not regard beauty as the unnecessary pursuit of an idle moment.

The Perversion of Beauty

All that I have said about the Bible's approval of beauty needs to be qualified. Many biblical passages make it clear that beauty can be used in evil and destructive ways. Beauty was created or given by God and is good in principle. Like any of God's gifts, it can be perverted to a bad end by fallen people. That is why one of Dostoyevsky's literary characters can say that beauty is the battlefield where God and the devil fight for the human heart and why Aldous Huxley can write that "as a matter of plain historical fact, the beauties of holiness have often been matched and indeed surpassed by the beauties of unholiness."[23] What we are talking about, though, is the abuse of something, not its inherent nature.

Beauty in Christian Perspective

The Bible treats beauty as something that has value because God made it and delights in it. If the modern secular mind scorns beauty, that is simply one more evidence of where it has gone awry. To people who reluctantly admit that modern art, music, and literature possess the usual elements of artistic form and beauty "if you want to see them there," my reply is simple: My Christian world view has given me "antennae" to notice and value artistic beauty.

A missionary who faced the question of how beauty related to her life in a foreign culture came to a similar conclusion. Did not a life of service in India mean living in squalor and ugliness? Margaret Ho wrestled with the issue and came to this conclusion:

> I believe my attitude toward beauty and order, as reflected in my home and lifestyle, says much to the people around me about the God I serve. Therefore, I want to reflect . . . something of the artistry, the beauty, the order of the one I'm representing, and in whose image I've been made. To me, sacrifice does not mean ugliness.[24]

If, in a Christian view of things, everything that God has created is not self-contained but points toward him, Ralph Waldo Emerson was not quite correct when he wrote that "Beauty is its own excuse for being."[25] But surely Emerson came much closer to the truth than have many segments of modern culture, Christian and secular alike.

The Enjoyment Of Art

> *Paradise Lost* is much more fun written in blank verse than it would be in prose, or is so to anyone capable of enjoying that particular kind of fun. Let us have all the delights of which we are capable.
>
> Charles Williams, *Reason and Beauty in the Poetic Mind*

It is an easy step from artistic creativity and beauty to the idea of the arts as enjoyment. The Bible endorses pleasure or enjoyment as thoroughly as it approves of beauty.

The Biblical Attitude toward Enjoyment

Pleasure and its synonyms are, for example, one of the recurrent themes in the Psalms. The writer of Psalm 16 rejoices in the fact that "the lines have fallen for me in pleasant places" (vs. 6), and he asserts that at God's "right hand are pleasures for evermore" (vs. 11). For another poet, the "harp with the psaltery is pleasant" (Psalm 81:2, KJV). Another psalm declares about God's people, "they feast on the abundance of thy house, and thou givest them drink from the river of thy delights" (Psalm 36:8).

One of the unifying themes of the book of Ecclesiastes is the contrast between the false, purely humanistic pursuit of pleasure and the legitimate, God-oriented quest for pleasure. Two of the key assertions about the legitimacy of pleasure when it is placed in a context of faith in God are these:

> I know that there is nothing better for them than to be happy and enjoy themselves as long as they live; also that it is God's gift to man that every one should eat and drink and take pleasure in all his toil (Ecclesiastes 3:12-13).
>
> Behold, what I have seen to be good and to be fitting is to eat and drink and find enjoyment in all the toil with which one toils under the sun the few days of his life which God has given him, for this is his lot. Every man also to whom God has given wealth and possessions and power to enjoy them, and to accept his lot and find enjoyment in his toil—this is the gift of God (Ecclesiastes 5:18-19).

These same sentiments are reiterated in Paul's instructions to Timothy concerning the wealthy: "Charge them that are rich in this world, that they be not highminded, nor trust in uncertain riches, but in the living God, who giveth us richly all things to enjoy" (1 Timothy 6:17, KJV). This key verse establishes three important principles: (1) God is the giver of all good things, (2) He gives people these things so they can enjoy them, (3) the misuse of them consists not in enjoyment of them but in trusting in them or making idols of them.

The biblical doctrine of heaven also exalts pleasure. If heaven is the place where there is no more pain (Revelation 21:4), C. S. Lewis can correctly assert that "all pleasure is in itself a good and pain in itself an evil; if not, then the whole Christian tradition about heaven and hell and the passion of our Lord seems to have no meaning."[26]

The Example of Jesus

No one could have lived a busier life than Jesus did during the years of his public ministry. Yet he did not reduce life to continuous work or evangelism. He took time to enjoy the beauty of the lily and the sky. If we could arrange the gospel accounts of Jesus' habitual activities into a series of portraits, one of them would be a picture of Jesus attending a dinner or party. Jesus turned water into wine to keep a wedding party going (John 2:1-10). By his example, Jesus consecrated pleasure and enjoyment.

Is God Opposed to Fun?

The Bible makes it clear that we must be ready to sacrifice our pleasures for the sake of God and people in need, but the Bible is not against enjoyment itself. Nowhere do we get the impression that God considers people more virtuous if they do not enjoy themselves, even in their moments of self-sacrifice. Jesus endured the cross "for the joy that was set before him" (Hebrews 12:2).

A person's attitude toward pleasure is actually a comment on his or her estimate of God. To assume that God dislikes pleasure and enjoyment is to charge him with being sadistic toward his creatures. As Norman Geisler writes, "God is not a celestial Scrooge who hates to see his children enjoy themselves. Rather, he is the kind of Father who is ready to say, 'Let us eat and make merry; for this my son was dead and is alive again; he was lost and is found' (Luke 15:24)."[27]

We could come to that conclusion simply by looking at the world that God created. It contains much that is sheerly pleasurable. Surely John Calvin was right when he wrote that "if we ponder to what end God created food, we shall find that he meant not only to provide for necessity but also for delight and good cheer."[28]

Enjoying the Arts

What does the Bible's affirmation of beauty and pleasure have to do with the arts? Primarily it validates the enjoyment of the imaginative beauty of art as a Christian activity. Scripture tells us that people are created in the image of God. This means, among other things, that people possess the ability to make something beautiful and to delight in it.

Given this biblical aesthetic, when we enjoy the colors and design of a painting, the fictional inventiveness of a novel, the harmonious arrangement of a sonata, we are enjoying a quality of which God is the ultimate source and performing an act similar to God's enjoyment of the beauty of his own creation. We can participate in the arts to the glory of God by enthusiastically enjoying the arts, recognizing God as the ultimate source of the creativity and beauty that we enjoy. If artistic creativity is, as the Bible claims, a gift of God, we can scarcely demonstrate our gratitude for the gift any more adequately than by using and enjoying it.

If the act of enjoying the arts seems either blameworthy or trivial, it is because we have fallen prey to an unbiblical attitude, whether it be derived from asceticism (with its view that denying pleasure is inherently virtuous), a distorted work ethic in which only hard work is a legitimate use of time, or scientific utilitarianism (with its scorn for anything that is not useful in mastering the physical world or making money). It is a fallacy to suppose that pleasure is wrong or that an activity must be directly useful, in a utilitarian sense, in order to be considered worthwhile. God created people with the ability to enjoy life and beauty, even as God does.

The Arts as Recreation

The disparagement of enjoyment has even led to a serious misconception about the arts, namely, that they do not exist for enjoyment. A little reflection will show that this view of the arts is nonsense. The arts do not exist only for enjoyment, but they certainly do not exist for less than that.

Why do people hang paintings on the walls of rooms? Not to receive information or moral instruction, surely. Why do they listen to music? They do so because music gives them pleasure. When and where do people read novels and poetry? In the evenings or on weekends or vacations, and in an easy chair.

The arts have refreshment value. They add to the pleasure of life. The modern poet T. S. Eliot called poetry "superior amusement."[29] Aesthetic theorist and philosopher Jean-Paul Sartre wrote that "the writer, like all other artists, aims at giving his reader . . . aesthetic joy."[30]

Artists do not claim that art is only entertaining. Robert Frost spoke for most artists when he said that a poem "begins in delight and ends in wisdom. . . . It begins in delight . . . and ends in a clarification of life."[31] From delight to wisdom: that is in fact the order in which the two functions of art usually occur in our experience.

The overwhelming majority of people hang paintings or go to a concert or attend a play because they wish to be refreshed and to receive some type of enjoyment. In the process, they are usually edified or intellectually enriched as well. The entertaining and edifying functions of art are complementary, not incompatible.

But defenses of art are typically one-sided. They focus on the usefulness of art and ignore the thing that prompts people to go to art in the first place. There has been a lot of misunderstanding and some hypocrisy on this point, and we should not allow these to stand in the way of coming to understand why the arts exist and how we should value them. It defeats one of the main purposes of the arts to reduce them to their utilitarian function. To regard even our recreation as a form of work is, in the words of C. S. Lewis, to attempt "to get a work-time result out of something that never aimed at producing more than pleasure."[32]

Recreation And Leisure

> Leisure is a form of silence, of that silence which is the prerequisite of the apprehension of reality. . . . Because Wholeness is what man strives for, the power to achieve leisure is one of the fundamental powers of the human soul. . . . In leisure . . . the truly human values are saved and preserved.
>
> Josef Pieper, *Leisure: The Basis of Culture*

The only context within which the enjoyment of human creativity and beauty can flourish is a high view of leisure. If we dignify leisure as it deserves, the place of the arts in human life will be a lot clearer.

A Biblical Basis for Leisure

A Christian understanding of leisure begins with God's rest after his creation of the world. We read that

> . . . on the seventh day God finished his work which he had done, and he rested on the seventh day from all his work which he had done. So God blessed the seventh day and hallowed it, because on it God rested from all his work which he had done in creation (Genesis 2:2-3).

The primary meaning of God's rest on the seventh day is that it is the origin and model for a day of worship in every week.

But God's rest on the seventh day also suggests something of the nature of recreation for people. God did not, it is true, need to rest the way people do, but in his cessation from labor we can see a principle that is true for people also. To begin, recreation is a resting from work and acquisitiveness. Much of the restorative effect of recreation comes from the way in which a person is freed from utilitarian ends and can perform a pleasurable activity for its own sake. As God's rest after creation suggests, life is built on a rhythm in which work and rest or recreation alternate.

At its best, recreation is a quality of mind and soul. Its goal is human joy and satisfaction. As God contemplated the work of his creativity, he found it good. Made in God's image, we too can be satisfied by the creative work of artists and can find it good. Josef Pieper has stated the Christian case for leisure thus:

> Leisure . . . is a mental and spiritual attitude—it is not simply the result of external factors, it is not the inevitable result of spare time, a holiday, a weekend or a vacation. It is, in the first place, an attitude of mind, a condition of soul. . . . Compared with the exclusive ideal of work as toil, leisure appears . . . as an attitude of contemplative "celebration.". . . We may read in the first chapter of Genesis that God "ended his work which he had made" and "behold, it was very good." In leisure, man too celebrates the end of his work by allowing his inner eye to dwell for a while upon the reality of the Creation. He looks and affirms: It is good.[33]

Leisure as a Human Necessity

Aristotle in the *Politics* has an important insight into leisure. The Spartans, according to Aristotle, remained strong while they were at war, but they collapsed once they had acquired an empire. Their fatal flaw was that they did not know how to use the leisure that peace brought to them. Is our own culture really any different?

One of the great tragedies of our own day is that people do not know how to use their leisure time in enriching ways. Paul Elmen, in his book *The Restoration of Meaning to Contemporary Life*, analyzes the cultural malaise that is perhaps most evident in many people's leisure time: boredom, the search for distraction, the fear of spending time by oneself, sensuality, escape into comedy, violence, and the appeal of horror ("the fun of being frightened").[34] Blaise Pascal found already in his day that "all the unhappiness of men arises from one single fact, that they cannot stay quietly in their own chamber."[35]

What is particularly distressing is the mindlessness of leisure pursuits in our culture. Several years ago a Gallup poll found that 58 percent of Americans had never finished reading a book.[36] The most common form of leisure activity in American culture, watching television, is also one of the most passive forms (rivaled only by sleeping). Several psychologists have documented the trance-like fixation of television viewers that destroys the ability to engage in conscious thought. Several studies of brainwave activity have shown how inactive the brain is while a person watches television. One of them found that "the mode of response to television is . . . very different from the responses to print."[37]

How important is the crisis in people's ability to find enriching forms of recreation at a time when they have an unprecedented amount of leisure time? Viewing the problem from a Christian perspective, Robert Lee writes,

> Leisure is a part of man's ultimate concern. It is a crucial part of the very search for meaning in life, inasmuch as the social malaise of our time has been diagnosed as anxiety and boredom, alienation and meaninglessness. . . . It is in the realm of free time that these conditions will be brought into bold relief, bringing man to the depths of despair or to the heights of ecstasy and creativity. Increasingly it is in our leisure time that either the meaningfulness or the pointlessness of life will be revealed.[38]

How Should Christians View Leisure?

In the Christian community the problem seems to be that we have no adequate theory of leisure and play. Regarding recreation as something frivolous or ignoble, Christians often sink to mediocrity by default.

For Christians, the wise use of leisure is part of the stewardship of life. Stewardship of our bodies and minds means, first of all, that we will find time for leisure. People who do not take time to recreate themselves have nervous breakdowns.

Stewardship of time, moreover, means that we are responsible for the time that God has given us. Frank Gaebelein once wrote that "the very word 'leisure' implies responsibility. . . . Leisure and working time are equally to be accounted for to the Lord."[39] The first step toward exercising good stewardship is to invest the idea of recreation and leisure with dignity and worth. To act as if recreation is unworthy of a Christian, or to pretend that we do not engage in entertainment when in fact we spend a major part of our lives filling our non-working time with activities, is to allow our leisure pursuits to remain at a low level by default.

Leisure time presents us with choices, and "even a non-choice amounts to a choice by default."[40] Choosing leisure pursuits wisely is a moral issue. As C. S. Lewis puts it, "Our leisure, even our play, is a matter of serious concern. There is no neutral ground in the universe; every square inch, every split second, is claimed by God and counterclaimed by Satan. . . . It is a serious matter to choose wholesome recreations."[41]

Education for Leisure

Aristotle in his *Politics* claimed that the aim of education was the enlightened use of leisure time. That is no doubt an overstatement, but one of the best tests of whether people are truly educated is what they do in their free time.

The key to the wise use of leisure time is education, broadly defined. We do in our leisure time what we have learned to do. Left to ourselves, the law of mental laziness takes its course and our horizons remain rather narrow. The reclamation of our leisure pursuits, therefore, will have to begin with our willingness to learn about new areas, including artistic ones.

The English thinker and poet John Milton defined an adequate education as one that equips a person to perform "all the offices, both private and public," that life affords.[42] In our economically oriented society we know all about education for our public roles, chiefly our job. But what about the private role of living an enriching life of the mind and imagination and spirit?

An education is adequate only if it equips a person to spend an evening doing something more than listening to the kind of music or watching the type of television program with which most people in our culture are satisfied. While it is undoubtedly true that our college years afford the greatest luxury of opportunity to develop our capacity for meaningful kinds of recreation, ultimately all education is self-education. People can learn to enjoy the arts on their own. All they need is a commitment to learn, some books that will open the door to the arts, and time spent with music, literature, and visual art. Now is the time to begin.

Summary

Artistic creativity and beauty are the gifts of God. Their function is to glorify God and refresh people. As gifts of God, they have value in themselves. Artists labor to perfect the technical excellence of their art, and audiences should admire that excellence.

Christians have no reason to feel guilty about enjoying the arts. God has created people with a need for leisure. Leisure time is a gift that requires responsible stewardship, and the arts at their best are an enriching leisure pursuit.

Further Reading

Dorothy L. Sayers, *The Mind of the Maker* (1941).

Jacques Maritain, *Creative Intuition in Art and Poetry* (1953).

Roland A. Delattre, *Beauty and Sensibility in the Thought of Jonathan Edwards* (1968).

Harold D. Lehman, *In Praise of Leisure* (1974).

F. Duane Lindsey, "Essays Toward a Theology of Beauty," *Bibliotheca Sacra,* (1974) 131:120-136.

Leland Ryken, ed., *The Christian Imagination: Essays on Literature and the Arts* (1981).

Chapter Three, Notes

1. Oscar Wilde, "The Decay of Lying," in *The Modern Tradition: Backgrounds of Modern Literature,* ed. Richard Ellman and Charles Feidelson, Jr. (New York: Oxford University Press, 1965), p. 20.

2. Dorothy L. Sayers, *The Mind of the Maker* (1941; reprint ed. Cleveland: World, 1956), p. 34.

3. Abraham Kuyper, *Calvinism* (Grand Rapid: William B. Eerdmans, 1943), p. 142.

4. Laurence Perrine, *Sound and Sense: An Introduction to Poetry,* 5th edition (New York: Harcourt, Brace and World, 1977), p. 217.

5. C. S. Lewis, *Christian Reflections* (Grand Rapids: William B. Eerdmans, 1967), p. 7.

6. Sir Philip Sidney, "Apology for Poetry," in *Criticism: The Major Statements,* ed. Charles Kaplan (New York: St. Martin's, 1964), p. 114.

7. Chad Walsh, "The Advantages of the Christian Faith for a Writer," in *The Christian Imagination: Essays on Literature and the Arts,* ed. Leland Ryken (Grand Rapids: Baker, 1981), p. 308.

8. Kuyper, p. 156.

9. Ibid., p. 156.

10. Denis de Rougemont, "Religion and the Mission of the Artist," in *The New Orpheus: Essays Toward a Christian Poetic,* ed. Nathan A. Scott, Jr. (New York: Sheed and Ward, 1964), p. 64.

11. Calvin Seerveld, *A Christian Critique of Art* (St. Catharines, Ontario: Association for Reformed Scientific Studies, 1963), pp. 31-35.

12. Gerard Manley Hopkins, "Poetry and Verse," as quoted in *Gerard Manley Hopkins: The Major Poems,* ed. Walford Davies (London: J. M. Dent and Sons, 1979), p. 38.

13. Max Dessoir, *Aesthetics and Theory of Art,* trans. Stephen A. Emery (Detroit: Wayne State University Press, 1970), pp. 149-159.

14. James S. Hans, *The Play of the World* (Amherst: University of Massachusetts Press, 1981), p. 123.

15. Dylan Thomas, "Poetic Manifesto," in *The Poet's Work,* ed. Reginald Gibbons (Boston: Houghton Mifflin, 1979), pp. 185-186.

16. Wassily Kandinsky, *Concerning the Spiritual in Art* (New York: George Wittenborn, 1947), p. 75.

17. Nicolas Poussin, "Observations on Painting," in *Artists on Art,* ed. Robert Goldwater and Marco Treves (New York: Pantheon Books, 1945, 1958), p. 156.

18. Norman Foerster, "The Esthetic Judgment and the Ethical Judgment," in *The Intent of the Critic,* ed. Donald A. Stauffer (Princeton: Princeton University Press, 1941), pp. 69-70.

19. H. R. Rookmaaker, *Modern Art and the Death of a Culture* (Downers Grove: InterVarsity, 1970), p. 233.

20. John Milton, *Apology for Smectymnus,* in *John Milton: Complete Poems and Major Prose,* ed. Merritt Y. Hughes (New York: Odyssey Press, 1957), p. 693.

21. Werner Jaeger, *Paideia: The Ideals of Greek Culture,* trans. Gilbert Highet (New York: Oxford University Press, 1939), 1:34.

22. Matthew Arnold, "Literature and Science," in *Prose of the Victorian Period,* ed. William C. Buckley (Boston: Houghton Mifflin, 1958), pp. 493-494.

23. Fyodor Dostoyevsky, *The Brothers Karamazov,* trans. Marc Slonim (New York: Modern Library, 1950), p. 127; Aldous Huxley, *Brave New World* (New York: Harper and Row, 1958), p. 52. Huxley goes on to observe that Hitler's rallies "were masterpieces of ritual and theatrical art" and to quote an observer's statement that "for grandiose beauty I have never seen any ballet to compare with the Nuremberg rally."

24. Margaret Ho, "Reflecting a God of Beauty," *Eternity,* November, 1982, p. 29.

25. Ralph Waldo Emerson, "The Rhodora," line 12.

26. C. S. Lewis, *Christian Reflections,* p. 21.

27. Norman Geisler, "The Christian as Pleasure-Seeker," *Christianity Today,* 25 September 1975, p. 11.

28. John Calvin, *Institutes of the Christian Religion,* ed. John T. McNeill (Philadelphia: Westminster), 1:720.

29. T. S. Eliot, "Preface" to *The Sacred Wood* (London: Methuen 1920, 1960), p. viii.

30. Jean-Paul Sartre, *What Is Literature?* trans. Bernard Frechtman (New York: Philosophical Library, 1949), p. 58.

31. Robert Frost, "The Figure a Poem Makes," in *Writers on Writing,* ed. Walter Allen (Boston: The Writer, Inc., 1948), p. 22

32. C. S. Lewis, *Christian Reflections,* p. 34.

33. Josef Pieper, *Leisure: The Basis of Culture* (New York: New American Library, 1963), pp. 40-43.

34. Paul Elmen, *The Restoration of Meaning to Contemporary Life* (Garden City: Doubleday, 1958).

35. Blaise Pascal, *Pensees,* II, 139.

36. Cited by Arthur Schlesinger, Jr., "Implications for Government," in *Technology, Human Values, and Leisure,* ed. Max Kaplan and Phillip Bosserman (Nashville: Abingdon, 1971), p. 77.

37. My information for this paragraph comes from Jerry Mander, *Four Arguments for the Elimination of Television* (New York: William Morrow, 1978), pp. 205-211.

38. Robert Lee, *Religion and Leisure in America* (Nashville: Abingdon, 1964), pp. 25-26.

39. Frank E. Gaebelein, "The Christian Use of Leisure," in *The Christian, the Arts, and Truth: Regaining the Vision of Greatness,* ed. D. Bruce Lockerbie (Portland, Ore.: Multnomah Press, 1985), p. 228.

40. Harold Lehman, *In Praise of Leisure* (Scottdale, PA: Herald Press, 1974), p. 147.

41. C. S. Lewis, *Christian Reflections,* pp. 33-34.

42. John Milton, *Of Education.*

Chapter 4

The World of the Imagination

An Alternate World

> The world of literature is a world where there is no reality except that of the human imagination. . . . The constructs of the imagination tell us things about human life that we don't get in any other way.
>
> Northrop Frye, *The Educated Imagination*

"My love is a red, red rose." "Lilies that fester smell far worse than weeds." "And they lived happily ever after." Is there any doubt that the world of the imagination is, from a literal viewpoint, nonsense? Why, we might wonder, has this make-believe world held such a grip on the human race throughout history?

We might even ask, with C. S. Lewis, "What then is the good of—what is even the defence for—occupying our hearts with stories of what never happened . . . ? Or of fixing our inner eye earnestly on things that can never exist . . . ?"[1] Are our excursions into the imaginary world of the arts frivolous? Or are they indispensable to our well-being? Are they an escape, or a doorway to reality?

The Imagination: Maker of Worlds

We should avoid the perennial attempt to minimize the extent to which the arts create their own world. The world of the imagination, despite all its resemblances to the real world in which we live, is an alternate world. "Worldmaking" is a prime activity of the artistic imagination.

Even the materials out of which the imagination creates its world are intangible compared to the world we touch and on which we stand. Music, for example, creates its reality out of sound, and literature out of words. The face or scene painted on a canvas has none of the tangible properties of a real landscape or person.

The realities of art exist only in our minds and imaginations, though they of course remind us of the world in which we live. Someone has said regarding literature (and it applies equally to music and art) that its realities

> are not "out there" in the world around us. They are all in your head. You cannot study literature with a telescope or a microscope: you can only study it with that combination of reason and emotion we call the imagination. . . . Its realities are inside men's minds.[2]

There is emancipation in the imagination: It frees us in an instant from our time and place and transports us to another world. There is power in the imagination: As the English author and critic Oscar Wilde said, it "makes and unmakes many worlds."[3] And there is mystery in the imagination: It transcends the limitations of external reality in a manner that seems magical.

The Separateness of Art from Ordinary Reality

As a separate world with its own "rules" of reality and its own ways of operating, the world of the artistic imagination invites comparison with games. In both art and games, we temporarily remove ourselves from ordinary reality in order to cope with it better.

Games, moreover, have a self-contained quality in which we expect behavior that we do not allow in ordinary life. In some games deceit is considered a virtue, as when a basketball player "fakes out" the opponent guarding him or her. Football players push each other around with abandon on the field but would be arrested for similar behavior at a shopping center.

The world of the imagination—the world that we enter when we sit down to read a novel or stand before a painting—is also a world having its own identity and integrity.[4] Throughout history, and in the Christian community today, a lot of mischief has been done when people fail to grant validity to the separate world of the imagination. At one extreme we find the perennial attempt to deny the distinctiveness of the world that the imagination creates and to value the arts only for their supposedly realistic or lifelike qualities. At the other extreme are people who, while granting the imaginative quality of the arts, regard that world as a trivial one we should outgrow as we do childhood.

The Imagination as Part of God's Reality

Studying the world of the artistic imagination will tell us things that are just as crucial to human well-being and to God's glory as an exploration of the physical world around us. My conviction as a Christian is that to explore the world of the imagination is to explore part of God's created reality. The Bible tells us that it is God who created people and who endowed them with a creative imagination. People and their imaginings, we can infer, are part of God's universe. "The sphere of imagination," writes someone, "is as much part of God's creation as the sun, moon, and stars. They are given, like all gifts, for His glory and our good."[5]

A World of Concrete Images

From Homer, who never omits to tell us that the ships were black and the sea salt, or even wet, . . . poets are always telling us that grass is green, or thunder loud, or lips red.

C. S. Lewis, *Christian Reflections*

The most obvious quality of the imagination is suggested by the word itself. The imagination works by means of images. Dorothy Sayers has said that art exists "to image forth something or the other."[6] This is most obviously true with music and the visual arts. Music consists of sounds that we hear with our ears. Visual artists use thoroughly tangible materials as the medium by which they embody reality, and we assimilate works of visual art primarily with our eyes.

The fact that literature is made out of words should not obscure that it, too, depends on the image (broadly defined) as its vehicle. Stories and plays consist of people in physical settings performing physical acts. Poets likewise fill their poems with images of physical reality. Northrop Frye comments that "literature's world is a concrete human world of immediate experience. The poet uses images and sensations much more than he uses abstract ideas; the novelist is concerned with telling stories, not with working out arguments."[7]

The human mind tends to formulate its knowledge in two distinct ways—through abstract propositions and through images. We can identify these with the theoretic or rational intellect and the imagination, respectively. For example, one way to describe human mutability is to assemble actuarial data about life expectancies and psychological profiles on aging. By contrast, here is how Shakespeare describes his awareness of human mutability (Sonnet 12):

> When I do count the clock that tells the time,
> And see the brave day sunk in hideous night;
> When I behold the violet past prime,
> And sable [black] curls all silvered o'er with white;
> When lofty trees I see barren of leaves,
> Which erst from heat did canopy the herd,
> And summer's green all girded up in sheaves
> Borne on the bier with white and bristly beard,
> Then of thy beauty do I question make
> That thou among the wastes of time must go. . . .

For the poet, the phenomenon of human aging is not an abstraction but a series of images from nature applied to the human situation.

The storyteller relies just as thoroughly on concrete images of reality, as fiction writer Flannery O'Connor explained with particular clarity:

> The beginning of human knowledge is through the senses, and the fiction writer begins where human perception begins. He appeals through the senses, and you cannot appeal to the senses with abstractions. . . . The first and most obvious characteristic of fiction is that it deals with reality through what can be seen, heard, smelt, tasted, and touched. . . .[8]

Why do artists communicate with images? Because it is the most effective way to convey the truth about actual human experience. One of the best introductory essays on the subject is by C. S. Lewis, and his final conclusion expresses well the premise on which the arts rest:

> Now it seems to me a mistake to think that our experience in general can be communicated by precise and literal language and that there is a special class of experiences (say, emotions) which cannot. The truth seems to me the opposite: there is a special region of experiences which can be communicated without [concrete images], . . . but most experience cannot. To be incommunicable by Scientific language is . . . the normal state of experience.[9]

The World of Make-Believe

> Literature was born not the day when a boy crying wolf, wolf came running out of the Neanderthal valley with a big gray wolf at his heels: literature was born on the day when a boy came crying wolf, wolf and there was no wolf behind him."
>
> Vladimir Nabokov, *Lectures on Literature*

The word *imagination* implies the act of imagining things. To imagine is to call into being something that does not literally exist in the real world around us. The world that the imagination creates is a fictional world.

This is readily apparent if we stop to analyze the conventions that prevail in the arts. Every area of human experience has its recognizable rules and conventions. When people eat dinner, they ordinarily sit on chairs around a table and use spoons and forks to get the food from plates to their mouths. There is a conventional order in which foods are eaten, with meat and potatoes preceding ice cream. If we observe street traffic from a high view, we can see at once that the flow of traffic is regulated by a definite set of rules. Cars move in opposite directions on the two halves of the street, they stop at points where roads intersect, and so forth.

The arts also have conventions—lots of them. These conventions are part of the order that the imagination imposes on reality. "Literature and life," writes Northrop Frye, "are both conventionalized, and of the conventions of literature about all we can say is that they don't much resemble the conditions of life."[10] The arts are filled with things that happen constantly in art but rarely or not at all in real life.

Unreality in the Visual Arts

Consider some of the unlifelike conventions of painting. Even the subjects that painters select for portrayal are usually unrealistic. Judged by the standards of what we see in daily life, the content of paintings is usually (though not always) implausible and often preposterous: skies and mountains and gardens heightened beyond ordinary reality, combinations of objects not normally seen together, characters and events from classical mythology or the Bible that neither the painter nor we ever had a chance to see in person, and characters placed in symbolic surroundings that we know they never really set foot near.

At first glance, John Constable's painting *The Haywain* may strike us as realistic, but in fact it is based on some common conventions of painting that are thoroughly artificial.

The Haywain by John Constable
Reproduced by courtesy of the Trustees, The National Gallery, London

To begin, the scene that we look at is framed, giving it a quality of being whole and complete in itself. The sights and experiences of real life are never self-contained in this way; they always merge with surrounding objects and experiences.

The picture is also unlifelike in its design and composition. Constable has used one of the oldest of all principles of design to place the central focus on the haywain (hay-rack or wagon) in the stream. The principle is called the golden mean and is achieved by drawing an imaginary horizontal line one-third of the way up from the bottom and a vertical line one-third of the way from the right border. The intersection of these lines becomes the focal point of the painting. Even when painters do not use this specific convention, most paintings have a central focus. But when we look at a scene in real life, we are not aware of such a focus. This, too, is one of the unlifelike conventions of painting.

Constable's painting captures movement in the scene. In the center of the foreground is a stream, suggesting movement of water. The haywain is in the middle of the stream, alerting us that it is in a process of crossing the stream. Clouds are prominent in the picture, and clouds epitomize change. Even the dog is moving. But the paradox of the painting is that it captures all this movement in still form. This ability to "freeze" human activity is another of the unlifelike aspects of art. In real life, events keep flowing. Art, however, has the magical power to make moments permanent.

The very fullness and completeness of the scene makes it heightened beyond ordinary life. The painting does equal justice to height, depth, and width. It combines water, trees, meadow, and sky in a single view. It encompasses home (rest) and work, animal and human, light and dark, in a single composite view. Where in real life do we find such concentration of diverse elements? Paintings customarily compress an unlifelike abundance into a single space in an obviously posed arrangement.

The unity of mood in the painting also surpasses ordinary life. The dominant mood is one of harmony and tranquility (given vitality by the movement noted earlier). The mood is achieved by Constable's portrayal of a "harmonious interaction of diverse life processes" and "a complex system of interdependencies."[11]

To summarize, Constable's painting illustrates the basic fact of all art: Art takes real life as its subject, but the imagination of the artist transforms those materials in keeping with the conventions of art. We are not surprised to learn that Constable worked on *The Haywain* for months in his studio. If even as realistic a painting as *The Haywain* uses the unlifelike conventions of art, we can rest assured that more imaginary paintings will do so even more.

Conventions in Music

Music has its own unique "language," too. It gives us combinations of sounds and a structure of regular rhythm that we do not find in nature. Various musical forms such as sonatas and symphonies and fugues are artificial arrangements of sounds and motifs that belong to the realm of music itself, not to life.

The imaginary conventions of music are equally apparent if we consider works that use structures of sound to suggest real-life events. The biblical sonatas for harpsichord that Bach's predecessor Johann Kuhnau wrote offer a good illustration. Sonata I portrays the combat between David and Goliath. Using musical sounds and patterns as his materials, Kuhnau captures the spirit of such events as Goliath's stamping and ranting, the trembling of the Israelites, the steadfastness of David, and the rejoicing of the Israelites.

We all know that the sounds produced by the harpsichord are not literally what the ranting of Goliath sounded like. Nor was the youthful courage of David literally a musical melody. The general rejoicing of the Israelites at the end is couched in the frolicsome dance known as the minuet, a form unknown to the Israelites.

The whole composition consists of conventions that, when compared to actual life, are unreal. Using the conventions of music, Kuhnau has created a world of the musical imagination. It would be folly to treat that world as identical with the physical world in which we live. We do not mistake the world of the imagination for reality. The fictions of the imagination do, however, bring that reality to mind.

Unlifelike Conventions in Literature

Literature is also replete with unlifelike conventions. Poets, for example, expect us to believe that people can go around speaking in rhyme and regular meter. Love poets are always busy praising their beloved as ideally beautiful or handsome. They picture themselves as ideally ardent lovers. Their rivals are ideally villainous. Self-respecting love poets fill their poems with vows of eternal constancy (they will love until the moon deserts the sky or until the twelfth of never), and they will of course compare their beloved to beautiful objects in nature (roses or the sun or springtime).

Stories also have their conventions. Jesus told stories about three passersby who encountered an injured man on the road, about three stewards, and about three people who found excuses to avoid attending a banquet. Why three? Because the story pattern of threefold repetition is one of the most universal narrative conventions. Have you ever noticed the tendency of stories to end with poetic justice (good characters rewarded and bad ones punished)? This, too, is a convention of literary narrative, different from what often prevails in real life.

Drama has its own conventions as well. The passage of time is greatly compressed in a play, so that we witness a complete courtship or tragedy in the space of one or two hours. The placing of events is far more structured than the random flow of events in everyday life: characters take turns speaking (often in poetry), events are divided into self-contained scenes, the whole action moves to a climax, and so forth. As for the characters on the stage or screen, we know that they are playing a role and that after the performance is over they will return to their real selves.

Even forms of literature that are often praised for their closeness to life depend on literary conventions. Consider some of the artificialities of tragedy, for example. In tragedy, the hero's downfall is always caused by some flaw of character or error in judgment, but in real life suffering is not always the sufferer's fault. In literary tragedy, suffering leads to insight and is accompanied by a certain grandeur. Literary tragedy also omits much of what accompanies suffering in real life. In the words of C. S. Lewis, literary tragedy omits "the clumsy and apparently meaningless bludgeoning of much real misfortune and the prosaic littlenesses which usually rob real sorrows of their dignity"; instead, tragedy portrays suffering that is "always significant and sublime." "Next to a world in which there were no sorrows," writes Lewis, "we should like one where sorrows were always significant and sublime. But if we allow the 'tragic view of life' to make us believe that we live in such a world, we shall be deceived. Our very eyes teach us better."[12]

Even realistic literature, which aims to create the illusion that it is a "slice of life," is filled with imaginary conventions. Have you ever noticed the ease with which one car can follow another in detective movies? Or the coincidences of certain people being in certain places at certain times in so-called realistic fiction and drama? Realistic stories are structured on the time-honored principle of beginning-middle-end, although events do not have this self-contained quality in real life.

The Middle English storyteller Geoffrey Chaucer made use of virtually all the literary conventions one might name in his masterpiece *The Canterbury Tales*. In the "General Prologue" to the tales, the narrator tells us that he has copied down the very words of the pilgrims. How could he have done that while riding on horseback from London to Canterbury? The stories, moreover, are told in poetic form. The best of the stories features a talking rooster and hen (who could, however, be any husband and wife). Another famous tale includes an aged wanderer (death) who cannot die even though he has tried to do so for years.

Shakespeare's plays are equally suffused with imaginary conventions. To enter into the spirit of his plays, we must grant the premise that people can speak in blank verse, go around baring their inner souls in set speeches called soliloquies, and become instantly virtuous when they enter the Forest of Arden. It is no wonder that one scholar praises Shakespearean drama, not for its realism, but "because the inhabitants of its artificial world are constantly consistent in their remoteness from life."[13]

Like painting and music, literature is filled with unlifelike conventions. The corresponding rule for approaching the arts is simple: We must expect works of art to have an imaginary quality to them. There is always a cleavage between art and life. They do not exist on the same plane of reality, even though they are vitally connected, as we shall see.

The Uses of Unreality in the Arts

Some degree of unreality is the very basis of the arts. The classical tradition called it imitation to denote that the world of the artistic imagination, for all its correspondence to reality, is actually a fictional rearrangement of the materials of life. More recent aesthetic theory has seized upon the word *imagination* to express the same insight. Someone summarizes the situation thus:

> Though all art implies an element of "imitation," without which it cannot interest or touch us, it is never quite a copy or transcript. . . . Literature [for example] . . . requires . . . a transformation of the raw material: condensation and contrast; emphasis or exaggeration here, slurring or understatement there; and the observance of certain traditions and conventions. Tragedy must be tragic, comedy comic, with . . . death at the end of the one, marriage at the end of the other. . . . For the essential and vital material of art is not actual experience, but . . . an imaginative one, from the actual often remote.[14]

Why does the imagination gravitate toward a world of make-believe? For one thing, we find that world entertaining.

There is no other way to account for the persistence with which writers and painters through the centuries have perpetuated these conventions and with which audiences have enjoyed them. If given the chance to choose between the random sounds of external reality and the artificially arranged sounds of music, the human race chooses the latter as more interesting and pleasing.

The unreality of the imagination has another quality to commend it. It has arresting strangeness—a strangeness that compels our attention because it is something other than the ordinary. One of the main functions of the arts is to overcome the deadening effect of the routine, the commonplace, the cliché. The imagination is always searching for freshness of expression. The English Romantic poet Samuel Taylor Coleridge diagnosed the problem very well: The greatest truths "are too often considered as so true, that they lose all the life and efficiency of truth." The imagination, claimed Coleridge, "rescues the most admitted truths from the impotence caused by the very circumstance of their universal admission."[15]

By creating a form of unreality, art defamiliarizes experience. The imagination rearranges the ideas and objects of our everyday experience so we take note of them. Still life painters focus our attention on a bowl of fruit or bouquet of flowers when our harried daily routine has obscured them. Human faces become an anonymous blur to us, but a painted portrait suddenly leads us to see the uniqueness and expressiveness of every human face.

Why does the psalmist command us to "sing a new song" to the Lord? Don't the old songs express the truth adequately? They do, but they also gradually lose their power through sheer repetition and familiarity. According to the English poet Percy B. Shelley, the imagination "lifts the veil from the hidden beauty of the world, and makes familiar objects be as if they were not familiar. . . . It purges from our inward sight the film of familiarity which obscures from us the wonder of our being. It compels us to feel that which we perceive, and to imagine that which we know."[16]

The Illumination of Reality

The imaginary conventions of the arts do more than entertain and captivate us. They also help to illuminate reality. It is not only the arts that rearrange the external world in order to see it more precisely. What a scientist sees under the microscope is not what we see around us. The facts in a psychological profile are not what we see when we talk with a person sitting in front of us. The generalizations made in a history book are different from the immediate events that happened to a person living in a given age. The artistic imagination does something similar. The goal of its imaginary qualities is to help us see life more clearly. The exaggerated coldness of the lady in courtly love poems, or the unrelieved misery of naturalistic literature and painting, or the untainted piety of the speaker in devotional poetry, allows us to see the precise nature of these human experiences better.

The conventions of the imagination thus give us a heightened sense of reality. Sometimes they are simply an index to human longings—longings for grandeur in tragedy or justice in life. Sometimes the unlifelike conventions of the imagination express things that are real but hidden from ordinary view. If, for example, it is true that God will ultimately judge evil, even though such justice is often absent from real life, then stories that are based on poetic justice can be truer than "real" life.

A Simplified and Heightened World

> The deeds of Achilles or Roland were told because they were exceptionally and improbably heroic; . . . the saint's life, because he was exceptionally and improbably holy. . . . Attention is fixed . . . on the more than ordinary terror, splendour, wonder, pity, or absurdity of a particular case.
>
> C. S. Lewis, *An Experiment in Criticism*

Once upon a time there was a son who asked his father for his share of the family inheritance. After his father gave him the money, he took a journey to a distant land where he quickly wasted all that he had on wine, women, and song. Then he came to himself and returned to his father, asking to be forgiven.

This brief story typifies an important feature of the world of the imagination, namely, that it is a simplified world in which all of the irrelevant details have been omitted and only the essential pattern remains. We know exactly who the son is: he is the young prodigal who squanders his money on riotous living and then is initiated into the world of suffering. The shape of the plot is also clear, consisting of such motifs as the journey, the initiation into evil and its consequences, transformation through ordeal, and homecoming. Even if the story were elaborated into a novel, the underlying patterns would still stand out fully illuminated.

The artistic imagination is highly selective as it molds the materials of life into a work of art. Works of art always represent a distillation of human experience or external reality. Artists, in other words, silhouette the essence of their subject so that we see it with heightened clarity.

Highlighting in Literature

Consider the following poem entitled "The Lamb" by William Blake:

Little lamb, who made thee?
Dost thou know who made thee?
Gave thee life and bid thee feed
By the stream and o'er the mead;
Gave thee clothing of delight,
Softest clothing, wooly, bright;
Gave thee such a tender voice,
Making all the vales rejoice?
Little lamb, who made thee?
Dost thou know who made thee?

Little lamb, I'll tell thee,
Little lamb, I'll tell thee:
He is called by thy name,
For He calls Himself a lamb.
He is meek, and He is mild;
He became a little child.

I a child, and thou a lamb:
We are called by His name.
  Little lamb, God bless thee!
  Little lamb, God bless thee!

Blake's poem distills all that is desirable and innocent in human experience—childhood, nature, God, gentleness—and presents it in the form of a child's address to a symbolic lamb. The poem gives us a poetic version of innocence.

Literature is obviously not a journalistic report of everything that happens. It is not a recording of the mere flow of human experience. Rather, a writer distills from human experience what fits the story's pattern or theme. A love poet, for example, distills the beauty and attractiveness of the beloved. The writer of tragedy selects details that fit the tragic pattern of the particular story or the pessimism of his or her view of life. The writer of satire distills what is ugly or foolish in life and omits what is virtuous. Homer's *Odyssey* gives the essence of the family man, Shakespeare's Romeo is the ideal lover, and so forth.

The world of the literary imagination is a highly organized version of the real world. It is a world in which images, characters, and story patterns are presented stripped of distracting complexities. What C. S. Lewis says of Sir Philip Sidney's *Arcadia* is true of most art: "its inhabitants are 'ideal' only in the sense that they are either more beautiful or more ugly, more stately or more ridiculous, more vicious or more virtuous, than those whom we meet every day. The world he paints is, in fact, simplified and heightened."[17]

Heightened Reality in Music and Visual Art

Music and the visual arts also heighten reality beyond what we find in real life. Music heightens our feelings of love or exultation or gloom. Painting can give us a heightened or concentrated perception of virtually any aspect of external reality, all the way from a tree to a human face to a side of beef hanging in a butcher shop. The distortions and omissions and juxtapositions in paintings usually serve the function of highlighting the subject being portrayed. We have all stood before statues of people that are obviously larger than the people really were. By their very unreality these statues capture the greatness of the people they represent.

The whole thrust of the artistic imagination is to silhouette a subject with clarity. It does so by devices of selectivity, omission, exaggeration, and positioning.

Imagination: The "Lie" That Tells the Truth

> We all know that Art is not truth. Art is a lie that makes us realize truth.
>
> Pablo Picasso, article in *The Arts*

Virtually everything I have said thus far has stressed the unlifelike qualities of the imagination. The imagination, I have said, plays the game of make-believe. It simplifies and heightens reality. It is a more highly structured world than the one in which we live.

Despite all its farflung fantasies, however, the artistic imagination is a window to reality. The imagination transforms the materials it takes from everyday life, but by means of that transformation we are led to see reality more clearly. No matter how unreal some of the conventions of the arts might be, the human issues portrayed are those of actual human experience. Our excursions into the imagined world of the arts are not an escape from reality but a journey into reality.

If we look only at a work of art, we see much that is literally a lie: talking animals, strange worlds, bigger-than-life statues, people who speak in poetry, patterns of sounds that we will never find in nature, human emotions rendered as musical sound, people and scenes made out of paint. But we are not intended to look only at this imaginative construct. We also look through it to our experience in the world. Works of music, literature, and art are a window or lens through which we perceive reality.

The Literary Imagination as a Window to Reality

Consider, for example, what happens in Coleridge's *Rime of the Ancient Mariner.* The protagonist is punished for his senseless killing of an albatross by having the dead albatross hung around his neck. In real life people do not wear a dead albatross around their necks, but they do go to work or to the psychiatrist haunted by the horror of unrelieved guilt. In fact, the image of the albatross around one's neck has passed into our storehouse of proverbs.

When the mariner in the story blesses the water snakes that he is watching in the middle of the ocean, the albatross slides from his neck into the sea, and he is able to pray. Nothing like this literally happens to people in the everyday world, but people do lose their guilt and experience the new life. In real life people do not have the powers of strength and immortality that the mariner does, but in real life there is something called heroism. So no matter how remote the world of the *Rime of the Ancient Mariner* may be from reality, it is also so much a part of reality that every person carries that world within his or her own soul.

The English Renaissance poet Edmund Spenser imagined a world so remote from everyday reality that he called it "Fairy Land." It consists of a magical and enchanted forest filled with monsters and knights and ladies in distress. But at the same time, like Coleridge's poem, it expresses the realities that lie within every person. In real life people do not journey into a dark forest and fight with a monster named Error, but they do journey to classrooms and television sets and find themselves forced to discern truth from falsehood. In real life we do not find (as we do in Spenser's story) witches who look beautiful 364 days of the year and ugly one day, but we do encounter malicious and evil people who conceal their moral ugliness when they find it advantageous to do so.

Only in Spenser's poem do people go to a place called the Schoolhouse of Faith, where they meet characters named Fidelia, Speranza, and Charissa; but in our world people do experience the new life of faith in Christ and attain the virtues of faith, hope, and charity. In the most famous episode in the *Faerie Queene,* Spenser places his hero in a garden called "the Bower of Bliss." The journey into the bower represents a temptation to excess, and although this is not the form that temptation takes in everyday life, C. S. Lewis is right when he says that "despite the apparent remoteness of his scenes, . . . the houses and bowers and gardens of the *Faerie Queene* . . . are always at hand."[18]

The same principle can be illustrated from broad categories of literature. In real life, lovers do not speak in rhyme, nor do they actually say or do the things that love poets imagine them doing. But people do fall rapturously in love and say things they would not otherwise say. In real life people do not perform the heroic feats that they perform in epics, but in real life there are such things as heroism and courage and perseverance. Newspapers do not carry stories like that of Homer's Odysseus, who spent seven years on the shore of Calypso's island crying for his home and wife, but there are people around us who resist temptations that would destroy their faithfulness to home and spouse.

Poetry as a Lens to Reality

There is an additional side to literature that will justify my claim that the imagination is a "lie" that tells the truth. The most basic ingredient in poetry is metaphor—an implied comparison between two things. A metaphor is always a lie at the literal level, inasmuch as it asserts something that is not literally true.

Consider these specimens from the Old Testament Psalms: "the LORD God is a sun and shield" (Psalm 84:11); "their teeth are spears and arrows, their tongues sharp swords" (Psalm 57:4); "the LORD is my chosen portion and my cup" (Psalm 16:5); "pride is their necklace" (Psalm 73:6). None of these statements is literally true. God is not really a sun or shield or portion of land or cup. You have never seen a person whose teeth are spears and arrows. Nor can anyone wear pride as a necklace. These are literal falsehoods.

Do they express truth? Yes they do. These metaphors are a lens through which we can contemplate the truth about God and people. In each instance, the thing to which a comparison is made possesses qualities that are true of the poet's actual subject. What we call "poetic license" is a form of fiction, just as surely as a made-up story. The prevalence of such figurative language in the Bible should leave us with no doubt that the imagination and its fictions can be a way of grasping reality and truth.

Music and Painting as a Window to Reality

What I have said about literature applies equally to music and the visual arts. They, too, use the imaginary to capture truth. For illustration, I turn to how a poet, a composer, and a painter used their imaginations to portray the sin of lust.

The medieval Catholic poet Dante told a fictional story about his journey through hell, where he observed various sins being punished. When Dante reaches the circle of the lustful, he sees shades being ceaselessly blown about by a wind (*The Inferno,* Canto 5).

The Russian composer Tchaikovsky transposed that piece of literary fiction into music in his *Fantasia on Francesca Da Rimini*. The piece uses rushing scales, tortured phrases for the stringed instruments, and violent exclamations for the brasses and woodwinds to create a continuous musical tension that quickly produces physical discomfort.

The English painter William Blake captured the same quality of uncontrolled motion in a painting based on Dante's story. He pictures a group of human figures moving through the air in a white stream-like flow. To heighten the effect of movement, the stream forms a circular loop.

At a literal level, all three artists have created an imaginary "lie." Lust is not really a wind that never ceases blowing. It is not literally rushing string music. Nor does anyone believe that hell is a stream of figures in constant motion. But these artistic "lies" are a window through which we understand something of the nature of lust. Lust is like a wind in the way in which it grabs control of a person's feelings and governs his or her behavior.

And as for the sense of physical discomfort these works produce in an audience, what could better suggest the revulsion that the sin itself produces and the nature of God's eternal punishment of sin in hell? The constructs of the artistic imagination, said the eighteenth-century critic Samuel Johnson, are not "mistaken for realities, but . . . bring realities to mind."[19]

For one more example, consider the famous lithograph by Edvard Munch (reproduced on p. 118), which also exists in a painted version.

In real life we will never see a face exactly like this. Does the picture express recognizable truth? It sums up a whole modern trend of existential despair. The piece is entitled *The Shriek,* and the painter wrote under the lithograph, "I felt the great scream through nature."[20] The loss of meaning in many people's lives here takes the sensory form of a sexless, emasculated figure with a skull-like face. Its twisted torso merges with the environment and loses its identity as a human form.

Are the Arts Escapist?

If the imagination produces art that differs from waking reality, should we not charge it with being escapist? The charge is often made and deserves to be taken seriously. Let us begin by noting what C. S. Lewis has said about literature:

> Now there is a clear sense in which all reading whatever is an escape. It involves a temporary transference of the mind from our actual surroundings to things merely imagined or conceived. This happens when we read history or science no less than when we read fictions. All such escape is from the same thing; immediate, concrete actuality. The important question is what we escape to.[21]

This is very enlightening. Entering the world of the artistic imagination is on an equal footing with reading *Time* magazine or watching the television news.

When, then, do these activities deserve the stigma of being called escapist? The test is very simple: If they alert us to

The Shriek (1895) by Edvard Munch
Collection, The Museum of Modern Art, New York. Matthew T. Mellon Fund.[22]

actual reality and make us better able to cope with it, they are not escapist. If, on the other hand, there is no significant connection between the world we temporarily enter and the world of our daily lives, we can legitimately speak of escapism. If reading literature or attending a concert or visiting an art gallery sends us back to life with a renewed understanding of it and zest for it they are certainly not escapist activities. The Catholic fiction writer Flannery O'Connor once commented, "I'm always highly irritated by people who imply that writing fiction is an escape from reality. It is a plunge into reality. . . ."[23]

It would be a mistake to think that literature or art that is highly unrealistic or unlifelike in its conventions is, at the level of its real subject, remote from human experience. And realistic literature or art that is close to the external appearances of life often has little significant relationship to actual human experience. The typical television detective mystery story is utterly realistic, but at what point does it touch upon the significant issues of life? By comparison, Chaucer's story about a talking rooster and hen ("The Nun's Priest's Tale") is in no sense escapist, despite all its fantasy, because it captures the essence of marital discord stemming from temperamentally opposite personalities.

Often it is the most obviously fantastic literature that touches most powerfully and at the most points on actual experience. In his classic essay entitled "On Fairy-Stories," J. R. R. Tolkien observes that "fairy-stories deal largely . . . with simple or fundamental things." It was in fairy stories that Tolkien first sensed the wonder of such things "as stone, and wood, and iron; tree and grass; house and fire; bread and wine."[24] In a similar vein, C. S. Lewis could claim that a fantasy story with animals as characters (*The Wind in the Willows*) sent him back to the real world with a renewed understanding of it because the story presented such realities as "food, exercise, friendship, the face of nature, even (in a sense) religion. . . . The whole story, paradoxically enough, strengthens our relish for real life. This excursion into the preposterous sends us back with renewed pleasure to the actual."[25]

The role of the imaginary in our lives can be clarified if we stop to think about the most universal form of imagining—the fantasy world in which we spend some time living every day. Our fantasy world is a make-believe world that we enter through our mind or imagination. What are our fantasies like? They differ from everyday reality, but they are made up of the materials of actual life. Our fantasies serve two basic functions: They allow us to compensate for the deficiencies of real life, and they enable us to cope with the problems of real life by letting us deal with them at a safe distance. In both cases, our excursions into an imaginary world have the potential to help us master life.

The function of the artistic imagination is similar. At the level of physical existence, the world of the imagination is an escape. But its connections with life are so vital that we can become better equipped for life by immersing ourselves in art.

Thinking Christianly About the Imagination

> The Christian . . . is free to have imagination. This too is our heritage. The Christian is the one whose imagination should fly beyond the stars.
>
> Francis Schaeffer, *Art and the Bible*

Christians have much to learn about the uses of the imagination. For one thing, they need to respect the primacy of the imagination in art. They need to build their practice as artists and audiences on the best aesthetic theory that is available. Modern aesthetic theory and practice are based on the imagination as the key to everything else. The imaginary quality of the arts has long been suspect in some Christian circles. I do not see why it should be. Why should Christians feel more comfortable with biography than fiction or fantasy, or with realism in painting rather than impressionism, or with a newspaper rather than a novel? Jesus told fictional stories. The Bible is filled with poetry and metaphor and with imaginary pictures of reality. If we doubt that the imagination can be a vehicle for the truth, we need only read the Old Testament prophets and the New Testament book of Revelation.

When we turn from the Bible to the Christian world today, we cannot help but be struck by the contrast. We rarely trust the power of metaphor or fiction or paint on canvas or musical sound to express the truth. And when Christians do respect the voice of the imagination, they have a tendency to reduce art to realism. The more realistic a painting or story is, the better it is, runs this line of argument. In the process, we settle for some decidedly mediocre and inferior art. After all, works that never violate external reality frequently say little that is significant about the issues of life, while art that is highly imaginary can touch upon life powerfully at many points. Nor should we forget that the Christian world view extends reality far beyond the external physical world.

A fictional story about a missionary can be as true to a missionary's experience in the world as a missionary biography. A good fictional drama can be as true to human experience in the world as the evening news. A biography tells us what happened, while a fictional story tells us what happens (what is true generally). The movie *Chariots of Fire* was as true to the Christian nature of Eric Liddell's life as a biography is.

If Christians need to revive their confidence in the ability of the imaginary to express truth, they also need to trust the power of the concrete image. In Christian circles generally, the theological abstraction and outline have replaced the imaginative boldness of the writers of the Bible. Jesus did not distrust the images of the imagination. When asked to define neighbor, he told a story. He constantly spoke in image and metaphor: "I am the light of the world"; "you are the salt of the earth." The Bible repeatedly appeals to the intelligence through the imagination. So should we.

SUMMARY

The imagination has its unique way of expressing truth and reality. It uses a language of concrete images and sensations to capture a sense of life and human experience. The world of the artistic imagination is essentially fictional. It is an imaginary world governed by conventions that only partly correspond to things in real life. In works of art, we find the materials of life simplified, rearranged, and heightened.

Despite the unlifelike qualities of art, works of music, art, and literature nevertheless illuminate life as we know it. At the level of human issues, works of art are a window to reality. Like a lens that "distorts" in order to enable us to see something more clearly, the artistic imagination creates imaginary worlds that allow us to see reality with heightened clarity.

FURTHER READING

George MacDonald, "The Imagination: Its Functions and Its Culture," in *A Dish of Orts* (1908).

E. H. Gomrich, *Art and Illusion* (1956).

C. S. Lewis, *An Experiment in Criticism* (1961).

Northrop Frye, *The Educated Imagination* (1964).

Roger Cardinal, *Figures of Reality: A Perspective on the Poetic Imagination* (1981).

Leland Ryken, ed., *The Christian Imagination: Essays on Literature and the Arts* (1981).

Chapter 4, Notes

1. C. S. Lewis, *An Experiment in Criticism* (Cambridge: Cambridge University Press, 1965), p. 137.

2. Alvin A. Lee and Hope Arnott Lee, *The Garden and the Wilderness* (New York: Harcourt Brace Jovanovich, 1973), p. 45.

3. Oscar Wilde, "The Decay of Lying," as reprinted in *The Modern Tradition: Backgrounds of Modern Literature,* ed. Richard Ellmann and Charles Feidelson, Jr. (New York: Oxford University Press, 1965), p. 20.

4. This is an insight I wish I had been introduced to much earlier in my artistic experience than I was. The scholar who, more than anyone else, gave me a conviction of this truth was Northrop Frye, to whose work I was introduced during my first year of graduate study and whose book *The Educated Imagination* is the indispensable source on the subject of the present chapter. Later I found the literary criticism of C. S. Lewis (especially his book *An Experiment in Criticism*) reinforcing my awareness that the world of the artistic imagination is a world having its own identity and worth.

5. John Wilson, *One of the Richest Gifts* (Edinburgh: Handsel Press, 1981), p. 6.

6. Dorothy L. Sayers, "Towards a Christian Aesthetic," in *Unpopular Opinions* (London: Victor Gollanz, 1946), p. 37.

7. Northrop Frye, *The Educated Imagination* (Bloomington: Indiana University Press, 1964), pp. 27-28.

8. Flannery O'Connor, *Mystery and Manners,* ed. Sally and Robert Fitzgerald (New York: Farrar, Straus and Giroux, 1957), pp. 67, 91.

9. C. S. Lewis, "The Language of Religion," in *Christian Reflections* (Grand Rapids: William B. Eerdmans, 1967), p. 138.

10. Frye, pp. 89-90.

11. The quoted phrases come from a source to which my interpretation of Constable's landscape paintings owes much: Karl Kroeber, *Romantic Landscape Vision: Constable and Wordsworth* (Madison: University of Wisconsin Press, 1975), pp. 19-20.

12. C. S. Lewis, *An Experiment in Criticism,* pp. 79-81.

13. Leo Kirschbaum, "Marlowe's Faustus: A Reconsideration," in *Christopher Marlowe's Dr. Faustus: Text and Major Criticism,* ed. Irving Ribner (New York: Odyssey Press, 1966), pp. 90-91.

14. Elmer Edgar Stoll, *From Shakespeare to Joyce* (Garden City: Doubleday, Doran and Company, 1944), p. 50. See also Stoll's book *Art and Artifice in Shakespeare* (New York: Barnes and Noble, 1933).

15. Samuel T. Coleridge, *Biographia Literaria,* Chapter 4, as excerpted in the *Norton Anthology of English Literature*, fourth ed., ed. M. H. Abrams et al. (New York: W. W. Norton, 1979), 2:394.

16. Percy B. Shelley, *A Defence of Poetry*, in *Criticism: The Major Statements,* ed. Charles Kaplan (New York: St. Martin's Press, 1964), pp. 362, 377. Shelley's essay is one of the best sources on the imagination.

17. C. S. Lewis, *English Literature in the Sixteenth Century Excluding Drama* (Oxford: Oxford University Press, 1954), p. 341.

18. C. S. Lewis, *English Literature in the Sixteenth Century,* p. 391.

19. Samuel Johnson, "Preface to Shakespeare," in *Criticism: The Major Statements,* ed. Kaplan, p. 264.

20. Edvard Munch, as quoted in Reinhold Heller, *Edvard Munch: The Shriek* (New York: Viking, 1972), p. 87.

21. C. S. Lewis, *An Experiment in Criticism,* p. 68.

22. Edvard Munch, *The Shriek* (1895, signed 1896). Lithograph, printed in black, composition: 13 15/16 x 10″. Collection, The Museum of Modern Art, New York. Matthew T. Mellon Fund.

23. O'Connor, pp. 77-78.

24. J. R. R. Tolkien, "On Fairy-Stories," in *Essays Presented to Charles Williams,* ed. C. S. Lewis (Grand Rapids: William B. Eerdmans, 1966), p. 75.

25. C. S. Lewis, "On Stories," in *Essays Presented to Charles Williams,* p. 100.

Chapter 5

Art and Truth

The Roman author Horace bequeathed a great formula to aesthetic theory when he said that literature (and by extension, art in general) has a dual function: it is both delightful and useful. We have already explored the first of these. But wherein lies the usefulness of the arts?

This is a complicated question, but ultimately the usefulness of the arts depends on their relationship to truth. If the arts can be shown to add significantly to our fund of truth, then their usefulness is secure. But do the arts tell the truth?

There is no single answer to that question. It all depends on what we mean by "truth." It is the burden of this chapter to differentiate levels or types of truth in the arts and to sound a caution against simplistic claims of the truthfulness of the arts. To begin, we need to clear the ground of some common fallacies about the relationship between art and truth.

Art and Truth: Five Fallacies

> The basis of art is truth, both in matter and in mode.
>
> Flannery O'Connor, *Mystery and Manners*

> I could not doubt that the sub-Christian or anti-Christian values implicit in most literature did actually infect many readers.
>
> C. S. Lewis, "Christianity and Culture"

Fallacy 1: Art by Definition Tells the Truth

One of the commonest charges against the arts through the centuries is that they are not useful. Faced with the charge, defenders of the arts have tried to meet the utilitarian challenge on its own ground by arguing that the arts by their very nature "teach truth."

Usually this defense has rested on a confusion between ideational content and intellectual truth. Most art—and certainly all literature—contains an implicit intellectual content. Works of art make implied assertions about reality.

The attractiveness of simply calling that content "truth" is obvious: in one fell swoop we demolish the utilitarian objection to the arts. After all, if by their very nature the arts express truth, they are obviously useful to the human race. Despite its appeal, this view rests on a great fallacy.

The fact that art has ideational content does not mean that it expresses truth. The ideas in a work of literature or art might be untruthful. In fact, they frequently are. People who make the equation of ideational content with truth have been much too facile and undiscriminating in their claims that the arts teach truth.

Fallacy 2: All Art Tells the Truth

Even when defenders of the arts have not mistakenly equated ideas and truth, they have often extended their claims for truth in art far too broadly. All art, they claim, asserts a common truth that everyone can accept. We are told, for example, that "we may say of the greatest pagan and Christian poets that they 'are folded in a single party.'"[1]

The appeal of this approach, too, is easy to see: it gets around the perennial charge that the arts teach error, and it eliminates any need to discriminate between truth and error when we read a story or visit an art gallery. Once again, however, the fact that a theory is inviting does not make it true. To make unqualified claims that all works of art tell a common truth is to be guilty of a double fallacy.

From a Christian viewpoint (as well as others), the arts in general have not embodied the truth. To verify this, all we need to do is reflect on the values that the arts have offered for our approval. This is an entirely legitimate approach because the thematic content of art often consists of implied comments about human values.

C. S. Lewis, in one of his most outstanding essays, has observed that "the values assumed in literature have seldom been those of Christianity."[2] The value structure of most literature (and of the other arts) is what Lewis quite correctly calls "sub-Christian." He goes on to say, "Some of the principal values actually implicit in European literature were . . . (a) honour, (b) sexual love, (c) material prosperity, (d) pantheistic contemplation of nature, (e) Sehnsucht [longing] awakened by the past, the remote, or the (imagined) supernatural, (f) liberation of impulses."

One can, it is true, make a case for the relative accuracy of the scale of values espoused in literature as a whole. If we arrange values on a hierarchy ranging from the lowest to the highest, we can conclude, with Lewis, that literature as a whole records "man's striving for ends which, though not the true end of man (the fruition of God), have nevertheless some degree of similarity to it, and are not so grossly inadequate to the nature of man as, say, physical pleasure or money."

Still, this does not alter the case substantially. If the arts as a whole do not present a Christian view of values and, in fact, frequently contradict them, no automatic claims can be made for the arts as a teacher of truth.

That theory runs afoul of another fallacy as well. The arts as a whole are contradictory in the values by which they urge people to order their lives. When an artist in the classical tradition urges people to conduct their lives by their reason, the romanticist by their emotions, and the naturalist by their drives and impulses, and when the Christian, believing all of these faculties to be fallen, urges people to order their lives by the moral law of God, the resulting picture is contradictory. All of these value structures cannot be true.

We should therefore reject the following model of what happens in the arts:

art = truth → readers, viewers, listeners → life, world view

According to this model, we can simply accept works of art as expressing the truth. As individual consumers of the arts, we need only accept and apply the truth that we get from art to our own lives and world view. The important thing about the diagram is where the ultimate standard of truth is located, namely, art rather than the Bible.

This model is based on the fallacies noted earlier: The arts as a whole are contradictory in their value structure and therefore cannot simply be equated with truth, nor can a person simply obey these contradictory statements; the arts as a whole are nonbiblical or sub-Christian in their value system, so that a Christian is unable to make a simple acceptance of the arts as true.

Fallacy 3: The Usefulness of a Work of Art Consists of Its Abstract Ideas.

Faced with the charge of nonusefulness, apologists for the arts have found another fallacy attractive: by stressing the ideas in art, they have attempted to find a place for art at least equivalent to such "thought" disciplines as philosophy, psychology, sociology, and even theology. In the process, the arts have invariably become the expendable stepchild of other disciplines.

To reduce works of art to their ideational content is to rob them of their power, distort their true nature, and make them finally unnecessary. If the ideas are the important thing in a work of art, we obviously do not need the work itself once we have deduced the ideas. To reduce a poem to its ideas, says C. S. Lewis, "is an outrage to the thing the poet has made for us. I use the words *thing* and *made* advisedly." A work of literature "is not merely logos (something said) but poiema (something made)."[3] In their landmark book *Understanding Poetry,* Cleanth Brooks and Robert Penn Warren made a similar comment about Longfellow's poem "A Psalm of Life:"

> If . . . advice is what the poem has to offer us, then we can ask why a short prose statement of this good advice is not as good as, or even better than, the poem itself. But even the people who say they like the poem because of its "message" will usually prefer the poem to a plain prose statement.[4]

Who would be willing to substitute the thrill of actually experiencing one's favorite novel or movie for a one-page summary of the ideas embodied in it?

Artists themselves are equally insistent that a work of art communicates more than ideas. Fiction writer Flannery O'Connor has said that "the whole story is the meaning, because it is an experience, not an abstraction."[5] When the composer Schumann played a new composition and was asked what it meant, he replied, "It means this," and played the piece again.[6] Musicians overwhelmingly agree that music begins where words leave off.

It is no wonder that T. S. Eliot insisted that literature should be approached as literature and "not defined in terms of something else,"[7] that is, not as philosophy, sociology, psychology, theology, or history, but as an art form with its own ways of expressing truth.

Fallacy 4: The Usefulness of the Arts Depends on the Truthfulness of Their Philosophic Viewpoint.

Wrong again. As I will argue more fully later, there are many benefits to be gained from works of art that do not agree with what the viewer, listener, or reader accepts as truth. Works of art clarify the human situation to which the Christian faith speaks, even if their interpretation of reality is wrong. Works of art also serve as a catalyst to thought, even if they assert falsehood. And they are certainly an invaluable index to the thinking and feeling of non-Christians who live around us.

Fallacy 5: Works of Art Make No Truth Claims.

This is exactly the opposite approach from the fallacies I have noted thus far. It, too, would lead us astray in our exploration of how art relates to truth. An influential modern attitude that sometimes goes under the title of "art for art's sake" has denied that works of art make claims to truth. They are a purely aesthetic phenomenon, says this theory. While this may be true of nonrepresentational art and music, it is not true of literature, nor of most art and music.

How do we know that works of art make claims to truth? We can begin by considering the nature of the arts themselves. The subject of the arts is human experience and human perception of the world. Like other people, artists have a view of the world and of what is important in it. Therefore, whenever writers set pen to paper or painters put brush to canvas, they are asserting something about the world and people. Those implied assertions deserve to be treated just as seriously as we treat the ideas of philosophers and theologians.

A second thing we should do is listen to the people who produce art. Do they intend to tell the truth? They do. Novelist Joyce Cary has written,

> All writers . . . must have, to compose any kind of story, some picture of the world, and of what is right and wrong in that world. And the great writers are obsessed with their theme.[8]

The French sculptor Auguste Rodin said that the artist's task is to reveal "the hidden truths beneath appearances."[9] John Constable considered landscape painting to be a science, and he claimed that the function of the painter was to instruct and guide the vision of others.[10]

Finally, as consumers of art we operate on the premise that works of art embody meanings and need to have their claims to truth assessed. That artists intend meanings is simply one of the interpretive assumptions with which we approach the arts. If we saw words scrawled on a rocky cliff we would try to determine their meaning on the assumption that someone wrote them there for a purpose. If we should happen to learn, however, that the markings were the result of erosion, we would no longer try to read the markings for their verbal meaning. We do not approach works of art as though they were caused by erosion. We assume an intended meaning.

One aesthetic theorist speaks of "the rule of significance" as the primary convention of literature. We should read works of literature, he claims, "as expressing a significant attitude to some problem concerning man and/or his relation to the universe."[11] And in the best essay on the subject, Gerald Graff argues that there are two good reasons for "accepting the claim that literary works make assertions. Briefly put, the arguments are that authors intend assertions and readers can scarcely help looking for them."[12]

The Arts as a Repository of Human Values

> The arts are a most important carrier of knowledge. . . . We derive from them an insight into human experience, and through that into human values, which to my mind makes this one of the fundamental modes of human knowledge.
>
> J. Bronowski, *The Visionary Eye*

Do the arts tell the truth? That question must receive multiple answers because there are four different levels of truth in art.

At the broadest possible level, the truth of the arts consists in what they tell us about human values. The arts are the most accurate index we have to basic human values—to human convictions about what is worth having, what is not important, and what matters most in life.

Whenever I visit an art gallery, I leave with two dominant impressions. One is the sheer devotion of the human race to artistry, craftsmanship, beauty, and creativity. The second is a renewed understanding of human values. What is most important to people? A walk through an art gallery tells us. Browsing through an anthology of literature produces a similar effect. The table of contents alone tells us what it means to be human. It alerts us to the preoccupations and values of the human race through the centuries.

The Arts as a Road Map to Essential Humanity

The arts, then, tell us the truth about foundational human experience. Simply at the level of content, they keep calling us back to bedrock humanity; they put us in touch with the great, universal images of life. Those images tend to fall into two categories, one ideal, the other unideal. What they give us, therefore, is a picture of human longings on the one hand and fears on the other. The arts tell us the truth about what people want and do not want.

The arts are the most accurate index to human preoccupations, values, fears, and longings that we possess. If we wish to know what it means to be a human in this world, we can go to the stories, poems, songs, and paintings of the human race.

The arts are a great organizing force in human life. In the rush of daily living, things become a meaningless blur of details. It is all too easy for the essential to become obscured by the immediate. The arts are therapeutic and corrective: They at once recall us to the essential patterns and values of life.

The reason we can often learn more from art than from life is that the arts awaken us to the central realities of living. A work of art is a distillation of experience in which the irrelevancies are stripped away. Novelist Joyce Cary puts it this way:

> The reader is often aware of learning more about the world from a book than he gets from actual experience, not only because in the book he is prepared to find significance in events that mean nothing in life, but because those events in the book are related to each other in a coherent valuation which sets them in ordered relation of importance, and this can reveal to him in what had seemed the mere confusion of his daily affairs new orders of meaning.[13]

The truth that the arts give us, we might add, is rarely new information; it tends to be a bringing to consciousness of what we already know but to which we have become oblivious in daily living.

This, then, is one level of truth in the arts: truthfulness to the fears, longings, and values of the human race. The arts possess such truth regardless of the philosophic or religious perspective of an artist.

A Type of Truth that Christians Need

Is this a valuable type of truth? Yes it is, especially for Christians. Christians are a minority within their culture and are subject to the tendencies of all minority groups: a sense of alienation from culture as a whole, an in-group mentality and vocabulary, an inclination to concentrate on how they are different from others and to slight what they share with them, a "we-they" outlook on the world. To this we should add that some forms of Christianity become so otherworldly that they have an unbiblical scorn for what is human and earthly.

The arts can serve as a helpful corrective to these tendencies. They put us in touch with ground level human experience and make us a member of the human race. One of the most common failures of sermons and Bible studies and Sunday school classes is that their vision is confined within the four walls of the church. Biblical truth needs to be related to life in the world. It was never meant to exist in isolation from the believer's experience in life and culture. Living with the arts is one way of staying in touch with the human race. To realize our full humanity is not frivolous. It is one of the things that God created us to do and something that he confirmed when he became human.

There is also a social and moral reason for Christians to value the truth about humanity that the arts can impart. Christian responsibility to society is both humanitarian and evangelistic. At the heart of the gospel is the belief that it is not enough to leave the human race where it is. In order to help people, however, we must understand their basic nature and needs, their longings and fears.

TRUTHFULNESS TO REALITY

> Fiction is an art that calls for the strictest attention to the real. . . . The writer should never be ashamed of staring.
>
> Flannery O'Connor, *Mystery and Manners*

Leaving aside nonrepresentational art (art that is purely artistic and makes no claim to represent some aspect of human experience or the external world), we can say that the subject matter of the arts is human experience. Within their chosen artistic medium, artists aim to capture some recognizable human experience. It might be an emotion, an event, a perception of the external world, a relationship. Whenever a writer or composer or visual artist accurately captures the contours of human experience or external reality, we can say that the resulting work of art is true to reality

The second level of truth in art, then, is representational truth. It consists of truthfulness to the way things are in the world. Art is capable of such truth because artists are, among other things, sensitive observers of reality.

Art as an Incarnation of Truth

To recognize how the arts express this type of truth will require that we grant their unique way of embodying truth. The arts do not state truth abstractly and propositionally. They embody it in concrete form.

We all know about theoretic or conceptual truth. It is stated in the form of abstract propositions, such as "people are sinful beings" or "the family is a basic human institution." But this is not the only way in which we understand and express the truth. Contemporary psychology has given us such terms as "preconceptual sensing" and "nonverbal cognition" and "the right side of the brain" to identify the type of nonpropositional truth by which we also live and communicate.

The knowledge that the arts give us is different from the ideas that the "thought disciplines" give us. The latter work largely by abstraction and labels. These are essential to our mastery of the world. But the trouble with these abstract labels—

table, love, sun, death, rose—is that they never do justice to the reality of those things. They help us to organize and quantify experience, but they do not capture the quality of experience.

The truth that the arts give us is different from that of the scientific and intellectual disciplines. The artist aims to present human experience, not simply to theorize abstractly about it. The truth that the arts give us is a "living through" of an imaginative experience. It is an experiential knowledge or truth.

Consider the parable that Jesus told when asked to define *neighbor:*

> A man was going down from Jerusalem to Jericho, and he fell among robbers, who stripped him and beat him, and departed, leaving him half dead. Now by chance a priest was going down that road; and when he saw him he passed by on the other side. So likewise a Levite, when he came to the place and saw him, passed by on the other side. But a Samaritan, as he journeyed, came to where he was; and when he saw him, he had compassion, and went to him and bound up his wounds, pouring on oil and wine; then he set him on his own beast and brought him to an inn, and took care of him (Luke 10:30-34).

Jesus here refuses to give an abstract or propositional definition of *neighbor*. Instead he puts the listener through an experience. This is how the arts operate: They incarnate meaning in concrete form. With Jesus' parable, we do not need a definition of *neighbor;* the story shows what it means to be a neighbor.

The truth that works of art communicate is experiential, concrete, sensory. A survey of why college students read literature reveals that

> students value literature as a means of enlarging their knowledge of the world, because through literature they acquire not so much additional information as additional experience. . . . Literature provides a living-through, not simply knowledge about: not the

> fact that lovers have died young and fair, but a living-through of Romeo and Juliet; not theories about Rome, but a living-through of the conflicts in Julius Caesar. . . .[14]

For "literature" in that statement we could easily substitute "art" and "music."

Images of External Reality

How can a painting or piece of music or poem express truth if it avoids propositional statements? I suggest that we allow some examples to answer that question.

Look again at the Constable landscape painting on page 24. Although it differs from a photograph of the same landscape, it makes us aware of certain truths about reality—the beauty of nature, God's intended harmony between people and nature, the persistence of time and human development. We "know" these realities as we look at the painting even if we do not focus our consciousness of them into abstract ideas. A good piece of advice is Flannery O'Connor's observation that "the longer you look at one object, the more of the world you see in it."[15]

Literature pictures external reality in words. Although it cannot rival the visual effects of painting when describing nature, it can use the resources of language to add a more specific note of human response to a landscape. Consider the following description of sunrise on the Mississippi River by Mark Twain:

> The dawn creeps in stealthily; the solid walls of black forest soften to gray, and vast stretches of the river open up and reveal themselves; the water is glass-smooth, gives off spectral little wreaths of white mist; there is not the faintest breath of wind, nor stir of leaf; the tranquillity is profound and infinitely satisfying. . . . Well, that is all beautiful; soft and rich and beautiful; and when the sun gets well up, and distributes a pink flush here and a powder of gold

> yonder and a purple haze where it will yield the best effect, you grant that you have seen something that is worth remembering.[16]

The truth that such a passage conveys is incarnated in the description itself. No propositional statement of theme—for example, "sunrise is beautiful and awe-inspiring"—does justice to the meaning of the passage. It is easy to see, too, why the English novelist Joseph Conrad wrote, "My task . . . is, by the power of the written word to make you hear, to make you feel—it is, before all, to make you *see*."[17]

The Truth about Human Feelings

If the arts are adept at expressing experiential truth about the external world, they are also good at capturing the inner weather of human emotions. This is preeminently true of music. Music does not always ask to be tied to the realm of human experience in the world, but when it does, it usually expresses an emotion or an emotional response to reality.

This is often true of painting as well. Constable said that "painting is with me but another word for feeling."[18] Or consider again Edvard Munch's lithograph entitled "The Shriek" (p. 118). What is the nature of the truth that it communicates? Not the literal truth of what we see in an actual landscape. Instead, it expresses an emotional experience of emptiness, despair, loss of human identity, and alienation. These feelings are expressed in visual, sensory form, in keeping with the medium of visual art. This, surely, is what existential despair feels like.

Literature is equally adept at expressing the truth about human feelings. The following sonnet ("Silent Noon") by Dante Gabriel Rossetti captures an emotional experience—the contentment and security of happy romantic love:

> Your hands lie open in the long fresh grass—
> The finger-points look through like rosy blooms
> Your eyes smile peace. The pasture gleams and glooms
> 'Neath billowing skies that scatter and amass.

All round our nest, far as the eye can pass,
  Are golden kingcup-fields with silver edge
  Where the cow-parsley skirts the hawthorn-hedge.
'Tis visible silence, still as the hour-glass.
Deep in the sun-searched growths the dragonfly
Hangs like a blue thread loosened from the sky:
  So this winged hour is dropt to us from above.
Oh! clasp we to our hearts, for deathless dower,
This close-companioned inarticulate hour
  When twofold silence was the song of love.

What is all that nature description doing in a poem about love? we might ask. It is there to contribute to the emotional truth of the poem. Only as the poem creates a mood of beauty, security, and contentment can it embody that truth.

Human Character and Society

Another area in which the arts express truth powerfully is human character and society. Stories are a particularly effective medium for capturing these realities. They portray characters in action, confronting the world, expressing human character, grappling with social problems and moral dilemmas. Homer's *Odyssey,* for example, leads a reader to contemplate important dimensions of home, the social order, justice, romantic love, and human temptation. Aldous Huxley's *Brave New World* explores in narrative form the horrors of the technological society.

In stories such as these, it is the actual presentation of the subject that constitutes the truth of the work. Even when the subject of a literary work is something as intangible as "evil" (as in Shakespeare's *King Lear*) or "guilt" (as in Shakespeare's *Macbeth*), literature allows a reader to "know" its subject as a concrete experience, not as a philosophic proposition. It is precisely when we state the truth of a work in the form of a proposition that we realize how much of that truth gets lost when compared with the impact of the total work.

Art and music, too, express the truth about human character and society. In Kuhnau's sonata on the David and Goliath story, musical sounds capture human arrogance and courage. Portrait paintings usually capture some aspect of human character. Narrative paintings that portray human activity in a social setting convey an experiential understanding of human endeavor or social ideals that leads us to assent that "this is true to the way things are."

Spiritual Reality

The arts can also tell us the experiential truth about spiritual reality, as a later chapter will explore in more detail. Music like Handel's *Messiah* uses sound combined with words to capture the truth about redemption. Rembrandt's painting of the prodigal son expresses the truth of God's forgiveness in picture form. John Bunyan captures it in the story of pilgrim's journey through a physical landscape.

Why Truthfulness to Human Experience is Important for Christians

At this second level of truth in art, Christians need to take special note of some things. Given their theological bent, Christians have often operated on the premise that the only truth that matters is abstract or philosophical truth. They have assumed that a person's world view, including their own, consists only of ideas. This is a dangerous fallacy.

The truth by which people live is partly a truth expressed in images, symbols, stories, and characters. People are as much image-perceiving creatures as they are rational ones. A noted theologian has said that "we are far more image-making and image-using creatures than we usually think ourselves to be." We "are guided by images in our minds," he states, adding that the human creature "is a being who grasps and shapes reality . . . with the aid of great images, metaphors, and analogies."[19]

What are the implications of this? If we ourselves wish to express the truth to others, we must utilize all the means we have at our disposal. The arts are one of these means. I find a rather disturbing gap between young people and older generations on this score. Young people are generally attuned to the visual, aural, and literary media of their surrounding culture, and they show by their very actions that these media convey a tremendous amount of meaning to people who have the right "antennae" to receive it. Older people seem so often to believe that ideas are the only vehicle for truth.

We also become good candidates for self-deception when we act as though our world view consists solely of abstract ideas. In fact, we are influenced by images at least as much as ideas. That is why advertising has such a strong influence on people. We may assent to the proposition that the true end of life is not to make money and accumulate possessions, but if our minds are filled with images of big houses and fancy clothes, our actual behavior will run in the direction of materialism. We may theoretically believe in the ideals of chastity and faithful wedded love, but if our minds are filled with images of exposed bodies and songs that recommend the liberation of our impulses, our sexual behavior will have a large admixture of lust in it.

It worries me to see a noted Christian philosopher assert that "only propositions can be true" and then to ask scornfully, "How could a nocturne or one of Rodin's sculptures be true?"[20] To view the matter thus is to write off a whole aspect of our culture that wields enormous influence in people's lives. A song or sculpture does, in fact, express the truth about reality in terms appropriate to a given art form. And people are influenced by that truth, whether they realize it or not.

General Truth in the Arts

> All great artists have a theme, an idea of life profoundly felt and founded in some personal and compelling experience. . . . The writer selects his facts. He arranges their order to suit his own conception of values, his own theme.
>
> Joyce Cary, *Art and Reality*

The first two levels of truth in the arts—truth about human values and representational truth about reality—are levels at which the artist's philosophic perspective makes little difference. It is in the very nature of art to express truth at those levels.

But artists do more than simply present human experience. They also interpret it. They see reality from their own perspective and mold their vision around their own opinions. The common way to express this is to say that works of art have one or more themes. They make implied comments about life.

Consider, for example, this poem by William Wordsworth:

> It is a beauteous evening, calm and free,
> The holy time is quiet as a Nun
> Breathless with adoration; the broad sun
> Is sinking down in its tranquilty;
> The gentleness of heaven broods o'er the Sea:
> Listen! the mighty Being is awake,
> And doth with his eternal motion make
> A sound like thunder—everlastingly.
> Dear Child! dear Girl! that walkest with me here,
> If thou appear untouched by solemn thought,
> Thy nature is not therefore less divine:
> Thou liest in Abraham's bosom all the year,
> And worship'st at the Temple's inner shrine,
> God being with thee when we know it not.

This is not simply an objective description of nature. Instead, we look at nature through the "filter" of the speaker's consciousness.

The first five lines are almost all response, with only a brief sketch of the external scene that is eliciting the response. These lines picture nature as positive, nurturing, healing—a "romantic" interpretation of nature that is far different from the modern "naturalistic" one. Then the speaker moves to a religious interpretation of the scene. He deifies nature with words like "mighty Being," "eternal motion," "everlastingly." Finally he offers a perspective on children as intuitively enjoying communion with God and nature, while adults do so only occasionally and as a result of "solemn thought."

Except for nonrepresentational art and music, virtually every work of art, music, or literature makes an implied interpretation of reality. We can arrange these themes on a scale or continuum from the very general to the more specific. On one side of the scale, we can state the themes of artistic works in such a general form that virtually anyone would agree with them, including Christians.

Stated in sufficiently general terms, the poem by Wordsworth can be said to express several important themes. One is that nature is a source of beauty and psychic health in human experience. Nature, moreover, is viewed in a religious light. So are people: Both the speaker in the poem and his daughter who is on the seashore with him are pictured as experiencing communion with the divine.

Even nonrepresentational art conveys a sense of life. At this end of the thematic spectrum, artistic perspective consists of such attitudes as order or lack of it, hope or despair, the presence or absence of a supernatural reality, meaning or futility.

When we interpret the arts in terms of their most universal and vaguely defined assertions, we are identifying what I call general truth (as distinct from ultimate truth and a world view, which I will discuss shortly). John Milton said that truth is like the body of Osiris, fragmented and scattered as a result of the Fall. As seekers after truth, our task is to collect pieces of the truth. We can make use of the scattered insights that artists put into their work, even though we might reject their ultimate vision of reality.

Without belittling these pieces of truth gleaned from the arts, it should also be evident that to remain at this level is to be content with a superficial understanding of what works of art are really saying. We do no service to either artists or consumers of art when we state the content of a work so generally that virtually everyone would agree with the assertion. Works of art usually offer very specific perspectives on the topics they portray. And part of the task of every artist is to build a total canon of work that expresses the whole truth as the artist sees it. This should propel us, then, to press the issue of truth in art to a fourth level.

ULTIMATE TRUTH AND WORLD VIEW IN ART

> The artist . . . can transmute . . . reality into the order of significant form only in accordance with what are his most fundamental beliefs about what is radically significant in life.
>
> Nathan A. Scott, "The Modern Experiment in Criticism: A Theological Appraisal"

At one end of the thematic scale, the implied assertions of works of art take the form of individual comments about life. At the other end, they pass from general truth to ultimate truth. That is, works of art also make comments about the fundamental beliefs and ultimate values of the artist. When molded into a coherent whole, moreoever, this vision can be called a world view.

Basic Premises about God, People, and the Universe

A world view consists of the basic beliefs or premises that someone makes about reality. It includes foundational principles about God, the person, nature, society, and the supernatural world. It is the intellectual "furniture" of an artist's mind.

These basic premises fall into three main categories, as follows:

1. Reality. What really exists?
2. Morality. What constitutes good and bad conduct?
3. Values. What is of worth in experience? What really matters?

These foundational assumptions add up to the artist's "world." Determining the ingredients of that intellectual and moral world is a large part of what we mean by a world view in a work of art. Flannery O'Connor has said that "it is from the kind of world the writer creates, from the kind of character and detail he invests it with, that a reader can find the intellectual meaning of a book."[21]

A Central Value

In addition to basic premises, a world view is built around a central value that gives meaning to everything else. The most helpful source on the subject is an out-of-print book by Richard Stevens and Thomas J. Musial.[22] According to their framework, a reader must make two assumptions about a work of literature: "First, he must assume that any world view has a central concept, or value. . . . Second, the reader must assume that all the other elements in the world view will derive their significance and worth from their relation to the central concept or value."

This means that the essential ingredient of a world view is a concept or value that integrates and gives meaning to all aspects of experience. The highest value might be God, a person (self, a specific individual, humanity in general), an institution (state, church, home), an abstract quality (love, truth, beauty, order, reason, emotion), or nature. Literary critic Nathan Scott speaks of a work's "ultimate concern" and about "some fundamental hypothesis about the nature of existence which . . . introduces structure and coherence . . . into the formless stuff of life."[23]

A theistic world view, for example, makes God supreme and central to all of life. To a person living by this world view, God is the ultimate reality and the one who integrates everything that exists. People are thus defined as creatures made by God. The self is viewed as the image of God. Moral goodness consists of doing God's will. Time and history are identified as the working out of God's purpose. The state is viewed as a divinely ordained social institution established by God. Knowledge, in a theistic world view, is the truth that God reveals, and reality itself is defined as God's creation. In short, a theistic world view is one in which God is the point of reference for all experience—the one who gives meaning and identity to every aspect of life.

Identifying a World View in Works of Art

A world view is a map of reality. It is the framework of beliefs, values, and images within which a person makes decisions and conducts the business of living. Someone has said that "every person carries within his head a mental model of the world—a subjective representation of reality."[24]

To identify a world view in works of art and in the total canon of an artist, we can ask a few questions that get at the heart of the matter. They include the following:

1. According to this work, what really exists? The physical world? A supernatural world? Moral qualities like goodness or love or courage? Do relationships among people or loyalties to institutions exist, or is only the individual regarded as real? What is true about human nature?

2. What is the highest value and integrating core in life?

3. How should life be lived? What constitutes the good life? What is good and bad moral behavior in people?

4. What brings human fulfillment or meaning? Virtue? Pleasure? Sex? Physical objects? Money? God?

5. What is assumed to be true about God, human nature and destiny, and the physical world?

For particular art forms, especially literature, the questions might be framed more specifically. In literature, for example, a reader should ask in each case what the characters in the story or poem (as well as the author) regard as really existing, elevate to the highest value, etc. Stories, moreover, have the ability to portray characters who undertake an experiment in living that comes to a certain end, and here especially, the question of world view emerges strongly.

The best rule to follow as a reader, viewer, or listener is to regard oneself as brought into an encounter—with characters, with the artist, with values, with basic premises about life. In this encounter, the artist is saying something about reality and values through his or her work. Reading the hidden or expressed signs is the best procedure to follow.

For example, what world view is implicit in the poem by Wordsworth quoted above? The fundamental premises about life include a belief in the existence of God, the value of nature, the worth of social bonds, and the possibility of human rapport with the divine. The world view is one that I would call pantheistic. Briefly put, pantheism equates God, people, and nature. This is what Wordsworth does in the poem. He deifies both nature and the little girl walking with him.

The Value of Knowing about World Views

A knowledge of various world views as we encounter them in works of art is a worthwhile knowledge for several reasons. To begin, it gives us a historical perspective. Such a perspective is important because it is necessary to know how we got where we are before we can truly understand our own civilization and culture, and even our own world view. We need a historical perspective because we cannot afford the naivete of beginning anew with each generation.

A second reason for concerning ourselves with the world views of art is that they help us understand people. The great world views are not simply historical specimens of a bygone age. They are enduring responses to permanent issues. A hedonistic or materialistic or humanistic world view articulated hundreds of years ago can help us understand a neighbor or acquaintance who lives by the same world view today.

Third, knowing the important world views gives us a knowledge of the alternatives by which we may order our lives. Anyone's world view should arise from considered and responsible deliberation, and this necessitates an awareness of alternatives. When Jesus told his potential followers to sit down and count the cost before placing him at the center of their lives, was he not saying that people should compare the Christian world view with the other values by which they might order their lives?

There is a sense in which everyone, regardless of his or her world view, shares an identical task—that of coming to an understanding of the truth about reality in an intelligent awareness of the alternatives. C. S. Lewis has written that "to judge between one ethos and another, it is necessary to have got inside both, and if literary history does not help us to do so it is a great waste of labour."[25] I wonder if young people who abandon their Christian faith after high school or college might not have been better able to withstand the appeals of a secular world view if they had explored the world views in art and literature more seriously when they had the chance to weigh them with a measure of intellectual detachment.

There is yet another value of studying world views and one that may hold particular appeal for a Christian. Interacting with the world views that we encounter in works of art affords an opportunity to exercise and expand an already formulated world view. That world view is given by God in the Bible and the incarnation of Christ. Often a person's knowledge of that revelation is enhanced by the study of Christian theology as it has been articulated by gifted people through the centuries. In no sense, however, does the Christian go to art to find his or her world view.

Studying the important world views increases a Christian's sense of discrimination as he or she compares the Christian world view with the world views expressed in the arts. The model of analysis that I am advocating is this (and should be contrasted to the one I rejected earlier):

		reader,		works
biblical truth	→	viewer,	→	of
		listener		art

That is, Christians find their world view in Christian revelation. They apply that world view to works of art and use it to measure the truthfulness of the world views they encounter there. The important aspect of the model is where the authority for truth and belief is located, namely, the Bible as God's reliable revelation.

This model implies at least two important principles. The first is that we assimilate works of art in terms of what we bring to them. Works of art test and bring out what we already believe. This is not a conclusion I have reached theoretically but one that I have come to as I listen to people talk about the literature they have read or paintings they have seen or music they have heard. It is also one of the best documented views of recent audience-centered theories of art. It is as true of the general population as it is of Christians.

Secondly, according to this model the value of the arts is not that they necessarily or always teach truth. This model claims instead that encountering world views in art is profitable because it presents for our understanding and analysis the significant world views of history, thereby supplying the material upon which the Christian mind can apply Christian principles to human experience. The value of the arts, in this view, is that they are a catalyst to thinking.

Common Grace and the Arts

> All truth is from God; and consequently, if wicked men have said anything that is true and just, we ought not to reject it; for it has come from God.
>
> John Calvin, commentary on Titus 1:12

A discussion of the doctrine of common grace would have been appropriate at many points in this book, but this is perhaps the best place to explore the topic. The test of whether a work of art expresses truth is not the Christian orthodoxy of the artist. We can say this with confidence on the basis of the doctrine of common grace.

That doctrine claims that God endows all people, believers and unbelievers alike, with some good qualities and with his natural blessings. One biblical foundation for the doctrine is that God created people in his own image. Human nature therefore has a capacity for goodness, truth, creativity, and so forth. With the Fall, God's image in people was marred and became directed to a bad end. But it was not destroyed (see Genesis 9:6).

The continuing presence of the image of God in people led John Calvin to comment,

> Whenever we come upon [truth] in secular writers, let that admirable light of truth shining in them teach

> us that the mind of man, though fallen and perverted from its wholeness, is nevertheless clothed and ornamented with God's excellent gifts. If we regard the Spirit of God as the sole fountain of truth, we shall neither reject the truth itself, nor despise it wherever it shall appear. . . . Those men whom Scripture calls "natural men" were, indeed, sharp and penetrating in their investigation of inferior things. Let us, accordingly, learn by their example how many gifts the Lord left to human nature even after it was despoiled of its true good.[26]

The gifts of the artist are something that God dispenses as he chooses. Christians are free to enjoy and be edified by works of art regardless of who produced them, just as they are free to eat food cooked by unbelievers and live in houses built by them. When Solomon needed artisans for the temple, he did not ask whether the workers were believers. He was interested in excellence and concluded that "there is no one among us who knows how to cut timber like the Sidonians" (1 Kings 5:6). And so Solomon wrote for help to the pagan king Hiram, who sent craftsmen to work on God's temple (1 Kings 5:18).

Passages in the New Testament point in the same direction and allow us to conclude that all people, including unbelievers, are capable of true moral insight and right conduct. Jesus, for example, said, "And if you do good to those who do good to you, what credit is that to you? For even sinners do the same" (Luke 6:33). In the opening chapters of Romans, Paul not only argues that everyone falls short of attaining his or her own moral standards, whatever they are, but also that unbelievers have the capacity, part ot the time, to "do by nature what the law requires . . . even though they do not have the law. They show that what the law requires is written on their hearts" (Rom. 2:14- 15).

If unbelievers are capable of this kind of right moral behavior, we should expect to find in some of their writings and art true insights into human experience. The relevance of the doctrine of common grace to the arts and to human culture in general is obvious; Christians can and should spend time reading and looking at and listening to the artistic expressions of non-Christians because we can find there, too, the truth and beauty of God.

TRUTH IN HAWTHORNE'S *THE SCARLET LETTER*

Literature . . . extends the range of vision, intellectual, moral, spiritual; it . . . sharpens our discernment.

Charles G. Osgood, *Poetry as a Means of Grace*

Nathaniel Hawthorne's classic *Scarlet Letter* will help us synthesize the four levels of truth in the arts. What types of truth do we encounter as we read this great story?

Truth about Human Values

To begin, the book presents for our contemplation some of the powerful archetypes of literature and human experience. At the center of the story are two important character types—Hester, the martyr figure who by her courage and love wins eventual victory over social prejudice, and Rev. Dimmesdale, the great sinner who at last stands purified before God. The plot likewise revolves around two great archetypes—crime and punishment, and redemption through suffering.

The story also makes memorable use of some of the master images of the human imagination. Light and darkness become virtual actors in the story and assume their common meanings of revelation and concealment, respectively. Equally prominent are the forest and the town, but Hawthorne introduces a complexity by making both of these images ambivalent. The forest is a place of both natural freedom and moral error (being the scene of Hester and Dimmesdale's adultery and of their ill-fated plan to run away from their moral responsibility). The town represents social oppression, but it is also where Hester and Dimmesdale achieve their redemption (though in different ways).

The Scarlet Letter is a vision of human longings and fears. As we participate vicariously in the action, we feel the natural human longing for love and compassion, for relief from guilt, for truth and honesty, for union with God, society, and nature. We are also made to feel what we most wish to avoid: alienation from God and people, social ostracism, hatred among people, guilt and its effects.

What kind of truth does the story embody? First of all, the truth about basic human values, longings, and aversions. The usefulness of reading the story lies partly in its ability to organize some familiar aspects of our own experience and to bring them to our consciousness so we can act upon them.

The Truth about Human Experience

The story also presents significant aspects of human experience for our contemplation. The knowledge that it offers is not a series of abstract propositions or logical arguments but a living through of an experience. What human experiences does the novel enable us imaginatively to recreate?

Hawthorne gave American literature its classic anatomy of human guilt (as Shakespeare did for English literature in *Macbeth*). In the account of Dimmesdale's life we experience the reality of the guilty conscience, the isolation and self-torture that it engenders, the psychological anguish and aberrations that it induces, the physical suffering that it produces in its extremities, as well as the self-defeating impulse to perpetuate it through concealment. In this story we "know" all this experientially, not as abstract theory. In fact, I am always somewhat shocked when I reach the last chapter (the fireside chat with the author, in effect) and read Hawthorne's moralizing statement, "Be true." What an emaciated piece of advice that is compared with the experiential reality of the story itself.

The story also embodies the truth about human isolation or alienation. Beginning with Hester's exposure on the scaffold in the second chapter, we are made to feel what it is like to be rejected by society. The ostracism that the village members extend to Hester's daughter Pearl pushes the phenomenon in a social direction as well.

Other truths are also rendered as experiential realities in the novel. To know what self-righteousness is, we can read Hawthorne's descriptions of the Puritans. To feel the reality of hatred, both for the perpetrator and the victim, we can vicariously enter the life of Chillingworth. For a new awareness of the truth about God's forgiveness, we can read the great confession scene that comprises the story's climax.

Pieces of General Truth

What I have said thus far has already suggested some of the general truths that the book embodies. As we read the story, we recover truths that are the common wisdom of the human race: that people need love, that society can be unjust and oppressive, that feeling can be a better moral guide than unfeeling reason, that (however) feeling without rational judgment can be destructive of both self and others, that hatred and concealed guilt are self-destructive, that sin produces consequences.

Stated in these general terms, the morality of the story is a point at which most people can meet on a common ground. More needs to be said, obviously, but Christians should value the moral consensus that they can often find with people generally. It is a blessing of God's common grace and the basis of morality in society. The arts are a great humanizing agent and (not surprisingly) one of the first things that tyrants and totalitarian governments try to suppress.

World View in *The Scarlet Letter*

One of the most helpful frameworks for grasping the world view embodied in a story is to look upon the characters in the story (especially the protagonist) as people who make an experiment in living—who undertake some course of action that exemplifies and tests the kind of life in which they believe. This way of reading considers literary characters as persons who pursue an experiment in living "to its final stages within a situation of ultimate meaning. Meaning in fiction is thus viewed as what an action leads to, results in, or implies."[27] If the experiment in living succeeds, the work can be said to affirm that world view.

If the experiment fails, the work denies that view of reality and by implication usually suggests an alternative.

Hawthorne's story is an especially useful work with which to illustrate how works of art embody world views because it gives equal treatment to three distinct world views: the Puritan, the romantic, and the Christian.

The Puritan Community

The Puritan community is the first group of characters whose world view emerges in the story. Theirs is a legalistic world view that exalts a moral code to supremacy. The narrator describes them as "a people amongst whom religion and law were almost identical" (chapter 2).[28] Their elevation of moral law to the integrating factor in their experience explains the Puritan community's tendency to view Hester Prynne, the mother of the illegitimate child Pearl, not as a person but as the violator of a moral code. For example, the impressive scene that opens the story describes how the community brings Hester out of the prison to the scaffold of the pillory in order to hold her up as an example of moral sin.

The same propensity to define Hester in terms of the moral code is underscored in chapter five when we read that through the years, "giving up her individuality, she would become the general symbol at which the preacher and moralist might point, and in which they might vivify and embody their images of woman's frailty and sinful passion. Thus the young and pure would be taught to look at her . . . as the figure, the body, the reality of sin." The same thing is established by the letter "A" that the Puritan community compels Hester to wear. The symbol recurs in the book more than once every two pages and is a running reminder of the community's practice of defining Hester as an adulteress, a violator of the moral code.

The members of the Puritan community also take their own identity from the moral code that dominates their world. The spectators of Hester's exposure on the scaffold identify themselves as the self-righteous keepers of the code. Governor Bellingham, Reverend Wilson, Reverend Dimmesdale, and the city magistrates are the official guardians of the moral law. Throughout the story these characters illustrate how the moral code is the mainspring of action and governing principle for the Puritan community.

How does the Puritan community's experiment in living fare in the story? It fails, to put it mildly. The Puritans are portrayed as uniformly unsympathetic. Hawthorne secures a negative reaction to them by making them the object of satiric attack throughout his story. He also pays his readers the compliment of assuming that their world view and morality are healthy, so that we have no hesitation in condemning the bigotry, self-righteousness, sadism, and unforgiving nature of the Puritans' legalism.

The final task is to evaluate the Puritan community's legalistic world view by the Christian standard. Too many readers equate the Puritans in Hawthorne's story with Christianity (and with the real Puritans of history, which Hawthorne never intended) and conclude that Hawthorne is condemning Christianity. This is surely an inaccurate interpretation. *The Scarlet Letter,* when it attacks Puritan behavior, is not attacking Christianity because Puritan behavior in the story is not Christian. The attitudes and behavior of the Puritan community are condemned by a truly Christian standard, as contained in the Bible and the life of Christ.

The Christian ideal is one that forgives and restores the sinner. Christ forgave the woman taken in adultery (John 8:2-11); he did not excuse her, nor did he neglect to call adultery a sin, as evidenced by the fact that he told the woman, "Go, and do not sin again" (v. 11). Paul reinforced the same ideal of forgiveness when he wrote, "Brethren, if a man is overtaken in any trespass, you who are spiritual should restore him in a spirit of gentleness. Look to yourself, lest you too be tempted. Bear one another's burdens, and so fulfil the law of Christ" (Galatians 6:1-2).

In a Christian world view, then, the standard by which people are called to order their lives is a forgiving God who calls people to forgive their fellow humans. The Puritans in Hawthorne's story have substituted for that standard a moral law that only condemns (rather than restores) the sinner.

The Romantic World View

The second world view dramatized in the story is the romantic world view. Romanticism, that intellectual movement that became dominant early in the nineteenth century and has been influential ever since, elevated emotion, impulse, and human freedom from all civilized restraints as the highest of all values. If there is a single term that covers this complex of values, it is nature.

Hester, as all the commentators point out, is the great exponent of romantic values in the story. As the narrator says, "For years past she had looked from this estranged point of view at human institutions, and whatever priests or legislators had established; criticizing all with hardly more reverence than the Indian would feel for the clerical band, the judicial robe, the pillory, the gallows, the fireside, or the church. The tendency of her fate and fortune had been to set her free" (chapter 18). The great conflict in romantic literature is the individual against society, and by that standard Hester is a thoroughgoing romantic heroine.

In the view of Hester, as also of critics who share her romantic values, Hester and Dimmesdale are the victims of society. If only they could escape from the restrictions of civilization and Christian morality, they would be free. This is exactly the view that Hester espouses in the climactic forest meeting with Dimmesdale when she urges their escape with these words: "Whither leads yonder forest-track? . . . Deeper it goes, and deeper, into the wilderness, less plainly to be seen at every step; until, some few miles hence, the yellow leaves will show no vestige of the white man's tread. There thou art free! . . . Or there is the broad pathway of the sea! . . . What hast thou to do with all these iron men, and their opinions?"

Hester's attitude toward the adultery also reveals her romantic impulse when she says to Dimmesdale, "What we did had a consecration of its own. We felt it so!" (chapter 17). This is the romantic attitude that feeling is the norm.

What becomes of the romantic world view in the story? Early in the story, when Hester and the Puritan community are the only antagonists on the scene, the Puritans appear in such an ugly light that for at least half of the story we sympathize rather completely with Hester and regard romantic values as the normative viewpoint in the work. But as the story progresses we come to readjust our view of what constitutes reality. Hawthorne has employed what one critic calls "the technique of the guilty reader,"[29] in which the author leads readers to sympathize initially with a character and viewpoint that the readers later come to see as wrong. Such a strategy involves readers directly in the moral action of the story, forcing them to become critics of their own moral responses. There is no more brilliant example of the technique than *The Scarlet Letter*.

One commentator has documented "the progressive moral dereliction of Hester" late in the story.[30] The reader is meant to sympathize with Hester in her suffering and in the human redemption that it wins for her in the community, but late in the story her romantic outlook is juxtaposed to a Christian world view and is shown to be lacking. Hawthorne does not allow his two protagonists to escape from a world of moral consequences into a world of amoral freedom.

In the climactic confession scene at the end of the story, it is not society that destroys Dimmesdale. We read that the Puritan community "remained silent and inactive spectators of the judgment which Providence seemed about to work." In fact, the Puritan society cannot have judged Dimmesdale because it is ignorant of his sins of adultery and hypocrisy.

The Christian World View

There is, finally, the Christian viewpoint in the story, embodied in Reverend Dimmesdale. Dimmesdale's quest throughout the story is for forgiveness and renewed communion with God and with his fellow humans. This quest reflects the Christian priority of values. Throughout the story, Dimmesdale sees his problem all too clearly: He must be forgiven by God and must make a public confession of his sins of adultery and hypocrisy. James's statement, "Confess your sins to one another . . . that you may be healed" (5:16), is the great truth dramatized in the final salvation of Dimmesdale.

The Christian world view, which places the Christian God of forgiveness at the center of reality, emerges as the normative viewpoint at the end of the story with Dimmesdale's public confession, one of the greatest climaxes in all of literature. In that scene, Dimmesdale sees himself not simply as the violator of a social code, as the romanticist would have it, but in a relationship to God. "God's eye beheld it!" shouts Dimmesdale regarding his sins of adultery and hypocrisy. Furthermore, Dimmesdale espouses a Christian view of reality when he asserts that his confession and the renewed communion with God that it brings are the highest values that he can attain. As he mounts the scaffold, he turns to Hester and asks, "Is not this better than what we dreamed of in the forest?" And Hester, the true romanticist who had conceived of happiness as escape from civilized restraints, replies, "I know not! I know not!"

Why, in Dimmesdale's view, is it better to make a public confession of sin than to escape? Because in his world view, forgiveness of sin is the highest state that a person can achieve. It is a wholly Christian view of things. That, incidentally, explains why Dimmesdale says in his moment of exposure, "Thanks be to Him who hath led me hither!" and why he calls his confession an act of "triumphant ignominy."

To the romanticist Hester, the adultery had "a consecration of its own." Dimmesdale takes the Christian view toward moral sin and says regarding the adultery, "We forgot our God. . . we violated our reverence for the other's soul." In his concluding words, which resolve the plot of the entire story, Dimmesdale repeatedly defines his quest in life in terms of his relationship to God, with forgiveness and salvation as the highest values: "God . . . hath proved his mercy, most of all, in my afflictions. By giving me this burning torture to bear upon my breast! . . . By bringing me hither, to die this death of triumphant ignominy before the people. Praised be his name! His will be done! Farewell!" Dimmesdale ends his life praising God, and therein lies the key to the story's final meaning.

Someone writes regarding this conclusion, "Thus in his profoundest character-creation, and in the resolution of his greatest book, Hawthorne has employed the Christian thesis, 'Father, not my will, but thine be done.' "[31] Someone else correctly notes that "the protagonist of the novel is Arthur Dimmesdale and . . . the progress of the novel is the working out of Dimmesdale's redemption."[32] "The last scene on the scaffold," notes yet another critic, "is a complete vision of salvation."[33] Christian conversion has never been portrayed with greater conviction than in this great chapter of Hawthorne's novel.

The story ultimately affirms the Christian world view and contains within itself the antidote to the Puritan and romantic world views. As might be expected, critics with romantic values themselves have not read the novel this way.[34] But critics with Christian sensitivities have gotten the point. As one of them has said, "More than any other writer of his time, Hawthorne was a God-centered writer. He was innately religious, as his profound reverence for the mysteries of Christianity demonstrates."[35]

SUMMARY

The arts can embody truth in four different ways. The arts tell us the truth about human preoccupations, values, longings, and fears. Art is also true to life when it adheres to the reality principle—when it accurately pictures the contours of external or inner reality.

Because artists interpret the experiences that they present, the truthfulness of art can also be assessed at the level of perspective or slant on life. Considered in very general terms, the ideas in works of art often constitute truthful insights into life. At its most specific, the intellectual content of works of art consists of a world view—basic premises about reality, morality, and values, as well as a central integrating value that gives coherence to all of life.

Works of art do not automatically tell the truth at every level. But they always have a high potential to tell us the truth at one or more levels.

FURTHER READING

Flannery O'Connor, *Mystery and Manners* (1957).

John W. Dixon, *Form and Reality: Art Communication* (1957).

Joyce Cary, *Art and Reality: Ways of the Creative Process* (1958).

Roland M. Frye, *Perspective on Man: Literature and the Christian Tradition* (1961).

Rene Huyghe, *Art and the Spirit of Man* (1962).

Leland Ryken, ed., *The Christian Imagination: Essays on Literature and the Arts* (1981).

James W. Sire, *The Joy of Reading: A Guide to Becoming a Better Reader* (1978).

Chapter 5, Notes

1. Douglas Bush, "Tradition and Experience," in *Literature and Belief*, ed. M. H. Abrams (New York: Columbia University Press, 1958), p. 52.

2. C. S. Lewis, "Christianity and Culture," in *Christian Reflections* (Grand Rapids: William B. Eerdmans, 1967), pp. 12-36; reprinted in *The Christian Imagination: Essays on Literature and the Arts*, ed. Leland Ryken (Grand Rapids: Baker, 1981), pp. 23-36.

3. C. S. Lewis, *An Experiment in Criticism* (Cambridge: Cambridge University Press, 1965), p. 82.

4. Cleanth Brooks and Robert Penn Warren, *Understanding Poetry*, 3d ed. (New York: Holt, Rinehart and Winston, 1960), p. 10.

5. Flannery O'Connor, *Mystery and Manners*, ed. Sally and Robert Fitzgerald (New York: Farrar, Straus and Giroux, 1957), p. 73.

6. The incident is cited by Donald Whittle, *Christianity and the Arts* (London: A. R. Mowbray, 1966), p. 52. I have seen a similar incident ascribed to Beethoven.

7. T. S. Eliot, *The Use of Poetry and the Use of Criticism* (Cambridge, Mass.: Harvard University Press, 1933), p. 147.

8. Joyce Cary, *Art and Reality* (New York: Harper and Brothers 1958), p. 158.

9. Auguste Rodin, "On Sculpture," in *Artists on Art*, ed. Robert Goldwater and Marco Treves (New York: Pantheon Books, 1945, 1958) p. 325.

10. The views of Constable are summarized by John Walker, *John Constable* (New York: Harry N. Abrams, Inc., 1978), pp. 29, 86.

11. Jonathan Culler, *Structuralist Poetics: Structuralism, Linguistics, and the Study of Literature* (Ithaca: Cornell University Press, 1975), p. 115.

12. Gerald Graff, "Literature as Assertions," in *American Criticism in the Poststructuralist Age*, ed. Ira Konigsberg (Ann Arbor: University of Michigan Press, 1981), p. 161.

13. Cary, p. 137.

14. Louise M. Rosenblatt, *Literature as Exploration*, 3d ed. (New York: Noble and Noble, 1976), p. 38.

15. O'Connor, p. 77.

16. Mark Twain, *Life on the Mississippi*, Chapter 30 (New York: New American Library, 1961), p. 190.

17. Joseph Conrad, "Preface" to *The Nigger of the Narcissus* (New York: Collier Books, 1962), p. 19.

18. John Constable, in C. R. Leslie, *Memoirs of the Life of John Constable* (London: Phaidon, 1951), p. 86.

19. H. Richard Niebuhr, *The Responsible Self* (New York: Harper and Row, 1963), pp. 151-2, 161.

20. Gordon H. Clark, "Art and the Gospel," *The Trinity Review*, March/April 1982. To add to the confusion, the very next page contains a review by another writer praising the ability of the movie *Chariots of Fire* to express Christian truth in the form of narrative and visual images.

21. O'Connor, p. 75.

22. Richard Stevens and Thomas J. Musial, *Reading, Discussing, and Writing about the Great Books* (Boston: Houghton Mifflin, 1970).

23. Nathan A. Scott, Jr., "The Modern Experiment in Criticism: A Theological Appraisal," in *The New Orpheus: Essays toward a Christian Poetic* (New York: Sheed and Ward, 1964), pp. 156, 163.

24. Alvin Toffler, *Future Shock* (New York: Random House, 1970) p. 139.

25. C. S. Lewis, *English Literature in the Sixteenth Century Excluding Drama* (Oxford: Oxford University Press, 1954), p. 331.

26. John Calvin, *Institutes of the Christian Religion*, ed. John T. McNeill (Philadelphia: Westminster, 1960), 1:273-275.

27. Musial and Stevens, p. 24.

28. All quotations from *The Scarlet Letter* have been taken from *The Scarlet Letter and Other Tales of the Puritans*, ed. Harry Levin (Boston: Houghton Mifflin, 1960).

29. Joseph Summers, *The Muse's Method: An Introduction to Paradise Lost* (New York: W. W. Norton, 1962), p. 30.

30. Darrel Abel, "Hawthorne's Hester," *College English,* 13 (1952): 304.

31. Randall Stewart, *American Literature and Christian Doctrine* (Baton Rouge: Louisiana State University Press, 1958), p. 88.

32. James Ellis, "Human Sexuality, the Sacrament of Matrimony, and the Paradox of the Fortunate Fall in *The Scarlet Letter,*" *Christianity and Literature,* 29, no. 4 (Summer, 1980): 53.

33. W. Stacy Johnson, "Sin and Salvation in Hawthorne," *Hibbert Journal,* 50 (1951): 44. The most complete reading of the conclusion of the novel as a drama of salvation is by Darrel Abel, "Hawthorne's Dimmesdale: Fugitive from Wrath," *Nineteenth-Century Fiction,* 11 (1956): 81-105.

34. Ellis correctly observes that "what one sees in a novel is to some extent determined by what one brings to it. Accordingly, if one's view is either romantic or transcendentalist, one is likely to see Hester as the protagonist in *The Scarlet Letter* and her assertion of individual freedom as frustrated by a stagnant Puritan morality and the cowardly disavowal of her lover. If, however, one's view is either traditionally moral or Christian, then he is likely to see Arthur Dimmesdale as the protagonist and his suffering as a source of new moral growth, wherein he denies himself and chooses his God" (p. 53).

35. Joseph Schwartz, "Nathaniel Hawthorne, 1804-1864: God and Man in New England," in *American Classics Reconsidered: A Christian Appraisal,* ed. Harold C. Gardiner (New York: Charles Scribner's Sons, 1958), pp. 126-127. Despite Hawthorne's aloofness from the institutional Christianity of his day, Amos Wilder describes him as a writer "freely at home in the Hebraic-Christian tradition."— *Modern Poetry and the Christian Tradition* (New York: Charles Scribner's Sons, 1952), p. 30. Louis O. Rubin, Jr., calls Hawthorne a Protestant writer and views *The Scarlet Letter* as the nearest American equivalent to the novels of the French Catholic writer Francois Mauriac.—*The Teller in the Tale* (Seattle: University of Washington Press, 1967), p. 30.

Chapter 6

Perspective and Interpretation in the Arts

The previous chapter discussed the ways in which the arts can embody truth. In this chapter, I intend to analyze the related subject of how to determine whether a work embodies truth. The key element in this discussion will be perspective. The truth or falsehood that a work of art contains depends on the perspective of the artist; the ability of viewers, listeners, or readers to discern the truth and falsehood in works of art depends on the application of their perspective to a work.

As an organizing framework, we should note that artists perform three related activities: (1) they employ the techniques of art to create aesthetic form and pattern; (2) they present human experience for our contemplation; (3) they offer an interpretation of the experiences they present. The same three elements engage the attention of the audience of art. Perspective affects all three activities of the artistic enterprise in an ascending order of prominence. I will discuss artists and their audiences together, noting how the perspective of each operates in these areas.

Artistic Form and the Question of Perspective

True painting . . . is full of the spirit that moves the brush.
George Sand, letter to Gustave Flaubert.

Artistic form by itself is not strongly influenced by perspective, and therefore requires the least amount of interpretation from a listener, viewer, or reader. By themselves, the forms of art are relatively neutral in ideational content or philosophic perspective. The sonnet or sonata form is itself philosophically neutral. Whether a painter uses water colors or oil paints does not tell us anything about his intellectual allegiances. Stories and paintings can be used in the service of virtually any world view.

How, then, can artistic form bear any relationship whatsoever to the perspective of an artist or audience? At a very general level, the form itself of a work of art, literature, or music implies either order or disorder, meaning or the denial of meaning.

This is perhaps most evident in nonrepresentational art and music. An abstract painting can, by its very arrangement, suggest order and harmony, as in a Persian tapestry, or chaos and meaninglessness, as in much modern abstract art. I know an abstract sculptor who was asked by colleagues why his nonrepresentational sculptures possess clean lines and an order and gracefulness that are so atypical of prevailing contemporary trends. His answer was that his sculpture expressed a Christian view of the world as ultimately orderly. So, too, with musical compositions: A symphony in which organization dominates conveys a different sense of life from a symphony in which disorganization dominates.

Artists reveal themselves even in the style with which they handle their subject matter. A Renaissance painter commented that "if a painter is choleric he will show fury in his works; . . . if devout, religion; if lecherous, sensuality."[1] The nineteenth-century German illustrator Ludwig Richter tells in his autobiography of an occasion when he and three fellow artists spent a day drawing the same landscape "as objectively as possible." When the artists compared pictures in the evening, they found that the mood, color, and outline differed according to the dispostions of the painters. The melancholy painter, for example, had straightened the exuberant contours and had emphasized blue tinges.[2]

Some literary forms (though not all of them) carry a great deal of inherent perspective. Comedy (a U-shaped plot that descends into tragedy but rises to a happy ending) has long been regarded as the form that best embodies the Christian gospel. There has been a long debate about whether the conventions of tragedy (which presupposes, for example, a hero with greatness of spirit and the power of choice, grandeur in suffering, death as the final defeat) are amenable to Christianity and modern naturalism/pessimism. Satire (an attack on human vice and folly) at once implies a view of people and institutions as prone to evil.

Assessing the Perspective Implied by an Artist's Form

Simply at the level of form, therefore, a viewer or listener or reader is forced to an assessment of the implied perspective of a work. Already here, it seems to me, Christians will assimilate the formal meaning of a work in terms of their own world view. What is the Christian perspective on the question of order and design in the world? Surely that the universe makes sense. It does so, first of all, because God created everything that exists. The universe therefore has a meaning, for good or ill. Things are not out-of-control. They are under God's redemption and providence and final judgment.

No Christian will deny that there is disorder in the world. But it is a disorder that has a cause (the Fall and human evil consequent to the Fall). It can be defined as disorder only because there is a norm of order by which we can measure the deviation. To the extent to which a disordered or random artistic form expresses a denial of design in the universe, from a Christian perspective it does not tell the truth.

Implied Attitudes about the Value of Artistic Form

There is an additional way in which artistic form itself implies a perspective. It concerns the way in which an artist or audience regards artistic form. We might think that every artist values and respects the form or medium in which he or she has chosen to work. But one of the modern trends I will discuss in a subsequent chapter has been the revolt against form and artistic convention. Artists deliberately destroy artistic form to show their scorn for it. They put toilet stools and black canvases in art galleries. They require a pianist to sit motionless in front of a piano. They write stream-of-consciousness novels that defy understanding.

The ways in which an audience regards artistic form are even more crucial. On this issue, perspective enters the life of everyone. Does a person value or ignore the arts? Does he or she show a respect or disrespect for beauty and artistry? Is human creativity valuable or worthless? These are questions that we all answer by our very actions, and they are inherently laden with perspective.

What, then, constitutes a Christian perspective on artistic form? I have already answered that question in detail in earlier chapters. Artistic form has value in itself. It is one of the gifts of God, reflecting the quality of creativity that he himself possesses and that he conferred on the human race. On the other hand, artistic beauty is not, itself, divine. It can be overvalued as well as undervalued.

Perspective at the Level of Subject Matter

> Literary reality is a carefully framed and controlled kind of actuality, with every element displaying the artist's own beliefs, his own values. His choice of subject and his treatment of it are evidence of his attitudes.
>
> Keith McKean, *The Moral Measure of Literature*

The arts take human experience as their subject. They are above all the expression of human response to reality. When a poet writes a poem, he or she is expressing a human response to nature or love or God or one of a dozen other things. When painters portray a human face or landscape, they are capturing their response to human character and to nature. Music is adept at expressing the inner weather of the human emotions and moods. So rooted are the arts in human experience and the world in which it occurs that the oldest and most influential of all aesthetic theories has regarded the arts as an imitation of reality.

At the very outset, therefore, the arts imply a commitment to the value of human life in this world. To paint a human face is to imply that people are important and worthy of attention. To tell a story about people is to assert that human experience is worthy of study and understanding. To enter into the spirit of Aaron Copland's *Appalachian Spring* is to celebrate human experience.

How Important Is Human Life?

Artists by definition treat human experience as something worth observing, understanding, and recording. Their perspective is obvious. If they did not value human experience in this world, they would not compose works that portray it.

The same is emphatically not true of the audience of art. The arts, I have said, stay close to the way things are in the human and natural worlds. The knowledge that they convey is an experiential knowledge of the physical and human worlds. Whether or not this is a knowledge worth having depends on one's values and perspective. The Greek philosopher Plato had a negative attitude toward the physical world and, not surprisingly, banished the poets and storytellers from his ideal republic. Many people have agreed with Plato.

A Christian viewpoint disagrees with this denigration of physical and human reality. It does so partly on the basis of the doctrine of creation. Things are real because God made them. And because he made them, they are worthy of study and celebration and love. The Christian doctrine of Incarnation points in the same direction. When Jesus took on human form in order to redeem people, he demonstrated that earthly, human experience is of immense worth. Christianity is not escapist. It does not substitute a heavenly world for the earthly one, though it brings spiritual reality into the earthly sphere.

Simply at the level of subject matter, a Christian perspective has a good deal to say about the arts. Visual artists are assured that their preoccupation with the scenes and people and colors they paint are worthy of such attention. Musicians need not doubt the significance of the human feelings and attitudes embodied in their sounds. Poets and storytellers and dramatists can be convinced that their portrayal of the whole range of human experience in the natural and social worlds is a worthwhile endeavor.

Choice of Subject and Selectivity of Material

We might think that the mere subject matter of an artistic work is philosophically neutral and that perspective enters only when artists add their interpretive slant to the subject of portrayal. But the world-picture and values of creative artists emerge even from the subjects they select for portrayal.

In the previous chapter I spoke of the principle of significance in art. By it I mean that we should approach a work of art with the premise that the artist intends it as a comment on some significant aspect of human life or reality. The same principle applies to artists. The details that they include within the limited confines of a single work carry a burden of meaning larger than themselves and are understood to be representative of a bigger sense of life.

Artists choose their subjects carefully. They are on the lookout for scenes and characters and stories and situations in which "the deep significance of life reveals itself" (as the modern French poet Baudelaire put it).[3] Artistic subject matter implies a statement about both values and reality. "To tell a story," someone has said, "is to create a world, adopt an attitude, suggest a behavior."[4]

Subject Matter as a Comment about Human Values

In the realm of values, artists imply what they regard as worthy of human attention whenever they put brush to canvas or pen to paper. When painters in the Middle Ages painted madonnas with child and scenes of heaven, they were implying a world view in which the otherworldly or spiritual was the only reality that mattered. The Dutch realists of the seventeenth century were also Christian in their outlook, but when they painted everyday scenes and landscapes they embodied their belief that the reality of God does not belong only to another world but also enters this world. By their very subject matter, these painters rejected the sacred-secular dichotomy that dominated the Catholic Middle Ages.

When artists choose their subjects, they gravitate toward what is important to them. What, for example, did the Christians worshiping in the catacombs choose to paint on the walls? Not surprisingly, they painted Daniel in the lions' den—the person faithful to God suffering for his faith. They painted Jonah, a figure of hope and resurrection, a person delivered by God. Painters of the Protestant Reformation gravitated toward subjects that emphasized the idea of grace to the unworthy—the calling of Matthew, the prodigal son, the conversion of Paul, Christ healing the sick.[5]

What is true of painters is also true of composers and writers. Bach wrote church music on religious themes because he valued supremely the worship of God. Wordsworth's nature poems, simply at the level of subject matter, express his attitude toward what is important in human experience. When modern novelists and playwrights focus on the misery and injustice in the world, their choice of subject indicates their commitment to ideals of justice and human well-being.

Sometimes the implied statement of an artistic work must be understood against the background of the artistic conventions and expectations that prevailed in the artist's own time. The nineteenth-century French painter Courbet violated the artistic norms of his day by painting common stonebreakers and a peasant burial. Why was this shocking? Because the French Academy was aristocratic in its values and regarded commoners as unworthy of attention. By its very choice of subjects, the nineteenth-century romantic movement embraced the value of the commonplace.

Subject Matter as a Comment about Reality

What an artist chooses to portray is a comment about reality as well as values. Speaking as a storyteller, C. S. Lewis wrote,

> Everything in the story should arise from the whole cast of the author's mind. . . . The matter of our story should be a part of the habitual furniture of our minds.[6]

One of the chief conventions of the arts is that they express a sense of life and reality for the contemplation and celebration of an audience. The artist's function is partly to give shape to our own experiences, thereby leading us to affirm our conception of what is real.

When artists create a whole world of simulated reality out of the habitual furniture of their minds, what they exclude from that world is as important as what they include. Writers whose stories or poems never portray God, spiritual reality, or Christian values show their secular viewpoint by that very exclusion. By contrast, the oratorios of Handel and Mendelssohn exhibit a Christian world view by the very things that the composers accept as part of reality. The only caution I would urge in this regard is that an artist can hardly be expected to put everything into a single work of art. An artist's whole canon is the best barometer of what he or she believes about reality.

The Audience's Picture of Reality

Viewers, listeners, and readers also have a picture of what constitutes reality. If artistic subject matter is inherently laden with perspective, so is the person who receives an artist's vision. The audience of art, too, has habitual furniture of the mind. This partly explains why individuals resonate with some works of art and not with others. It partly explains the works that teachers of the arts decide to include in a syllabus, and those that performers of music choose to include in programs. It even explains what aspects of a work critics and teachers choose to discuss and emphasize.

This of course includes Christians, though they are not unique in this regard. Christians have a picture of reality and a value system stemming from their Christian world view. As they assimilate works of art, therefore, they should self-consciously assess the adequacy of artistic pictures of the world in terms of a Christian framework. The central tenets in that world picture are the existence of God and an unseen spiritual world, the worth of physical reality, the value of the individual person and social institutions, the fact of human evil and fallenness, the availability of God's redemptive grace, and a view of human history as being under God's purposeful providence.

As Christians look at the subject matter of artistic works through the lens of their convictions, some of what they see comes into focus. Other things remain out of focus. In either case, art has served its useful purpose: it has furnished the recipient with an occasion to exercise intellectual discrimination on questions of values and reality. Although some value systems and views of reality are wrong, Christians have an obligation to understand the world in which they live and to which they minister.

The Interpretation of Reality in Works of Art

> All great artists have a theme, an idea of life profoundly felt and founded in some personal and compelling experience. . . . A novelist, therefore, can give only . . . truth with an angle.
>
> Joyce Cary, *Art and Reality*

Artists do more than present human experience; they also interpret it from a specific perspective. Works of art make implied assertions about reality. A leading literary theorist has said that "literature differentiates itself from other modes not by refraining from assertion but by making a stronger, more universalizable kind of assertion."[7] I suggested earlier that these assertions fall into three main categories; they are comments about reality (what really exists), morality (what consititutes right and wrong behavior), and values (what matters most and least).

Not all works of art are equally laden with thematic perspective. Literature, because it consists of words, is the most consistently perspectival. Music, being the most nonrepresentational, is least likely to carry intellectual meanings. The visual arts fall somewhere between the two.

Determining the Topic(s) of a Work

How can we know what a work of art asserts? Mainly by having a keen eye for the obvious, by staring at a work until patterns of meaning begin to emerge, by immersing ourselves in the arts, and by reading commentary on works of art. We can profitably divide the process of interpreting works of art into two phases: First we should identify what the work is about and then analyze what it says about that subject.

There are several ways in which works of art suggest what the artist has portrayed. Sometimes the title of the work and the very subject matter tell us what to look at. Repetition is one of the most universal ways by which a work of art will guide the interpreter. Highlighting or foregrounding is another common technique. So is proportionate space, since artists ordinarily give most space to what they regard as most important in a work.

Determining the Angle of Vision

Having determined what the work is about, the remaining task is to determine how the artist wishes us to think and feel about that subject. We must be aware that works of art have a persuasive element to them. Their aim is affective: They try to affect an audience in calculated ways. What someone has said about literature applies equally to music and painting: "the writer expresses what he knows by affecting the reader; the reader knows what is expressed by being receptive to effects."[8]

Artists aim to make the audience share their vision—to see what they see, feel what they feel, and interpret life as they do. They constantly try to make readers and viewers and listeners commit themselves as they absorb a work. As we temporarily place ourselves under the sway of a work, we look at reality from the perspective of the artist, thus:

audience ——————→ work ——————→ the world

That is, the work of art becomes the window through which we perceive reality. We share the artist's angle of vision and feel what it is like to view the world from that perspective. This, remember, is one of the values of the arts: It allows us to see with someone else's eyes.

Our best strategy in interpreting a work of art, therefore, is to look upon the artist as a presiding presence in the work. Although some recent forms of audience-centered criticism have tried to banish the artist from the scene, I would suggest that we can profitably view the artist as our traveling companion. Artists arrange what we will see and the vantage point from which we see it. They point out things about the subject matter they have assembled before us. The most fruitful interpretive question to ask and answer is therefore this one: What perspective does the artist get me to share with him or her as I assimilate this work of art?

One of the most universal ways in which an artist manipulates response is to guide an audience's patterns of sympathy and antipathy, approval and disapproval. As we read a story or watch a play or movie, for example, we automatically respond with sympathy or aversion to various characters, decide whether the things that characters do are good or bad, and respond positively or negatively to settings of the action. Virtually the first thing we do when looking at a painting is decide whether the painter intends us to approve or disapprove of the scene that is portrayed.

Responding to the details in a work is an interpretive act. A literary scholar who made a study of the "devices of disclosure" by which selected storytellers influenced how readers interpret the ethical meaning of their stories concluded that the meaning of a story "depended heavily on how successful its creator was in controlling our sympathy and antipathy toward, approval and disapproval of, characters, thoughts, and actions at every stage."[9]

Some Examples of Perspective in Art

One of the best ways to perceive how thematic perspective enters our artistic experiences is to compare various treatments of a common subject. The figure of Christ, for example, has been painted throughout the Christian centuries, but the interpretation of him has differed widely. When the early Christians were a persecuted minority, they painted Christ with simple materials as the good shepherd—a humble figure tenderly caring for his helpless followers. When the Roman Catholic Church became powerful in the Middle Ages, Christ was depicted with rich materials as an imperial ruler. Under the sway of Catholic theology, Christ became increasingly remote and otherworldly, requiring a mediator (the church).

Or consider what two visual artists did with the apostle Peter as their subject. The elaborate Baroque sculpture piece *The Chair of St. Peter,* by seventeenth-century Italian sculptor Bernini, was created for St. Peter's Cathedral in Rome. It is a gigantic design built between columns of the cathedral and reaching to the ceiling. The throne of St. Peter is flanked by statues of the Doctors of the Church. This is a Catholic paradigm of Christianity: institutional, wealthy, monolithic, powerful, awesome, remote, appealing to long tradition.

In the same century the Protestant painter Rembrandt used the biblical figure of Peter to capture quite a different view of what it means to be a Christian. In his painting, *The Apostle Peter Denying Christ,* Rembrandt gives us a thoroughly human Peter: wrinkled, fearful, anguished, weak, the flawed individual failing Christ and totally dependent on God's grace for forgiveness.

That artists inevitably offer an interpretive slant on their subject is equally evident in literature. Consider three poetic treatments of the common subject of nature. The sonnet by

William Wordsworth quoted on page 141 expresses the romantic myth of nature. In this perspective, nature is deified. The goal of life is to become one with nature.

Later in the nineteenth century, Gerard Manley Hopkins wrote a sonnet entitled "God's Grandeur" in which he interpreted the beauty and permanence of nature in a disinctly Christian light:

> The world is charged with the grandeur of God.
> It will flame out, like shining from shook foil;
> It gathers to a greatness, like the ooze of oil
> Crushed. Why do men then now not reck his rod?
> Generations have trod, have trod, have trod;
> And all is seared with trade; bleared, smeared with toil;
> And wears man's smudge and share's man's smell: the soil
> Is bare now, nor can foot feel, being shod.
>
> And for all this, nature is never spent;
> There lives the dearest freshness deep down things;
> And though the last lights off the black West went
> Oh, morning, at the brown brink eastward springs—
> Because the Holy Ghost over the bent
> World broods with warm breast and with ah! bright wings.

The interpretation of nature in this poem shares much with Wordsworth's romantic viewpoint. Hopkins, too, is rapturous over the beauty and permanence of nature. He, too, sees nature in a religious light. Yet even the title alerts us that Hopkins is viewing nature from a Christian perspective. Nature is not divine. It declares the grandeur of a Creator. The poem even ends with a theological statement about the role of the Holy Spirit in the creation of nature.

Thomas Hardy, writing on the very last day of the nineteenth century, gives yet another interpretation of nature in his famous poem "The Darkling Thrush." The first two stanzas of the poem paint a landscape of death, the third introduces a contrast into the setting, and the last stanza interprets the experience:

I leant upon a coppice gate
  When Frost was specter-gray,
And Winter's dregs made desolate
  The weakening eye of day.
The tangled bine-stems scored the sky
  Like strings of broken lyres,
And all mankind that haunted nigh
  Had sought their household fires.

The land's sharp features seemed to be
  The Century's corpse outleant,
His crypt the cloudy canopy,
  The wind his death-lament.
The ancient pulse of germ and birth
  Was shrunken hard and dry,
And every spirit upon earth
  Seemed fervorless as I.

At once a voice arose among
  The bleak twigs overhead
In a fullhearted evensong
  Of joy illimited;
An aged thrush, frail, gaunt, and small,
  In blast-beruffled plume,
Had chosen thus to fling his soul
  Upon the growing gloom.

So little cause for carolings
  Of such ecstatic sound
Was written on terrestrial things
  Afar or nigh around,
That I could think there trembled through
  His happy good-night air
Some blessed Hope, whereof he knew
  And I was unaware.

This is obviously the naturalistic interpretation of nature. It denies meaning or hope in the universe. It sees in nature the symbol of an existential pessimism about life. The poem is an implicit rebuttal to both the romantic and Christian views of nature. The rejection of Christianity is made explicit in the next to last line. Exactly what Hope (capitalized) does Hardy reject? Surely the "blessed hope" of Titus 2:13—"the appearing of the glory of our great God and Savior Jesus Christ."

Christian Criticism of Art

> Literary criticism should be completed by criticism from a definite ethical and theological standpoint. . . . It is . . . necessary for Christian readers to scrutinize their reading, especially of works of imagination, with explicit ethical and theological standards.
>
> T. S. Eliot, "Religion and Literature"

If works of art are themselves value-laden, so is the assimilation of art. As readers, viewers, and listeners, we absorb works of art within the framework of our personal experiences and world view. Experiencing and interpreting works of art are subjective activities. It is a commonplace that the personal viewpoints of artists permeate their work, but we need to be reminded that the same thing is true of critics. "Literary criticism," writes someone, "is as much a personal matter, as much the product of a personal sense of life and value as literature itself."[10]

If experiencing and interpreting art are this subjective, we are free as consumers of art to be ourselves when we listen and look and read. We do not need to repress our values or apologize for having a world view when we assimilate works of art. We do, however, need to be self-aware about our responses. We also need to acknowledge the presuppositions that lead us to see certain elements in a work of art.

Current aesthetic theory stresses the idea of "interpretive communities"—groups of people who view the arts from a common set of interests and assumptions and values. Christians are such an interpretive community. They are not inherently better artists or critics than other people. But they have their own "agenda" of interests. They share beliefs and attitudes that they bring to their artistic and critical pursuits.

A Methodology for Christian Criticism

What, then, characterizes Christian criticism of art? My own conviction is that criticism is an activity or skill that is the same in kind for a Christian and any other person. The difference is simply that Christian critics, like Freudian or Marxist or humanist or any other critics, raise questions of an artistic work that may not interest people who do not share the same concerns.

What is the nature of the critical activity that a Christian shares with others? It is the ability to describe and interpret a literary work as accurately as possible. I accept Matthew Arnold's dictum that the aim of criticism "in all branches of knowledge, theology, philosophy, history, art, science" is "to see the object as in itself it really is."[11] The aim of biology, for example, is to see the plant or animal as it really is. The aim of sociology is to see society as it really is. The aim of criticism of the arts is to see works of art as they really are in themselves, "to put the [audience] in possession" of works of art.[12] The critic's "primary interest" writes T. S. Eliot, "is to help his readers to understand and enjoy."[13]

Christian criticism must first of all be respectable by the ordinary standards of the discipline. It should not abandon the ordinary tasks of description and interpretation and resort to esoteric or subjective evaluation of works of art. Good criticism, including that from a religious perspective, begins with painstaking scrutiny and interpretation of a work itself. It should be verifiable in the sense that it provides objective data from the painting or text or composition in support of interpretive generalizations.

What Differentiates Christian Criticism?

The distinctive feature of Christian criticism is that it takes the descriptive and interpretive process a step further than other criticism or a step in a particular direction that may not interest others. Having described the work of art as it really is in itself, a Christian critic describes the work in relation to Christian belief and biblical doctrine. This is not an esoteric activity, though it may be uninteresting to a non-Christian.

The methodology for criticism has been stated in kernel form by T. S. Eliot, who believes that criticism

> should be completed by criticism from a definite ethical and theological standpoint. . . . What I believe to be incumbent upon all Christians is the duty of maintaining consciously certain standards and criteria of criticism over and above those applied by the rest of the world; and that by these criteria and standards everything . . . must be tested.[14]

Notice that Eliot envisions a two-stage process for Christian criticism. First we must receive a work on its own terms and allow it to say what it really says. Then we must exercise our prerogative of agreeing or disagreeing with the artist's interpretation of reality and experience. Eliot also envisions a comparative process in which the viewpoint in works of art is compared to a Christian framework. The "explicit ethical and theological standards" of which he speaks are the Christian doctrines that are based ultimately on the Bible, the only final authority for belief in what is, after all, a revealed religion. The formulations of Christian creeds based on the Bible and of Christian thinkers who have codified and stated the implications of Christian doctrine are also useful statements by which the assertions of art can be measured. In this comparative process we can profitably ask three questions:

1. Does the interpretation of reality in this work conform or fail to conform to Christian doctrine or ethics? (The answer might well be mixed for a given work.)

2. If some of the ideas and values are Christian, are they inclusively or exclusively Christian? That is, are they ideas that include both Christianity and other religious or philosophic viewpoints, or do they exclude Christianity from other viewpoints? (We might visualize two circles, one representing

Christianity and the other representing other religious viewpoints. The overlapping area of agreement constitutes inclusively Christian material; the part of the circle representing Christianity that does not overlap is exclusively Christian material.)

3. If some of the ideas and values in a work are Christian, are they a relatively complete version of the Christian view, or are they a relatively rudimentary version of Christian belief on a given topic?

There is no need to mysticize what is commonly called the integration of faith and art. Christian criticism is a form of intellectually testing the spirits to see if they are from God. It is a rigorous intellectual exercise, calling for our best powers of scrutiny and discernment. The arts, for all their beauty and delightfulness and value as entertainment, are not intended as the occasion for us to take a holiday of the mind. The task of completing artistic criticism with a Christian assessment of an artist's perspective or world view needs to be informed by insights from philosophy, theology, ethics, and psychology. It can never rest on purely aesthetic considerations.

Some Implications

It is obvious from what I have said that whatever is distinctive about Christian criticism primarily concerns the content rather than the form of a literary work. Christian critics have little to say distinctively as Christians about sonnet form or narrative structure or pictorial composition or musical harmony. They have much to say relative to their interests about the ethical attitudes and world view and themes in works of art.

This means that the preoccupations that are distinctive to Christian critics cannot possibly be a complete act of criticism because content is not all there is to a work of art. If artistic form has value in itself, then it deserves the attention of Christians even though that attention is not distinctively Christian. The most obvious weakness of the religious movement in criticism is that in its most characteristic pose it concentrates on content to the exclusion of form and on the distinctively or exclusively religious dimension of art to the neglect of what Christians share with all readers and all critics. No wonder Christian criticism is read only by Christians and has little impact on the broader world of scholarship.

Although I do not believe that Christian criticism should be characterized primarily by an evaluative approach that pigeonholes works as Christian and non-Christian for purposes of approval and disapproval, it is also true that the comparative process I have described, while it is descriptive in nature, is also an evaluation in the sense that Christians are already committed to the truthfulness of the Christian faith that they set beside a work of art. This evaluative dimension should remain latent rather than prominent, however, especially in published criticism. If one's audience consists of Christians, the mere comparison of a work to Christian belief will be accepted simultaneously as an evaluation of the truth or falseness of the work's theme and world view. And if one's audience does not share the Christian viewpoint, accentuating the evaluative as distinct from the descriptive nature of the criticial process will unnecessarily alienate one's audience.

One of the most serious pitfalls to which any critic (including Christian ones) can fall prey is to allow one's personal perspective to determine the description or interpretation of what a work of art really says. When people like a work of art, for example, the temptation is strong to interpret the work as adhering to their own viewpoint. I noted in the previous chapter, for example, that Christian critics have tended to regard Dimmesdale as the hero of Hawthorne's *The Scarlet Letter*, while critics with a romantic bias have overwhelmingly regarded Hester as the protagonist and central concern of the story. A reader who disagrees with the hedonistic existentialism of Albert Camus's *The Stranger* is likely to find that the story exposes the inadequacies of its protagonist, while a reader who shares Meursault's outlook is inclined to think that Camus presents a sympathetic hero whose view of life is accurate. The ideal is first to allow a work to express its own perspective on life and then to exercise the prerogative of agreeing or disagreeing with that viewpoint.

The task of Christian criticism, in other words, is not (as some seem to think) to prove that a work is Christian but rather to determine *whether* it is Christian. Surely criticism that weighs the ethos or world view of a work in the scale of Christian belief and finds it lacking has performed its rightful service just as thoroughly as when it finds agreement between Christian doctrine and a work.

SHAKESPEARE'S *MACBETH* IN CHRISTIAN PERSPECTIVE

> A poem demands of its readers that they must come out to meet it, . . . so that their meaning may be added to its.
>
> Stanley Kunitz, comment in *Poetspeak,* ed. Paul B. Janeczko

To illustrate the process of Christian criticism that I have outlined, I have chosen a classic of English literature, Shakespeare's tragedy *Macbeth*. I have said that a Christian critic or reader performs the same type of descriptive and interpretive criticism that any good critic does. A Christian is not performing a different kind of criticism. To be a good critic, a Christian must first of all master the methods of explicating written texts. Before we relate the ethical ideas of Shakespeare's play to Christian belief, we must see the work as it really is in itself. This part of the critical act will account for at least three-fourths of what the Christian reader/critic does.

Without taking the time or space to develop these topics, I would list the following as those that deserve careful description:

1. The literary genre (drama), along with what this means in terms of setting, plot, and characterization.
2. The tragic pattern of the story, with all the implications that this has for characterization and plot.
3. An exploration of the powerful archetypes in the play, including the temptation motif, the crime and punishment pattern, the villain, the usurper, and the futile attempt to cheat the oracle.
4. The image patterns that are always an important part of the artistry of Shakespeare's plays.

5. The elements of artistry that raise Shakespeare's play above a television melodrama—the characterization (with emphasis on the psychology of the criminal mind and the psychology of guilt), the dramatic irony, the symbols, the figures of speech, the poetry, the use of foils and contrasts.

6. The relation of the play to the Renaissance world picture, with its emphasis on the great chain of being.

Having done all this, the Christian reader/critic will now want to describe the work in its relationship to Christian belief. The aim is still to identify the work, not as it is in itself this time, but as its content touches upon biblical truth and Christian experience. Critics generally agree that *Macbeth* is, in significant ways, a Christian play. The task of a Christian critic is to explore how this Christian identity manifests itself.

Identifying the Major Themes

A Christian approach to *Macbeth* must begin by discovering the major themes of the play. This is quite different from starting with a list of religious ideas that is then applied to the play, regardless of whether the play calls for application of a given doctrine. Works of art must be allowed to set their own agenda of issues. Identifying the major ideas in *Macbeth* is an inductive process that begins with ordinary literary criticism—with analysis of plot conflict and structure, characterization, and imagery. This means that we should not apply Christian categories to characters and events when the play itself does not raise the occasion for doing so.

G. R. Elliott, for example, interprets a number of episodes in *Macbeth* as warnings sent by divine providence to call Macbeth to repentance.[15] Now, it is true that Christians interpret events as being directed by God, but in many of the instances cited by Elliott there is nothing in the play to prompt us to interpret the events in such a manner. In such cases the critic imposes a Christian framework onto the play at points where the play itself does not invite such application of Christian doctrine. When the play is silent about the matter of providence, it strikes me as more accurate to say that it lacks a Christian perspective, but this is a dubious procedure because a writer is not obliged to cover the whole territory in every work. If the play does not commit itself on the issue of providence, there is no reason to measure it against that particular Christian doctrine.

When I say that a Christian analysis of *Macbeth* must begin by discovering the major themes of the play, the word *major* is important. Much religious criticism of Shakespeare has consisted of showing that specific phrases or lines in specific speeches of characters in the play have a theological or biblical content. All that such criticism shows is that a character in the play has uttered a Christian sentiment. In religious criticism of literature, there is entirely too much dipping into works for "proof texts," statements that have religious significance. It is a rule of interpretation that meaning resides in artistic wholes, not in isolated parts. It is customary for individual characters in a story to utter sentiments that the work as a whole repudiates.

Christian criticism becomes significant when it addresses itself to the major themes and ethical patterns of a work. In the case of *Macbeth,* we will be on the right track if we pay attention to what various critics have called the play's "mode of thought and feeling," "its implicit world view," its "fundamental moral principles," its "philosophical patterns," and its "moral vision."[16]

The Reality of Evil

A leading theme of *Macbeth* is the reality of evil and the implications this has for the view of human nature. Until the nineteenth century, Western thought was dominated by two views of human nature. The humanistic tradition, reaching back to ancient Greek thought, had a generally optimistic view of human nature. A major premise of humanism, from the time of Socrates forward, has been that people will ordinarily not do something wrong if they know better, that understanding will usually lead to virtue. If people do evil acts, proponents of this tradition argue, it is because they have not seen evil as it really is. In one way or another, they are victims of ignorance.[17] This view of knowledge as the doorway to virtue is summarized in the eighteenth-century poet Alexander Pope's aphorism that "Vice is a monster of so frightful mien, / As to be hated needs but to be seen."[18]

The Christian tradition, by contrast, has taken the view that people are sinful by nature and inclined to do evil regardless of how much knowledge they have. The writer of Psalm 19 prays to be forgiven not only of "hidden faults" but also for "presumptuous sins" (that is, sins committed against better knowledge). The theological basis of this view of human nature is elaborated in great detail by Paul in his New Testament Epistle to the Romans, where he argues that all people, whether or not they have access to the moral standards of the Bible, knowingly violate their own moral ideals.

Narrative embodiment of this belief can be found in most of the stories of the Bible, where a wholly idealized protagonist is a rarity and where characters who do what they know to be wrong are the rule. John Calvin, who exerted a major influence on the Christian milieu in which Shakespeare wrote, noted that whereas "the sum of opinion of all philosophers" had been that "reason . . . is a sufficient guide for right conduct, . . . all ecclesiastical writers have recognized both that the soundness of reason in man is gravely wounded through sin, and that the will has been very much enslaved by evil desires."[19]

Macbeth is a classic illustration of the human inability to live up to what a person's ideals and conscience tell him he should do. Throughout the early scenes of the play, we repeatedly get the impression that Macbeth and Lady Macbeth are caught in the act of doing something that they know to be monstrously wicked but which they are attracted to nevertheless. This explains Macbeth's titanic struggle with his own conscience, which torments him before, during, and after the murder. The thought of murdering Duncan is to Macbeth a "horrid image" that unfixes his hair and makes his heart knock at his ribs (I.iii.135-136).[20] The soliloquy in which Macbeth tallies up the reasons why he should not murder Duncan (I.vii.l-28) likewise shows how clearsighted he is about the sinfulness of the contemplated murder. As Kenneth Muir comments,

"Macbeth is never in doubt of the difference between good and evil; nor is Lady Macbeth, not even in the speech in which she deliberately chooses evil as a means of achieving the 'good' of the crown."[21] Or as Virgil Whitaker puts it, "Macbeth is the tragedy of a man who, in full knowledge of what he was doing, destroyed his own soul."[22]

The inclination of Macbeth and Lady Macbeth to evil is stronger than their ability to do it. Lady Macbeth prays for evil forces to unsex her and fill her, "from the crown to the toe, top-full/Of direst cruelty" (I.v.42-43). She must take the stimulant of wine before she can go through with the murder (II.ii.1-2). And Macbeth, it is clear, would never have perpetrated the murder if Lady Macbeth had not intimidated him into doing it.

Moral Responsibility

A second principle that the play enacts is that people are morally responsible for the evil that they do. In other words, the play challenges the naturalistic view that maintains that people are the helpless victims of psychological and environmental and cosmic determinism. Shakespeare's play, it must be granted, depicts all sorts of forces, both within Macbeth and outside of him, that push him in the direction of committing the murder. As in the Bible, however, external forces are not responsible for the evil that people do. External promptings to evil are only the occasion for what Dorothy Sayers has called "the drama of the soul's choice."[23]

Until Macbeth ceases to obey his conscience (it is misleading to say that he kills his conscience, since it continues to plague him after he violates it), he could have chosen the good. This is implied by the scenes in which he vacillates in his intention to kill Duncan. Early in the play, in fact, Macbeth elicits our sympathy because, although he is tempted by ambition, he resists the temptation. The presence of virtuous characters in the play is also a continual reminder that in the world of the play people are not forced to be criminal in their actions.

The play thus affirms the Christian, biblical view of human responsibility. Roland Frye summarizes the biblical teaching on the matter: "Man's difficulties do not arise out of the hostility of inanimate 'things,' but out of the operation of human choice in history. . . . This basic conception pervades the Bible: man's responsible choices in history are the heart of the matter."[24]

The Reality of Guilt

The play is also Christian in its insistence on the reality of guilt. Unlike so much modern psychological theory, Shakespeare's play does not treat guilt as an illusion that needlessly troubles people. On the contrary, there are few works of literature that depict with such clarity and conviction the experience of guilt stemming from moral evil. Shakespeare has given English literature its classic story of human guilt. The five episodes that dramatize the destructive effects of guilt in *Macbeth* are the dagger scene in which Macbeth's hallucinations picture to him a dagger that leads him to Duncan's chamber just before the murder (II.i), Macbeth's mental collapse immediately after the murder (II.ii), the scene in which Macbeth and Lady Macbeth share their mutual fears and misery (III.ii), the appearance of Banquo's ghost at the banquet (3.4), and Lady Macbeth's sleepwalking (V.i). Each of these scenes is, from the viewpoint of Christianity, impeccable in its theological premise that evil does something to the human psyche. For the biblical parallels one need only read some of the Old Testament Psalms.

Temptation

Macbeth is also an anatomy of temptation. In keeping with the Bible and Christian tradition, the play asserts, by means of the archetypal temptation motif, that there are forces both within and outside the individiual that tempt him or her to do what is wrong. As we read or view Shakespeare's play we are made to feel the force of the temptation. We feel it in the ladder-like series of prophecies that the witches make, in the circumstances of Macbeth's rising political fortunes, in the tug of ambition within Macbeth, and in the browbeating of Lady

Macbeth. The latter agent of temptation, particularly, makes us feel how terrible life will be around the Macbeth household if Macbeth resists the temptation to usurp the throne. But once we have been made to feel the weight of the reasons for succumbing to the temptation, the play comes down with its stern judgment against the crime.

This anatomy of temptation runs true to the teaching of the Bible, Christian theology, and Christian literature. Biblical stories that show the dynamics of human temptation include the stories of Eve, Samson and Delilah, Saul (who is tempted by circumstances to disobey Samuel's command), David and Bathsheba, Jesus (tempted by Satan in the wilderness), and Peter (tempted by circumstances to deny Jesus). The apostle James explains the theology of temptation when he writes that "each person is tempted when he is lured and enticed by his own desire. Then desire when it has conceived gives birth to sin; and sin when it is full-grown brings forth death" (James 1:14-15). This same attitude toward temptation to immorality is anatomized in imaginative literature by such giants of the Christian tradition as Edmund Spenser in the *The Faerie Queene* and John Milton in *Paradise Lost* and *Paradise Regained*.

Order as a Moral Good

Shakespeare's play has as one of its chief aims to affirm order, conceived largely in terms of the Renaissance concept of the great chain of being. According to this scheme, the whole scale of creation exists as a hierarchy that begins at the top with God and descends through the angels, the planets, people, animals, plants, and minerals. This principle of hierarchy extends to the state (where the king is expected to rule), the family (where the husband is the head), and the individual (where reason must rule the emotions and appetites).

In Shakespeare's play, order is affirmed, as it usually is in tragedy, by negative example. That is, we witness the destructive results that follow from its violation. We see the tragedy of the passion of ambition overcoming its rightful superior, reason. We observe the inversion of order in the family when

Lady Macbeth begins to dominate her husband, and in the state when Macbeth usurps the throne from the king, his natural superior in the great chain of being. In keeping with the idea of the corresponding planes of reality, disorder in the individual, family, and state produces disorder in nature and the cosmos as well.

This affirmation of order is consonant with biblical teaching. A glance at the moral commands of both the Old and New Testaments shows, for example, the pervasive biblical concern for adherence to the order that God has prescribed for human life. The enormity of rebellion against legitimate civil authority is a recurrent theme of the epic of the Exodus, and it is the main political theme in the story of the civil war instigated by Absalom against his father David (2 Samuel 14-18).

The idea of hierarchy in the family begins with Genesis 3:16 and culminates in statements by the apostles Paul and Peter. This is not to say, of course, that the specific formulation that the Renaissance gave to the ideal of order and hierarchy—the great chain of being—is biblical or Christian in its origin, although it is important to realize that contemporary Christian traditions in Shakespeare's day would have supported the great chain of being concept.

The Sanctity of Human Life

A final emphasis in the play, less central and more subjectively discerned, perhaps, is the horror of murder. The image pattern of blood that broods over the play dramatizes the special kind of guilt that attaches to the act of murder. The play captures the mysterious and profound principle of the sanctity of human life and the guilt that inevitably follows its violation.

Here, too, the play is Christian in its emphasis. Macbeth's famous aphorism, "It will have blood, they say: blood will have blood" (III.iv.121), is paralleled by the biblical principle, "Whoever sheds the blood of man, by man shall his blood be shed" (Genesis 9:6). The archetype of the blood that is shed in murder is nearly as pervasive in the Bible as it is in Shakespeare's play, beginning with the blood of Abel that cries from the ground (Genesis 4:10) and stretching to the spilled blood of the saints and martyrs in the book of Revelation.

Inclusively or Exclusively Christian?

Are these themes inclusively or exclusively Christian? Do they set Christianity off from other ethical and religious viewpoints? Or do they include both Christianity and other systems?

As we look at the list of Christian principles embodied in the play, it is clear they are inclusively rather than exclusively Christian. This is always the case with Shakespeare's plays, which arose from a generally Christian culture but which lack the explicitly Christian emphasis of Milton's work, for example. Christianity is not the only religion that recognizes the reality of evil, the crucial importance of moral choice, the reality of guilt and temptation, the importance of order, and the horror of murder.

This does not make these principles any less Christian, but it should serve as a caution to critics who apply the term "Christian literature" so broadly that it loses its usefulness as a term that distinguishes explicitly Christian artists from those who are simply in accord with Christian belief. Roland Frye correctly concludes that the Christian ideas in Shakespeare's plays are "not exclusively Christian, but universally human," and that Shakespeare's ethical ideas "might be drawn with equal propriety from non-Christian as from Christian sources."[25] If, on the other hand, the view of human nature in *Macbeth* is that people make free moral choices and are inclined to use that freedom to make evil choices, we have an idea that comes much closer to being distinctively Christian.

How Complete Are the Christian Patterns?

In addition to asking whether the Christian ideas in the play are exclusively or inclusively Christian, we should consider whether the play's version of these ideas is complete or rudimentary. This is an even more demanding exercise than simply discovering whether the ideas conform to Christian belief.

The play depicts the reality of evil. Yet it can hardly be said to suggest the Christian concept of evil, namely, that it is disobedience to the moral law of God. The play approaches evil and disorder in a rather utilitarian way. Disorder is bad because it leads to social problems and civil unrest, as well as to personal misery. In the soliloquy in which Macbeth considers the reasons why he should not murder Duncan (I.vii.1-28), he is "deterred only by the thought of the immediate, earthly consequences."[26] He cites the fact that Duncan is in double trust to him, since Macbeth is both subject and host to the king.

When the young Joseph was tempted in Potiphar's house, he rejected the solicitation to evil not only because it would be an act of treason against his master, but also because the act would be "sin against God" (Genesis 39:9). The biblical view that all sin, regardless of its obvious social effects, is ultimately sin against God is similarly captured in David's response after Nathan had confronted him with his sin of adultery. In his prayer of confession to God, David asserts, "Against thee, thee only, have I sinned" (Psalm 51:4).

Macbeth dramatizes the horror that evil brings to a society, and it may even be, as G. Wilson Knight calls it, "Shakespeare's most profound and mature vision of evil."[27] But the vision of evil stops short of being a biblically complete vision. It does not accurately perceive the sinfulness of sin.

It is much the same with the play's depiction of guilt. I have praised the play for its magnificent portrayal of the dynamics of human guilt. Yet it cannot be said to embody the whole Christian doctrine on the topic. Someone notes that Macbeth suffers from "a terrible anxiety that is a sense of guilt without becoming . . . a sense of sin. It is not a sense of sin because he refuses to recognize such a category."[28] The play, in other words, does not picture guilt as having a spiritual or supernatural identity as well as a psychological one.

The best illustration of this is the scene in which Macbeth and Lady Macbeth share their fears and insecurity and death wish (III.ii). Throughout this entire dialogue, neither character shows any awareness that the real enemy is guilt stemming from sin. In two scenes late in the play, the soliloquy in which Macbeth laments that his old age is not accompanied by the human values that should attend it (V.iii.22-28) and the "tomorrow, and tomorrow, and tomorrow" soliloquy (V.v.19-28), Macbeth similarly realizes that something has gone wrong without ever perceiving the deeper issue of guilt and sin. For contrast, one might profitably observe the analysis of guilt that David gives us in penitential psalms such as Psalms 32 and 51. Macbeth expresses remorse that he got caught, while David is devastated by his guilt before God.

If we took time to pursue the other ideas in the play to their logical conclusions, the results would be similar. The play seldom, if ever, relates the leading issues to God. This suggests that the Christian patterns in the play are incomplete, stopping short of the God-centered world view of the Bible. In part this is a comment on the nature of drama, since it is impossible to put God on stage and difficult to dramatize the inner thought processes of a character (though the Shakespearean soliloquy is one way to do it). Still, a comparison between Macbeth and Milton's *Samson Agonistes* will show the difference between a play that is inclusively and incompletely Christian in its thought patterns and one that is exclusively and thoroughly Christian.

Summary

Art inevitably involves the perspectives of both artist and audience. Even in their attitude toward artistic form and technique, people imply a philosophic perspective. The subject matter that artists choose for portrayal implies what they regard as real and significant. Works of art also embody the artist's interpretation of the subject matter that is portrayed.

Readers, listeners, and viewers assimilate works of art in terms of their own experiences and world view. Christians should complete their assessment of works of art by scrutinizing them with explicit ethical and theological standards.

FURTHER READING

Flannery O'Connor, *Mystery and Manners* (1957).

Nathan A. Scott, Jr., ed. *The New Orpheus: Essays Toward a Christian Poetic* (1964).

John W. Dixon Jr., *Nature and Grace in Art* (1964).

H. R. Rookmaaker, *Modern Art and the Death of a Culture* (1970).

Leland Ryken, ed. *The Christian Imagination: Essays on Literature and the Arts* (1981).

Leland Ryken, *Windows to the World: Literature in Christian Perspective* (1985).

Chapter 6, Notes

1. Vicente Carducho, "Dialogues on Painting," in *Artists on Art*, ed. Robert Goldwater and Marco Treves (New York: Pantheon Books, 1945, 1958), p. 140.

2. I have borrowed the description of this incident from E. H. Gombrich, *Art and Illusion* (New York: Pantheon Books, 1960), pp. 63-64.

3. Charles-Pierre Baudelaire, as quoted by J. Middleton Murry, *The Problem of Style* (London: Oxford University Press, 1922), p. 30.

4. John Shea, *Stories of God* (Chicago: Thomas More Press, 1978), p. 9.

5. See William H. Halewood, *Six Subjects of Reformation Art* (Toronto: University of Toronto Press, 1982).

6. C. S. Lewis, *Of Other Worlds: Essays and Stories*, ed. Walter Hooper (New York: Harcourt Brace Jovanovich, 1966), pp. 33-34.

7. Gerald Graff, "Literature as Assertions," in *American Criticism in the Poststructuralist Age*, ed. Ira Konigsberg (Ann Arbor: University of Michigan Press, 1981), p. 146.

8. David Lodge, *Language of Fiction* (London: Routledge and Kegan Paul, 1966) p. 65.

9. Sheldon Sacks, *Fiction and the Shape of Belief* (Berkeley: University of California Press, 1964), p. 249.

10. Vincent Buckley, "Criticism and Theological Standards," in *The New Orpheus: Essays toward a Christian Poetic*, ed. Nathan A. Scott, Jr. (New York: Sheed and Ward, 1964), p. 186.

11. Matthew Arnold, "The Function of Criticism at the Present Time," in *Criticism: The Major Texts*, ed. Walter Jackson Bate (New York: Harcourt, Brace and World, 1952), p. 452.

12. Cleanth Brooks, "Foreword" to *Critiques and Essays in Criticism, 1920-1948*, ed. Robert W. Stallman (New York: Ronald Press, 1949), p. xx.

13. T. S. Eliot, *On Poets and Poetry* (New York: Farrar, Straus and Cudahy, 1957), p. 130.

14. T. S. Eliot, "Religion and Literature," as reprinted in *The Christian Imagination: Essays on Literature and the Arts,* ed. Leland Ryken (Grand Rapids: Baker, 1981), pp. 142, 153.

15. G. R. Elliott, *Dramatic Providence in Macbeth* (Princeton: Princeton University Press, 1958).

16. These phrases come, respectively, from Harold S. Wilson, *On the Design of Shakespearian Tragedy* (Toronto: Toronto University Press, 1957), p. 212; Roy Battenhouse, *Shakespearean Tragedy: Its Art and Its Christian Premises* (Bloomington: Indiana University Press, 1969), p. 301; Virgil K. Whitaker, *The Mirror up to Nature* (San Marigno: Huntington Library, 1965), p. 273; Walter Clyde Curry, *Shakespeare's Philosophical Patterns* (Baton Rouge: Louisiana Sate University Press, 1937), passim; Irving Ribner, *Patterns in Shakespearian Tragedy* (London: Methuen, 1960), p. 9.

17. One source that documents this commonplace of intellectual history is Herschel Baker, *The Image of Man: A Study of the Idea of Human Dignity in Classical Antiquity, the Middle Ages, and the Renaissance* (1947; reprint ed., New York: Harper and Row, 1961).

18. Alexander Pope, *An Essay on Man,* Epistle III, 217-18.

19. John Calvin, *Institutes of the Christian Religion,* ed. John T. McNeill (Philadelphia: Westminster, 1960), 1:258.

20. All quotations from *Macbeth* have been taken from the new Arden Edition of William Shakespeare, 9th edition, ed. Kenneth Muir (New York: Random House, 1962).

21. Kenneth Muir, "Introduction" to the Arden Edition of *Macbeth,* p. lii.

22. Whitaker, p. 265.

23. Dorothy L. Sayers, "Introduction" to *The Comedy of Dante Alighieri: Hell* (Baltimore: Penguin, 1949), p. 11. Sayers uses the phrase in connection with Dante's *Inferno*.

24. Roland M. Frye, "Introduction" to *The Bible: Selections from the King James Version for Study as Literature* (Boston: Houghton Mifflin, 1965), p. xxv.

25. Roland M. Frye, *Shakespeare and Christian Doctrine* (Princeton: Princeton University Press, 1963), p. 8.

26. Wilson, p. 70.

27. G. Wilson Knight, *The Wheel of Fire* (1930; reprint ed., Cleveland: World, 1957), p. 140.

28. Wilson, p. 74.

Chapter 7

What Is Christian Art?

The Christian Vision in Art

> Books like *Resurrection* and *The Brothers Karamazov* give me an almost overpowering sense of how uniquely marvelous a Christian way of looking at life is, and a passionate desire to share it.
>
> Malcolm Muggeridge, *Jesus Rediscovered*

What is the nature of the Christian vision in art? Is it a matter of form, subject matter, or interpretive perspective? If Christian art is distinguished by its view of reality, what aspects of the artistic work reveal that view? Must art be exclusively or explicitly Christian before it can be considered Christian? Or does the term extend to art that simply avoids violating Christian belief? Must Christian art give the whole truth about its particular topic, or only partial truth? Is art Christian if it simply explores the problems of human existence? Or must it suggest a Christian solution?

The question of what constitutes Christian art is important for at least three reasons. As I noted in the previous chapter, measuring the world view of works by a Christian standard is the distinctive interest of Christian criticism. Secondly, the question of what constitutes the Christian vision in art has been important in academic criticism of the arts. The issue is already on the agenda in the world of scholarship at large. And thirdly, it is of course the perennial question facing Christian artists.

Some Fallacies

Before attempting to answer the question of what is Christian in Christian art, I wish to clear the air of some misconceptions. One of these is that art is totally neutral in its viewpoint and that there can be no such thing as Christian art. W. H. Auden's statement that "there can no more be a 'Christian' art than there can be . . . a Christian diet" is sometimes taken seriously, but it deserves to be dismissed.[1] For one thing, there is such a thing as a Christian diet: it consists of eating meals that are healthful, moderate, modest in cost, and delicious. Auden's comment betrays an elementary failure in logic. Trees, rocks, and cars are amoral and intellectually neutral. But ideas, opinions, attitudes, and statements about life are either true or false.

Since art not only presents experience but also interprets it—since it has ideational content and embodies a world view or ethical outlook—it will always be open to classification as true or false, Christian or humanist or Marxist or what not. In the long run, every artist's work shows a moral and intellectual bias. It is this bias that can be compared to Christian belief.

In talking about the Christian element in art, we are not concerned with style or form. Such stylistic and formal elements as metaphor, narrative, symphony, or still life painting can be used in the service of virtually any philosophic outlook. Francis Schaeffer correctly asserts that "there is no such thing as a godly style or an ungodly style."[2] This is something we need to hear in Christian circles. For many Christians, the right style of painting is that found in sentimental and pseudo- realistic Sunday school illustrations.

And in music, the issue of association has proved troublesome. That is, people interpret music in terms of the context in which they have heard it. Music heard in a roller rink, for example, is regarded as inappropriate for a religious setting, not on the basis of its innate qualities but because of where it is traditionally heard. Rossini's "Overture to William Tell" is associated in most people's minds with cowboys because it was the theme of the "Lone Ranger" radio and television shows. But we cannot regard a style of music as being either godly or wicked simply on the basis of the context in which we happen to have heard it. The melody of Bach's chorale, *0 Sacred Head Now Wounded*, came from a popular street song of the day.

If the Christian element in art is not stylistic, neither is it primarily a matter of subject matter. If, in a Christian view, all of life is God's, the Christian vision in art can encompass the whole range of human experience, just as the Bible does. Artists are free to portray the subjects they are best at portraying. Francis Schaeffer again expresses it well:

> Christian art is by no means always religious art, that is, art which deals with religious themes. Consider God the Creator. Is God's creation totally involved with religious subjects? What about the universe? the birds? the trees? What about the bird's song? and the sound of the wind in the trees?[3]

Freedom for the Christian artist, writes H. R. Rookmaaker, "means that there are no prescriptions for subject-matter."[4]

The only qualification I would make in this regard is that "out of the abundance of the heart the mouth speaks" (Matthew 12:34). Sooner or later, writers or composers or painters will say something about the things that matter most to them. If this is true, it is inevitable that the Christian vision in art will be characterized by the presence rather than the absence of such realities as God, sin, redemption, and God's revelation of himself in both Word and Son.

Yet another troublesome fallacy in the scholarly world is the loose equation of religious art with Christian art. Christian belief is only one kind of religious viewpoint. To ask what constitutes the Christian vision in art, therefore, is to undertake an inquiry that is much more specific than simply identifying the nature of religious art or "the sacred" in art. That is why criticism that discusses the phenomenon of religious art is usually of little practical use in an analysis of the Christian element in art, particularly when the word religious is vaguely defined in terms of deep thought or ultimate concern.

If "religious art" is too broad a category to do justice to the Christian element in art, the category "devotional art" is too narrow. By devotional art I mean art whose subject matter is the specifically religious aspect of human experience or the theological doctrines of the Christian faith. The contemporary Christian poet Chad Walsh describes literature of this type as "books in which such words as God, Christ, soul, etc., frequently occur; or books dealing with Church life, ministers, devout souls, etc."[5]

"Christian dogma will aid the artist," writes Roy Battenhouse, "not by giving him a privileged and special subject- matter but rather by defining for him a perspective from which 'full light' can be had on all subject matters."[6] Or as Flannery O'Connor confirms from her perspective as a Christian fiction writer,

> What we call the Catholic novel is not necessarily about a Christianized or catholicized world, but simply . . . one in which the truth as Christians know it has been used as a light to see the world by. . . . The Catholic novel can't be categorized by subject matter, but only by what it assumes about human and divine reality.[7]

A final fallacy is the maddening practice of many Christians to allegorize works of art, especially works of literature. The practice is deeply engrained in a certain type of Christian temperament. When I assign a Christian critique of a poem, I can confidently expect to find one or more attempts to allegorize the poem to make its details fit events in the life of Christ or Christian doctrine. Why is this so offensive? Because the doctrine of creation tells us that things have value and integrity in terms of what they are as created objects. We do not need to allegorize trees or windows or sidewalks in terms of Christian doctrine before they fulfill their God-given purpose in life. By the same token, we should not attempt to define Christian art in terms of how easily we can allegorize the details to fit Christian doctrines.

The Variety of Ways in which Art Can be Christian

In answering the question of what constitutes a Christian vision in art, we should avoid a simple criterion by which we categorize all works as either Christian or non-Christian. Instead of a "great divide" approach, we need a framework that identifies the variety of ways in which a work of art can show a Christian allegiance.

This framework, I would suggest, should be viewed as a continuum that ranges from the superficially or incidentally Christian at one end to the thoroughly and explicitly Christian at the other. Such a scale allows us to analyze, not whether a work is Christian or non-Christian, but the levels at which a work engages (if it does at all) the Christian view of reality. It is useful, in fact, to speak of the ways in which a work of art intersects with Christianity.

Christian Allusions

The first level at which works of art intersect with the Christian faith occurs when artists use allusions to the Bible and/or to Christian doctrine or symbolism. At the very least, such allusions show an artist's familiarity with the Christian faith. Unless the allusions are purely decorative or incidental, they enter into the meaning that the work of art communicates. In any case, such works of art require the Christian religion as a necessary framework for understanding them. Allusions can also be an index to a genuine Christian vision. By themselves, however, biblical allusions or Christian symbols are the least reliable index to whether the allegiance of a work is Christian.

For one thing, many artists are interested in the Bible and in Christian symbols in the same way that they are interested in classical mythology—for primarily artistic reasons. Allusion and symbol are, after all, part of an artist's language. They do not necessarily imply anything at the level of ideas or world view. When Shakespeare says regarding lust that "none knows well/To shun the heaven that leads men to this hell" ("Sonnet 129"), he is using the Christian images of heaven and hell as metaphors or symbols of pleasure and degradation, respectively, not in the sense employed by Christian eschatology. When the twentieth-century poet Wilfred Owen entitles an anti-war poem "At a Calvary near the Ancre," he is using the Christian image to represent military carnage, not as a way of saying something about the Christian doctrine of redemption.

Another reason why Christian references do not necessarily imply a Christian viewpoint in a work is that many artists, especially modern ones, reinterpret Christian images or biblical material to produce something entirely different from, and sometimes opposite to, the original meaning. This was never so clear to me as when my interest in the Bible as literature led me to undertake a systematic survey of poems and stories dealing with biblical characters and events. The following three examples typify much of the literature:

- A poem entitled "The Parable of the Old Man and the Young" by Wilfred Owen, in which the Abraham and Isaac story of Genesis 22 is inverted by having Abraham refuse to kill the "Ram of Pride" and kill instead his son, a killing that becomes a symbol for the carnage of World War I.
- Companion poems by Louis Untermeyer entitled "Goliath and David," in which Goliath regrets his destructive strength while David decides to throw aside his stone and invite Goliath to "come and play."
- Archibald Macleish's play, *J. B.*, in which the moment of epiphany is not, as in the biblical Job, an insight into the glory of God and the possibility of human fellowship with him, but an affirmation of human love as the highest value.

While it is no comment either positively or negatively on the quality of these works, we must be aware of the way in which their themes have been freed from their original source, the Bible, and been transformed into a viewpoint totally new.

Christian allusions do not imply a Christian perspective in such works.

Not only do artists feel free to reinterpret Christian symbols and biblical material, they are also capable of using a Christian idiom or vocabulary to express a content or world view far removed from Christianity. William Wordsworth, for example, was a master at using a biblical idiom to express a romantic world view and pantheistic religious experience. "The world is too much with us," writes Wordsworth, and the idiom comes from New Testament statements about "the cares of the world" that destroy true values (Matthew 13:22) and about how we should "not love the world or the things in the world" (1 John 2:15) and should "not be conformed to this world" (Romans 12:2). But by the time he reaches the end of the sonnet, Wordsworth has declared his preference for a pagan sensitivity to nature over the world of Christian belief.

A poem such as "Tintern Abbey" shows Wordsworth's characteristic use of "the vocabulary of religious devotion displaced into a naturalistic mode."[8] William Butler Yeats entitled one of his most famous poems "The Second Coming," but his poem does not imply an acceptance of Christian eschatology. Instead, Yeats uses the Christian terminology to express his own theory of history as a series of cycles or "gyres," and his poem is a speculation about what kind of age is in the process of replacing Christianity.

I do not wish to leave the impression that biblical or Christian allusions are never an index to an artist's Christian allegiance. For truly Christian artists, such allusions are full of Christian meaning. Rembrandt painted scenes from the Bible as part of his own deeply felt Christian commitment. The biblical references in Kuhnau's *Biblical Sonatas* and Handel's *Messiah* contribute to the Christian meanings of those works.

Christian writers, too, use allusions to signalize that they wish their work to be interpreted in a Christian way. For example, it is a commonplace of Spenser criticism that Book I of the *Faerie Queene,* which celebrates the distinctively Christian ideal of holiness, is filled with biblical allusions and Christian symbols, while Book II, devoted to the classical ideal of temperance, draws its allusions primarily from classical literature and philosophy. When Milton chose Genesis 1-3 instead of military warfare as his epic subject, his choice was more than a literary decision. And when the poetry of the seventeenth-century devotional poet George Herbert relies continuously on the Bible and Anglican liturgy, we naturally interpret such references as an expression of his Christian experience.

Christian allusions, however, do not by themselves say much about the degree to which a work has been shaped by Christian belief. Pornographic paintings and stories have been produced from the biblical story of David and Bathsheba. There are deeper levels of commitment within a work itself that tell us how to interpret an artist's use of Christian allusions and symbols.

Inclusively Christian Viewpoints

A second level at which art can show a Christian allegiance occurs when artists embody values or viewpoints that are inclusively Christian. An idea or viewpoint is "inclusively Christian" when it belongs to the large area where Christian belief overlaps with other religious or ethical viewpoints. It includes both art that exhibits Christian ideas without any explicitly Christian references and art that uses Christian terminology to express viewpoints that are, however, not the exclusive property of Christianity. The ways in which art can be inclusively Christian are many.

One big category is art that is content to hold the mirror up to life without much concern to interpret reality. Lyric poets, for example, have produced an enormous quantity of nature poetry and love poetry that attempts to reproduce as accurately as possible the sights and sounds of the landscape or the emotions of love. Unless such poetry violates Christian belief by revealing a pantheistic attitude toward nature or celebrating illicit love, for example, it can be said to be in accord with the Christian view of reality, regardless of whether the writer uses explicitly Christian terms.

A great deal of painting and music falls into the same category. In an earlier chapter I noted that one of the levels of truth in art is truthfulness to reality and human experience. A landscape or portrait painting, a love song or symphony, typically expresses such truth.

I do not wish to belabor the point that one of the ways in which art can show a Christian allegiance without being exclusively Christian is by embodying viewpoints that are in accord with Christian doctrine. Even the Bible, an avowedly religious or sacred book, contains this kind of art. The carvings at the temple included images from nature such as flowers and lions. The Song of Solomon does not place human love within a context of divine love or specifically religious values. The story of Esther contains a reference to the religious practice of fasting, but beyond that it does not relate the human action to any specifically religious or supernatural framework, refraining even from the mention of God's name. If the Bible itself contains works that I have termed "inclusively Christian," we should not be surprised to find such works in abundance in art more generally.

Nor should we be surprised when non-Christian artists produce works that express insights that are true to Christian belief. For one thing, the Christian world view has exerted a strong and steady influence over Western civilization through the centuries, so that the thought patterns of many (some would say most) non-Christian artists have naturally been molded to some extent by the Christian world view. But there is also a theological reason why Christians should accept non-Christian artists as capable of expressing Christian truth. That reason, as noted in an earlier chapter, is the doctrine of common grace.

Exclusively Christian Viewpoints

The final way in which art can reveal its Christian allegiance is by exhibiting viewpoints that are exclusively Christian. This category consists of art whose themes are distinctive to the Christian faith. I do not have in mind only art whose subject matter is distinctively Christian, that is, art about the person and work of Christ, or art about Christian doctrines such as providence or atonement or heaven, or works dealing with biblical characters and events. I also have in mind art that exhibits a Christian slant on whatever topic it happens to portray.

The subject of Gerard Manley Hopkins' nature poem "Pied Beauty" is not distinctively Christian. People of many persuasions have been rapturous over the variegated colors and shapes of nature. But when Hopkins begins the poem with the line, "Glory be to God for dappled things," and when he concludes it with the statement, "He fathers-forth whose beauty is past change: / Praise him," the poem becomes an explicitly Christian statement.

Edmund Spenser's *Epithalamion* (wedding poem) belongs to a tradition that includes both Christian and classical poets. There was nothing to surprise a classical poet in the prayer for progeny with which the poem concludes. But when Spenser prays for children "to increase the count" of "blessed Saints" in heaven, he is giving his poem a distinctively Christian cast that removes it from a purely humanistic framework. When Milton protests the slaughter of the Waldensians in a sonnet that is structured as a prayer addressed to the God of the Bible, his poem has a distinctively Christian meaning that makes it different from protest literature in general.

In an earlier chapter I spoke of a world view as a way of looking at reality in terms of a central value. In art that is distinctively and exclusively Christian, this center of coherence is the triune God of the Bible. Whenever a work of art or a given artist's corpus of works elevates God to a position of supremacy and relates all other areas of life to God, it can be identified as Christian art.

It is important to note that a work of art can be Christian in this way without making use of Christian terminology. Milton's elegy "Lycidas" is, on the surface, a thoroughly classical poem replete with allusions to classical mythology. This, however, is merely the poetic vehicle. At the level of theme and idea, the poem affirms such distinctively Christian doctrines as the life everlasting, heaven, God's personal providence, and the substitutionary atonement of Christ.

The Christian Vision in *Beowulf*

What I have said about the Christian element in art can be put into focus by a brief application to the Old English epic *Beowulf.* A leading issue in Beowulf scholarship continues to be the controversy over whether the epic merits the title "Christian." As I have suggested, we can expect the Christian data in the story to fall into several distinct categories.

I reject as legitimate data the details in the story that can be allegorized to make them fit Christian doctrine. M. B. McNamee, for example, interprets the story as an allegory of "the Christian story of salvation," with the story of the hero symbolizing "the very life of the Savior Himself."[9] Someone else regards the story as "a single allegorical song intimating the Divine Mystery of Redemption," concluding that "Beowulf, offering himself for others, is Christ redeeming man by self-sacrifice."[10]

The fact that the details in a rescue story can be allegorized in Christian terms proves nothing. Any rescue story, including the last one we have seen on television, is a Christian work by such logic. The Middle Ages allegorized pagan mythology in the same way, turning the *Aeneid,* for example, into a "Christian" work.[11] But we know that neither Virgil nor his epic was Christian in allegiance. The Christian element in a work of art must be judged by the kind of work it really is. The Christian doctrine of creation should lead us to respect the created nature of things. Nothing positive is gained by forcing works of art into something they are not.

I have seen an interpretation of "Humpty Dumpty" that allegorizes it to be "definitely a religious poem," re-enacting the falls of Adam and Satan. This is doubly wrong: It ignores the genre of the piece (and all that genre implies about intended meaning), and it robs criticism of its integrity as the discipline that elucidates the meanings that are genuinely present in works of art.[12]

Christian Allusions in *Beowulf*

One class of Christian data in *Beowulf* consists of allusions to the Bible and Christian doctrine. An early study of these allusions identified the total number as 68, with most of them consisting of "incidental allusions to the Christian God, to his attributes, and to his part in shaping the lives and fortunes of men."[13] The same study noted the omission of any references to Christ, the cross, the Virgin Mary, saints, the Trinity, or the Atonement. Later criticism also uncovered allusions to heathen practices and ideas that contradict the Chritian faith, reinforcing my earlier caution that writers who use Christian allusions tend also to use pagan sources.

By itself, therefore, the use of Christian allusions does not prove a Christian outlook in *Beowulf*. Still, the Christian allusions represent one indisputable level at which the epic interacts with the Christian faith.

The Hero and Ethos in the Story

Since *Beowulf* belongs to a literary family that I call heroic narrative (a story built around the exploits of an exemplary hero), we can expect the question of the degree to which the story is Christian to be decided most profoundly by the image of the hero in the story. The epic Beowulf idealizes a certain type of character. Does Christianity idealize the same type of conduct? To what extent does the epic ethos correspond to the biblical ethos?

If we look for evidence of a Christian perspective in the characterization of the hero, we will conclude that the story exhibits values that are inclusively Christian. The most important of these are hatred of evil, a spirit of self-sacrifice, loyalty in human relations, and belief in a personal God of providence. The first three of these were equally characteristic of the Germanic comitatus ethos that provides (with Christianity) the other ethical foundation of the story.

If there is anything distinctively Christian in the picture, it is of minor importance. For example, the forces of evil are occasionally associated with Christian ideas of devils and hell. Similarly, God is occasionally given attributes that make the theology not simply theistic but something that approximates Christianity (for example, God is almighty, ruler, and judge).

Elements that Contradict a Christian Outlook

In addition to displaying inclusively Christian virtues, the hero possesses traits that violate a Christian ethical ideal. The hero is proud and boastful and is governed by a desire for earthly fame, in a manner directly antithetical to Christlike humility. He shows a trust in military strength in violation of the psalmist's aphorism that "a warrior is not delivered by his great strength." And the story of the hero elevates material goods, especially treasure, to an exalted status in contradiction of Christ's command, "Lay not up for yourselves treasures on earth."

Some Telling Omissions

If, in addition, we pause to ask what things would have to be added to the list of Beowulf's character traits to make the portrait explicitly Christian, the list turns out to be rather revealing: something to show that the goal of human life is more than earthly success and fame; something to show the hero's consciousness of sin; something to indicate that the highest joy in life comes from being redeemed through the atonement of Christ; something to show that the proper motivation and power for virtuous conduct are supernaturally grounded.

Christian Artists

> Your beliefs will be the light by which you see, but they will not be what you see and they will not be a substitute for seeing. . . . I have found, . . . from reading my own writing, that my subject in fiction is the action of grace in territory held by the devil.
>
> Flannery O'Connor, *Mystery and Manners*

To theorize about the aims and methods of Christian writers, composers, and visual artists is to enter an arena of controversy. Why would we even try to theorize about the subject? Chiefly because the topic keeps coming up. It is already on the agenda. Christian artists themselves agonize over the issue because for them it is the question of vocation: How can they do their work to the glory of God?

Christian audiences inevitably have their own agenda of expectations for Christian artists. These expectations are partly conscious, partly unconscious, but they often come out in our conversations about art. Christians interested in the arts find themselves making statements that imply a theory about the task of the Christian artist.

To expect total agreement on the issue of the Christian artist is, I have found, quite futile. It is a controversial topic. I have also discerned something of a cleavage between Christian artists and Christian consumers of the arts. Artists themselves want freedom; they generally do not want prescriptive curbs put on their creativity. This is true chiefly because the process of artistic creativity is very intuitive and unconscious. Yet Christian artists will harm only themselves if they turn a deaf ear to the expectations of their audiences.

In the overview that follows, I have tried to balance the claims of artists with my insights as a critic. For those who disagree with my conclusions, I hope I will have at least raised the right questions.

Mastery of Artistic Form and Technique

Christian artists are first of all artists. They must master the craft of their art, just as a Christian basketball player must learn to shoot baskets and a Christian pianist must learn to play the keys on the keyboard. Christian artists must therefore be assured that meaning is conveyed through form. The Christian view of reality will never be transmuted into art—and it will never have great impact on an audience—unless Christian artists have managed to incarnate it in artistic form.

This means that Christian artists must be alert to the principle that art works by indirection. To be overly abstract or explicit in expressing one's viewpoint is to kill the artistic effect. The true artist perceives and describes the world as image and event, not as abstraction or system. The most common feature of weak writing, by Christians and by anyone else, is a failure to operate by concretion and indirection. Mediocre Christian art has a fatal tendency to Spell It Out. It is moralizing instead of simply moral, preachy rather than incarnational. Christian audiences are just as culpable, encouraging and even demanding such tendencies.

Cleanth Brooks has said that the writer "must be indirect, and as a consequence he always has to say to his audience: he that hath ears to hear, let him hear."[14] The terrifying question facing the Christian artist, therefore, is, Do I dare trust the resources of my art to express the truth? Am I willing to run the risk that my audience will do its half of the work of artistic communication?

What this means is that the Christian poet must master the poetic idiom—metaphor, image, and figures of speech. Simply to put Christian ideas into verse will not make one a Christian poet. A Christian writer of narrative must learn to invent the kinds of characters and events that will completely absorb the vision or theme. Christian dramatists must learn the knack of creating characters, dialogue, and dramatic situations that will incarnate what they are trying to communicate. The Christian painter must learn the principles of design and color.

Stylistic excellence should be a goal of every Christian artist for at least two reasons. As I have said many times in this book, a Christian world view values artistic beauty or form in itself. "What is good in itself," writes Flannery O'Connor, "glorifies God because it reflects God."[15] Secondly, as Francis Schaeffer correctly notes, "Art forms add strength to the world view which shows through, no matter what the world view is. . . . Good prose as an art form has something bad prose does not."[16] Christian content does not redeem a work that is technically mediocre; in fact, the lack of artistic excellence detracts from the impact of the Christian content.

Part of any artist's work is to observe life carefully and then capture it in art. This, too, is a skill the Christian artist must master just as any other artist does. Flannery O'Connor has expressed it very well:

> The beginning of human knowledge is through the senses, and the fiction writer begins where human perception begins. . . . Any discipline can help your writing: logic, mathematics, theology, and of course and particularly drawing. Anything that helps you see, anything that makes you look. The writer should never be ashamed of staring.[17]

The Subject Matter of the Christian Artist

If there is nothing distinctive about the artistic form of Christian artists, neither is there anything very different about their subject matter. Art that deals with specifically religious subjects—stories from the Bible, God, worship, Christian doctrines, prayer, the church calendar—is only one kind of Christian art. The seventeenth-century Anglican preacher and poet George Herbert devoted all of his poetic talents to this kind of poetry, partly, no doubt, because it was the kind of poetry at which he was best. But it would be tragic if every Christian artist chose only this part of reality for portrayal. That would be tantamount to turning over to non-Christian artists the other great areas of human experience.

The Christian faith has something to say about all of life, and Christian artists must subject all of life to the light of their faith. A Christian artist is Christian, not by virtue of his or her subject matter, but by virtue of the perspective that is brought to bear on the subject. The Bible itself points the way. In the Bible, spiritual reality reaches down into the very fabric of everyday life and touches upon every area of life, not simply a person's devotional life.

That is why Chad Walsh can say that a Christian novelist's "plots and characters may be precisely those one would find in a naturalistic or existentialist novel. . . . It is . . . the angle of vision, the nuances that a different pair of eyes can yield, a way of understanding, not subject matter" that differentiates a Christian writer's work.[18] "Christian art," writes Francis Schaeffer, "is the expression of the whole life of the whole person who is a Christian. What a Christian portrays in his art is the totality of life. . . . The art of an artist who never paints the head of Christ, never once paints an open tomb, may be magnificent Christian art."[19]

The Christian Perspective on Reality

What, then, will be distinctive about the perspective that Christian artists bring to their subject matter? Must their work be explicitly and distinctively Christian? Or should they be content if their work falls into the "inclusively Christian" category?

While it is no doubt undesirable to ask that every work written by a Christian exhibit a distinctively Christian identity, I believe that a Christian's overall production will show signs that label it as specifically Christian. This is simply the point at which Christian witness enters the Christian artist's vocation. The Christian faith is unique. Although Christian artists naturally share much with any other artist, they can scarcely avoid expressing the uniqueness of their Christian perspective.

In an earlier chapter I noted that artists create a whole world of the imagination that reveals their fundamental premises about life and a central integrating force. Christian artists are no exception. While their work should not preach a Christian world view, it should reveal it implicitly. And if artists inevitably express, at least part of the time, what matters most to them, a Christian artist's work will surely touch upon such realities as God, providence, forgiveness, salvation, and the life everlasting. This is perhaps truest for writers, since literature is the most ideational of the arts.

One reason why Christian artists will refuse to stay within the broad area where Christianity is like another moral or philosophic viewpoint is that by doing so they run the risk of having their own viewpoint misunderstood. Christians who produce social protest art, for example, may find their analysis of the social situation almost the same as that of a radical or Marxist, let us say. But their analysis of what causes social problems, as well as their solutions to human misery and depravity, will be distinctive. Will the Christian artist not wish to keep the record straight?

The "World" of the Christian Artist

Aristotle claimed that the artist "imitates nature," that is, observes reality and records its enduring qualities. For a naturalist or secularist, this means taking a look around and writing about the external world of nature and society. But if Christians live simultaneously in two worlds—if they believe that in addition to earthly reality there is a heavenly, spiritual world—then the reality they portray in art will be different from that of the non-Christian artist. In the words of Flannery O'Connor, "the Christian novelist lives in a larger universe. He believes that the natural world contains the supernatural." The Christian writer's "country," she says elsewhere, is not simply the countryside or a nation, but also "his true country, which the writer with Christian convictions will consider to be what is eternal and absolute."[20]

The "world" of the Christian artist also includes a view of people and human nature. Flannery O'Connor says about the Christian writer, "It makes a great difference to his novel whether he believes we are created in God's image" and "whether he believes that our wills are free."[21] And again, "The Christian novelist is distinguished from his pagan colleagues by recognizing sin as sin. According to his heritage he sees it not as sickness or an accident of environment, but as a responsible choice of offense against God which involves his eternal future."[22] To say that a Christian artist's view of humanity will display these characteristics is not to set up a checklist of items that must be put into a work. The task of the Christian artist is to portray human life, not to illustrate a list of doctrines. But it is to say that when Christian artists portray human nature, the portrait should be theologically accurate.

How Positive Must the Picture of Reality Be?

Will the overall thrust of Christian artists be positive? Will they suggest solutions in addition to exploring problems? I believe that they will.

A Christian's purpose in life is to be redemptive in the world. Someone who takes the example of Christ's life as a guide can tolerate neither a refusal to become immersed in the flow of actual human life in this world nor a willingness to leave fallen human life where it is. The Christian artist's mission is to add to the beauty, truth, and joy of the world, not its hopelessness. Flannery O'Connor put it concisely when she said, "I see from the standpoint of Christian orthodoxy. This means that for me the meaning of life is centered in our Redemption by Christ and what I see in the world I see in its relation to that."[23]

The best framework for resolving this issue is the one suggested by Francis Schaeffer. "The Christian world view," he writes, "can be divided into . . . a major and a minor theme." The minor theme is "the abnormality of the revolting world," which includes both the lostness of the world without Christ and the "defeated and sinful side to the Christian's life." The major theme "is the opposite of the minor; it is the meaningfulness and purposefulness of life." Its basis is the work of God. Christian artists have a responsibility to both themes:

> The Christian and his art have a place for the minor theme because man is lost and abnormal and the Christian has his own defeatedness. There is not only victory and song in my life. But the Christian and his art don't end there. He goes on to the major theme because there is an optimistic answer. This is important for the kind of art Christians are to produce.[24]

Notice that Schaeffer envisions a double emphasis in Christian art, just as there is in the Bible. The Christian vision of the world is comprehensive. It includes the bad news as well as the good news. Christian art does justice to both halves. Furthermore, great art earns the right to make its affirmations. It does so by giving a fair hearing to all sides of life, including the evil and misery in it. Mediocre Christian art provides easy answers and glosses over the misery of life.

How Self-Consciously Christian Should an Artist Be?

Will a Christian artist automatically produce art that reflects a Christian view of things? Is it true that a Christian cannot help but produce art that is Christian? Or should Christian artists consciously subject their work to Christian analysis?

In my experience, artists resist the idea of self-consciousness. It has become a hallowed rite for many of them to trot out T. S. Eliot's statement that he wanted "a literature which should be *un*consciously, rather than deliberately and defiantly, Christian."[25] A look at the context in which Eliot's statement appears shows at once that the statement does not mean what its quoters think it does and that, in fact, the word "unconsciously" was not an accurate word for Eliot's intended meaning. The statement appears in a passage where Eliot is denigrating overly obvious religious literature that "may come under the heading of Propaganda." What Eliot meant by "unconsciously Christian" was "sufficiently indirect, incarnational, and subtle to be true art."

I suggest that artists themselves know the most about the process of creativity. If they find that in the act of creating they cannot afford to be overly self-conscious about their beliefs we should grant them the freedom that they need. On the other hand, there is no reason to treat them as a special class of Christians.

We can clarify the issue if we simply view Christian artists like other Christians who speak publicly—Christian teachers or lecturers or neighbors, for example. What do we expect of such people? We expect that much of what they say will simply be the words of a person speaking to other people (to paraphrase Wordsworth's definition of the poet). We expect that they will not speak contrary to the truth of the Christian faith. And we expect that at least sometimes they will say things that are explicitly Christian. In order to do all these things, they will have to be thinking Christians who understand the content of Christian doctrine, and witnessing Christians who say what God means to them when the occasion arises. I see no reason why Christian artists should be exempt from this.

If Christian artists need freedom from self-conscious intellectual restraints in the act of creating, they must also be aware that revision and conscious analysis of the work, once it is standing, are also part of artistic composition. If artists find it helpful to be self-forgetful while they are inventing, they also find it necessary to be self-conscious when they revise. This may be the stage at which they need to test the accuracy of their perspective. If their Christian viewpoint has gotten into the work by intuition, they are to be congratulated. If not, they need to reconsider their work. For artists who find their Christian faith an artistic burden, who claim, for example, that "I find that as a poet I have had to shake loose some of what I learned in church and catechism class,"[26] the task of integrating faith and life is incomplete.

The Same Rules Apply to Critics

I should note that the responsibilities I have suggested for Christian artists apply equally to the audience of art and to the critics or teachers who write and speak about art. Christian consumers of art are sometimes more zealous to lay down rules for Christian artists than for themselves. If criticism is as much a personal expression as art itself is, everything I have said about the Christian artist is also true of Christian critics. Their analysis of art and public statements, too, should be true to their outlook as Christians.

The Artist's Calling

The Christian artist's calling is a great one. John Milton felt called from adolescence to be a poet, and he devoted long years of tireless preparation to fulfilling his calling. Although he had planned as a college student to enter the ministry, the corruptness of the church hierarchy and his Puritan leanings led him eventually to reject the church as his vocation. There is plenty of evidence that he did not regard himself as having settled for something second best by becoming a poet instead of a preacher.

Christian artists today deserve the support of the Christian church in a way that they do not come close to receiving. It is professionally disadvantageous to be a Christian artist, just as it is often disadvantageous to be a Christian in other professions.

The Christian church is suspicious of the artist, partly because the artist's task is to express the truth in perpetually fresh ways. But the task of closing the gap of suspicion between the artist and the believing community rests at least as much with the latter.

We need to see far more poetry and art in the church than we currently do. These are among the most powerful sources of Christian truth that we have available. Some of my most successful prayer meetings have come when, instead of discussing a Bible passage, the group explicated a Christian poem.

The Christian artist is, ideally, the speaker for the Christian view of things in the world of the arts and in society. If the Christian church extends its hands of blessing and support over its missionaries of the gospel, should it not do the same for those who speak the truth through art to an unbelieving world? And if Christian professors and sociologists and psychologists or those in business are given a platform to speak within the church, should not the Christian artist be encouraged to speak through art within the church? What the Christian artist has to say is fully as important as what another Christian professional has to say.

The time has come to hear the voice of the Christian artist in the worship service, in the sermon or small-group meeting, in church programs and special nights, in the hallway and church newsletter. The believing community portrayed in the Bible did not distrust the storyteller and poet and musician and visual artist. Neither should the Christian church today.

Summary

The Christian element in art is not primarily a matter of style, form, or subject matter. It consists rather of the perspective that a work embodies toward the subject matter that is portrayed.

There is a range of ways in which a work of art can embody Christian viewpoints or intersect with the Christian faith. The levels of involvement with Christianity include the use of Christian allusions and symbols, the embodiment of inclusively

Christian themes, and the expression of exclusively Christian concepts.

Christian artists must first of all be artists. The distinctively Christian element in their work is the perspective that they embody toward reality and the details of their imaginative world.

Further Reading

Flannery O'Connor, *Mystery and Manners* (1957).

John Killinger, *The Failure of Theology in Modern Literature* (1963).

John W. Dixon, Jr., *Nature and Grace in Art* (1964).

Madeleine L'Engle, *Walking on Water: Reflections on Faith and Art* (1972).

Leland Ryken, ed., *The Christian Imagination: Essays on Literature and the Arts* (1981).

Eugene Warren, "Speaking to Others: Christian Poet and Audience," *Christianity and Literature*, 32, No. 2 (Winter 1983): 15-18.

Chapter 7, Notes

1. W. H. Auden's statement appears in "Postscript: Christianity and Art," in *The New Orpheus: Essays toward a Christian Poetic*, ed. Nathan A. Scott, Jr. (New York: Sheed and Ward, 1964), p. 76.

2. Francis A. Schaeffer, "Some Perspectives on Art," in *The Christian Imagination: Essays on Literature and the Arts*, ed. Leland Ryken (Grand Rapids: Baker, 1981), p. 92.

3. Schaeffer, p. 95.

4. H. R. Rookmaaker, "Letter to a Christian Artist," in *The Christian Imagination*, ed. Ryken, p. 369.

5. Chad Walsh, "The Advantages of the Christian Faith for a Writer," in *The Christian Imagination*, ed. Ryken, p. 313.

6. Roy Battenhouse, "The Relation of Theology to Literary Criticism," in *Religion and Modern Literature*, ed. G. B. Tennyson and Edward E. Ericson, Jr. (Grand Rapids: William B. Eerdmans, 1975), p. 91.

7. Flannery O'Connor, *Mystery and Manners*, ed. Sally and Robert Fitzgerald (New York: Farrar, Straus and Giroux, 1957), pp. 174, 196.

8. Harold Bloom, *The Visionary Company* (Garden City: Doubleday, 1963), p. 148. One of the main thrusts of M. H. Abrams book *Natural Supernaturalism* (New York: W. W. Norton, 1971) is to show the extent to which the writings of Wordsworth "transpose . . . the design, concepts, and images of Biblical history and prophecy" from their original meanings.

9. M. B. McNamee, "Beowulf—An Allegory of Salvation?" *Journal of English and Germanic Philology,* 59 (1960): 190-207; reprint. *An Anthology of Beowulf Criticism,* ed. Lewis E. Nicholson (Notre Dame: University of Notre Dame Press, 1963), pp. 331-352.

10. Gerald G. Walsh, *Medieval Humanism* (New York: Macmillan, 1942), pp. 45-46.

11. For documentation, see, for example, Douglas Bush, *Mythology and the Renaissance Tradition in English Poetry,* revised edition (New York: W. W. Norton, 1963), pp. 5-22.

12. The interpretation of "Humpty Dumpty" is reprinted in *The Case for Poetry: A Critical Anthology,* 2d edition, ed. F. L. Gwinn et al. (Englewood Cliffs: Prentice-Hall, 1965), p. 13.

13. F. A. Blackburn, "The Christian Coloring in the Beowulf," *PMLA,* 12 (1897): 205-225; reprint. *An Anthology of Beowulf Criticism,* ed. Nicholson, pp. 1-21.

14. Cleanth Brooks, *The Hidden God* (New Haven: Yale University Press, 1963), p. 72.

15. O'Connor, p. 171.

16. Schaeffer, pp. 85-86.

17. O'Connor, pp. 67, 84.

18. Chad Walsh, p. 313.

19. Schaeffer, p. 96.

20. O'Connor, pp. 175, 27, respectively.

21. Ibid., pp. 156-157.

22. Ibid., p. 167.

23. Ibid., p. 32.

24. Schaeffer, pp. 93-94.

25. T. S. Eliot, "Religion and Literature," as reprinted in *The Christian Imagination,* ed. Ryken, p. 146.

26. Rod Jellema, "Poems Should Stay across the Street from the Church," in *The Christian Imagination,* ed. Ryken, p. 335. I do not wish to appear totally unsympathetic to Jellema's description of the artist's dilemma. His essay is superb on the subject of poetry. On the other hand, I found revealing the following critique in a review of the latest volume of Jellema's poetry: "By remaining totally nonconfessional, uncommitted to larger life issues, Jellema remains in toto what he, in fact, is as craftsman—superficial" (*Choice* Card).

Chapter 8

Recent Trends in the Arts

What should Christians do with contemporary literature, music, and art? This is the most problematical question that arises in any attempt to integrate art and faith. Christians cannot afford to ignore the contemporary scene. If they are to speak at all to their culture, they need to understand it and formulate a defensible response to it. But contemporary art is generally hostile to Christian values, and this naturally creates problems.

In the discussion that follows, I have attempted to delineate the leading contours in the landscape of current art. I have not included detailed analyses of specific works to illustrate my generalizations. My purpose is rather to provide an overview into which readers can fit what they already know about contemporary art. I assume that we all have enough encounter with our culture that illustrations would be superfluous. The quickest way to illustrate what I say would be to browse in an anthology of modern literature and visit the modern section of an art gallery.

The Secular Spirit

> What I . . . wish to affirm is that the whole of modern literature is corrupted by what I call Secularism, that it is simply unaware of, simply cannot understand the meaning of, the primacy of the supernatural over the natural life: of something which I assume to be our primary concern.
>
> T. S. Eliot, "Religion and Literature"

The decline of Christianity as the intellectual system that most Americans and Europeans accepted as truth is the biggest cultural movement of the last two centuries. The roots of that decline can be traced back at least as far as the eighteenth century, which is commonly known as "the Enlightenment" or "the Age of Reason." In the two centuries since then, a thoroughgoing secularism has replaced Christianity as the dominant intellectual and moral force in society.

Secularism in Art

One manifestation of the decline of Christianity as an intellectual force in Western culture is the absence of the Christian supernatural in works of art. During the Middle Ages and Reformation era, the Christian faith provided the most frequent subject matter for art, music, and literature. Even a roll call of the titles of works produced during those centuries reveals how such Christian realities as God, the person and work of Christ, sin, and salvation dominated the artistic imagination.

The decline of this Christian influence can be traced with greatest clarity in literature.[1] Until the end of the seventeenth century, writers wrote about God and Christian experience because these were the things that mattered most to them. There followed an era in which writers assumed the existence of the Christian faith but largely omitted it from their picture of reality. In the next phase, writers argued about the faith, lamented its passing, or defended it against assaults. In the twentieth century, most writers are either oblivious to Christianity or treat it as an anachronism—a museum piece from the dead past.

Modern art, literature, and music are thus characterized by

an alarming and blasphemous secularism. In the words of T. S. Eliot, "We must remember that the greater part of our current reading matter is written for us by people who have no real belief in a supernatural order, though some of it may be written by people with individual notions of a supernatural order which are not ours."[2] In our contacts with today's advertising, news media, television drama, or movies, where are we given any encouragement to believe that there exists a spiritual reality beyond what our senses can observe?

A Christian Critique of Secularism

How, then, should Christians respond to the phenomenon of secular culture? They should begin by acknowledging that it represents the mindset of most people living in our culture. Here, in short, is what it means to live without God in the world, and here, therefore, is an occasion for vicarious empathy with a lost world. Jesus was unfailingly patient in understanding the unregenerate mind and in hearing it out. We cannot do less.

But neither should Christians minimize the untruth of secular art. To ignore God and spiritual values as secular art does is a monstrosity in God's world. No matter how great an artist's technique might be, or how sensitive the portrayal of human experience is, a work of art is finally false if it limits reality to the temporal, physical world or omits God's existence from its picture of reality. As Francis Schaeffer notes, "Art may heighten the impact of the world view (in fact, we can count on this), but it does not make something true. The truth of a world view presented by an artist must be judged on grounds other than artistic greatness."[3]

If modern art is prevailingly secular, so is modern criticism. Academic presses and the review media are heavily biased against Christian viewpoints. Even where they are not hostile, they are simply uninterested in a Christian viewpoint. This, too, leads people into a distorted view of reality. If Christian artists are responsible to tell the whole truth, so are Christian critics and teachers.

Art as a Substitute Religion

The secularization of Western culture was accompanied by the elevation of art to the position of a substitute religion to replace Christianity. We may think this is a movement limited to artists and does not extend to the masses, but we should not quickly conclude this. The case has been made that in our own secular culture, movies and popular music have replaced the pulpit as the leading influence on people's thinking and values.

The self-conscious worship of art about which I am speaking here has belonged for two centuries to the artistic elite of the world. It is part of the institution of "high art." The French novelist Gustave Flaubert wrote, for example,

> Art is vast enough to take complete possession of a man. To divert anything from it is . . . a sin. . . . I am turning to a kind of aesthetic mysticism. . . , and I wish my faith were stronger. . . . We must love one another in Art, as the mystics love one another in God.[4]

The most influential statement of the view comes from the pen of Matthew Arnold, the English Victorian worshiper of culture:

> More and more mankind will discover that we have to turn to poetry to interpret life for us . . . ; and most of what now passes for religion and philosophy will be replaced by poetry.[5]

A Christian Response

There is a right and wrong Christian response to such idolatry. The most common response has been for Christians to say, in effect, "See—this is what contact with the arts leads to. A person had better stay away from art." But this is to adopt an unbiblical scorn for art and to turn the whole artistic enterprise over to the unbelieving segment in our culture.

Let us remember that the non-Christian mind elevates much besides art to the status of a substitute religion. We do not avoid cars or ball games or clothes or science or good works because some people have made idols of them. The Bible teaches us to value art. We can love it without worshiping it. The Christian doctrine of creation should spare us from both the worship and the rejection of art.

Christians should of course resist any cultural trend to elevate art above its creaturely status. It is not the ultimately important thing in life. When I have attended poetry readings on university campuses, I have been struck by the religious atmosphere of such occasions. People approach the event with all the reverence of a church service. Art can never hold such a place in the life of a Christian. As C. S. Lewis said,

> The Christian will take literature a little less seriously than the cultured Pagan. . . . The unbeliever is always apt to make a kind of religion of his aesthetic experiences. . . . But the Christian knows from the outset that the salvation of a single soul is more important than the production and preservation of all the epics and tragedies in the world.[6]

The Autonomy of the Artist

> The artist's work can have meaning for the society God put him in if he does not go to live in the ivory tower. . . . He has to make art while thinking of his neighbors in love, helping them, and using his talents in their behalf.
>
> H. R. Rookmaaker, "Letter to a Christian Artist"

The Artist as Superior Genius

Society at large has never held a single view of artists. Sometimes artists have been a neglected minority. At other times, such as during the Renaissance, they have held an exalted and admired position in society. Before the nineteenth century, however, there was an underlying agreement that what set writers, painters, and musicians apart from ordinary people was their skill with their chosen artistic medium. What distinguishes the artist, in this view, is an ability, just as cooks have the ability to prepare food and doctors to diagnose and treat illnesses.

But the romantic movement of the nineteenth century introduced an important shift by defining artists, not by their ability to manipulate the techniques of a given craft, but by their personal and moral qualities. In this theory, art is not a voluntary creative activity but an inherent superiority of person. Artists thus became viewed as a separate race of great souls.

The definition of the poet offered by the English romantic poet William Wordsworth is a typical illustration of what happened. The poet, said Wordsworth, is a person

> endowed with a more lively sensiblity, more enthusiasm and tenderness, who has a greater knowledge of human nature, and a more comprehensive soul, than are supposed to be common among mankind; a man . . . who rejoices more than other men in the spirit of life that is in him. . . .[7]

The superiority of the poet, according to this definition, is not skill with words or the inventive ability to discover metaphors or an ease with putting words into regular rhythm and rhyme. Instead it consists of a superiority to other people in such traits of character as "sensiblity," "enthusiasm," and "tenderness."

Once this attitude became entrenched, it produced some notable and unfortunate results in the lives of writers, painters, and musicians. Arrogance was only the beginning of woes. Much more troubling was a prevailing belief among artists that their genius put them above ordinary morality. The personal lives of artists, especially in the twentieth century, have frequently been sordid. Some of the best known of such artists have committed suicide. Reading their biographies reveals not only the moral aberrations of the artists themselves but also the assumption of some biographers that their subject's genius makes him or her exempt from ordinary morality.[8]

Naturally, the belief of artists that they could do as they pleased affected the works of art they produced. Art increasingly became an assault on traditional morality and a shock to conventional standards of good taste. The artist Hans Hofmann sounded the keynote when he wrote, "The encompassing, creative mind recognizes no boundaries."[9]

The Christian View of Art as God's Gift

A Christian world view finds no place for such a theory of the artist as superhuman. In my earlier survey of what the Bible says about the arts, I noted the passages in Exodus that describe how God endowed the artists who beautified the tabernacle. Here we find the Christian view of the artist in kernel form, and the important idea is that God is the ultimate source of artistic talent. He endows artists with the specific abilities that their art requires. Artists, like everyone else, are the recipients of grace. They are stewards of what has been given to them. God gave them the gift of artistic ability, not for unrestrained self-indulgence, but to glorify God and serve their fellow humans.

It goes without saying that the very idea that anyone is above morality is repugnant to everything we find in the Bible. No one, whether king, priest, or servant, is exempt from moral criticism in the Bible.

In short, a Christian world view stands opposed to prevalent modern assumptions about artists as superior creatures. That theory, as C. S. Lewis has correctly stated, was "first made by the arrogance of [artists] and since accepted by the misdirected humility of an irreligious age."[10]

The Isolation of the Artist

The romantic glorification of the artist at the beginning of the nineteenth century produced a related phenomenon at the end of the century. It was the isolation or alienation of artists from their surrounding culture. A substantial number of artists in any age have been temperamentally solitary figures. But generally, they have expressed the values and attitudes of their age and regarded themselves as members of their society.

Beginning late in the last century, however, writers, artists and musicians self-consciously cultivated their alienation from their society. They flaunted their scorn for the middle class masses. They lived in communities of artists (especially in Paris) in splendid exile from their native culture. "By example and reason," says one scholar,"they announced the independence of art, its freedom not only from society and moral convention but from nature itself."[11]

Such exile naturally affected the art, literature, and music that artists produced. Above all, it produced a new obscurity in the arts. Writing and painting for self-expression rather than communication, artists produced works that few can understand.

In literature, for example, twentieth-century writers have generally accepted the theory articulated by T. S. Eliot in 1921 that "we can only say that it appears likely that poets in our civilization . . . must be difficult. . . . The poet must become more and more comprehensive, more allusive, more indirect, in order to force, to dislocate if necessary, language into his meaning."[12] This theory has dominated twentieth-century literature.

In both poetry and the novel, writers have used a stream-of-consciousness technique in which events and images are thrown incoherently together in imitation of how the mind actually works. This structural disjointedness is matched by esoteric allusions and an absence of explanatory comment within poems and stories that might suggest an interpretive framework for the images and events. Equally prevalent has been the tendency of poets to develop their private mythology and system of symbols instead of relying on the inherited cultural framework of myths and symbols. The resulting obscurity has made most modern literature inaccessible to all but a handful of people who study it in college courses.

The Christian Ideals of Community and Servanthood

What does the Christian faith say about a movement that removes art from the population at large? More crucially, how can a contemporary Christian artist negotiate between the expectations of a Christian public that art communicate something to them and the demands of experts that contemporary art conform to current artistic styles and norms?

Before we denounce obscurity in modern art, we should acknowledge that not all modern art is equally inaccessible. Some of it is on a par with the poetry of Shakespeare and Milton or the symphonies of Beethoven or the paintings of Rembrandt. Great art is never transparent. It requires and then repays serious effort from a reader, listener, or viewer. Once a person has gone to the initial scholarly effort to master a piece of modern art, he or she can "walk into" the work and possess it at will.

Having said that, it is also true that most modern art, music, and literature does not aim to be accessible to society at large. I see no reason why a person should feel guilty about leaving such art untouched. Communication is a two-way street. There is enough great art from the past to go around. If modern artists are uninterested in communicating, they should be granted their wish. We can legitimately regard intelligibility in art as a qualifying exam: if it cannot even pass that criterion, we are relieved from inquiring further into its qualities.

But what about Christian artists who must choose a contemporary style in which to compose their works? They should begin with the premise that they are not exempt from the Christian ideals of community and servanthood. The Christian poet John Donne captured the essence of Christian belief about community when he wrote that "no man is an island, entire of itself."[13] The Bible never considers the possibility of an individual achieving full meaning apart from community. The obligation to serve one's fellow humans is written large in both Testaments.

For Christian artists to regard these as their foundational premises will naturally set them apart from prevailing trends. It is the glory of their Christian vocation to see themselves as serving a genuine social function. Artists are people who have been given a talent by God. The use to which they should put that gift has been beautifully stated in 1 Peter 4:10-11:

> As each has received a gift, employ it for one another, as good stewards of God's varied grace: whoever . . . renders service, as one who renders it

by the strength which God supplies; in order that in everything God may be glorified through Jesus Christ.

In a Christian scheme of things, no artist has a right to isolate himself or herself from the human race. The reverse is also true: Christians at large cannot exile the artist from their midst.

Subjectivism in Art

The arts have been dominated by a pervasive subjectivism for nearly two centuries now. When Christianity became just one intellectual force among others, artists could no longer base their vision of the world on a publicly-shared system of values. This was a great watershed in the cultural and intellectual history of the West. Private experience replaced public (shared) experience as the standard of reality.

This revolution of thinking about what constitutes reality is well illustrated in William Wordsworth's definition of poetry: "All good poetry is the spontaneous overflow of powerful feelings."[14] Prior to this time, artists believed that the subject of art was the external world of people and things. Wordsworth's definition is really revolutionary. It locates both the source and substance of literature within the mind of the poet.

The same theory has dominated art and music for the past two centuries. Artist Oskar Kokoschka writes, "The life of consciousness is boundless. . . . Therefore we must harken closely to our inner voice. We must strive through the penumbra of words to the core within. . . . Consciousness is the source of all things and of all conceptions."[15] Similarly, two cubist artists theorize that "there is nothing real outside ourselves."[16] This is obviously an artistic manifestation of philosophic relativism. Its working assumption is that truth is whatever is true for a given individual.

What were the implications for art? At its most innocuous, subjectivist theories simply produced a new interest in human psychology as a subject for art. In its more extreme forms, it became another impetus for obscurity in art. Painters, for example, filled their canvases with images that expressed their inner feelings and perceptions but that often represented nothing recognizable to the viewer. Poets developed their private mythologies in apparent indifference to whether the resulting poetry was intelligible to the world at large.

The Christian Conception of Truth

Subjectivist theories, of course, contradict the Christian conception of truth and reality. In a Christian scheme of things, God and everything he created are real and important. Truth moreover, is supernaturally grounded. Artists do not create truth; God is its source and revealer. Truth is not relative to every individual; it exists objectively as God creates and reveals it. Nor should artists deny their ties with the human race in their quest for a purely private reality.

Having criticized the more extreme theories of subjectivity in art, I should add that there is no reason to be as negative about the movement as some Christian critics are. There is always an element of subjectivity in art. Artists necessarily portray reality as they perceive it. Inner feelings and perceptions have been one of the richest subjects of art, from the Old Testament Psalms to the latest song. The crucial question is whether an audience can find anything recognizable and universal in what an artist produces.

Nihilism in Art

> We don't want to feel less when we have finished a book; we want to feel that new possibilities have been opened to us. We don't want to close a book with a sense that life is totally unfair and that there is no light in the darkness; we want to feel that we have been given illumination.
>
> Madeleine L'Engle, *Walking on Water*

The Denial of Meaning

Twentieth-century art has been dominated by a denial that the universe has meaning. In fact, modern artists have expended some of their best energy and ingenuity in devising forms that will express the meaninglessness they find in the universe. The arts have been the vehicle by which philosophic nihilism and despair have become the prevailing spirit of our age.

Because literature has such an obvious ideational content, it is the modern art form where we can find the denial of meaning in its most detailed expression. The typical modern novel or play is a calculated strategy to leave the reader with the feeling that the universe lacks a coherent purpose and meaning. The typical subject matter of modern fiction and drama is an assertion that human life in this world lacks the beauty and meaning that past centuries found in it. The fate of literary tragedy in our century is instructive. It ended in a whimper because tragedy requires a high view of people as capable of significant moral choice and a belief that we live in a morally intelligible universe in which human suffering has a human cause.

We catch the strains of futility virtually anywhere we turn in modern poetry. "I have measured out my life with coffee spoons," laments the speaker in T. S. Eliot's poem "The Love-Song of J. Alfred Prufrock" as he contemplates the emptiness of his life. "Anyone lived in a pretty how town" is the opening line of a poem by E. E. Cummings, a poem whose lack of ordinary grammar, punctuation, and syntax by itself epitomizes much about modern poetry. The concluding stanza of the poem clinches the point about the failure of human life to mean anything significant:

> Women and men (both dong and ding)
> summer autumn winter spring
> reaped their sowing and went their came
> sun moon stars rain

The literary tradition of nihilism appears in concentrated form in the so-called absurd movement. It began as "the theater of the absurd" in the middle of this century. What did playwrights mean by "the absurd"? Eugene Ionesco defined his understanding of it thus: "Absurd is that which is devoid of purpose. . . . Cut off from his religious, metaphysical, and transcendental roots, man is lost; all his actions become senseless, absurd, useless."[17]

Rooted in a philosophic belief that human life in this world has no ultimate meaning, writers in the absurd tradition applied their ingenuity to inventing plots and characters and literary structures that would stike an audience as absurd. Farfetched situations, bizarre characters, and disjointed jumping from one event to the next became the stock-in-trade of dramatists and novelists. Disorientation of the audience became a chief aim.

Nihilism in the Visual Arts and Music

There are parallels to the literary tradition of the absurd in the visual arts and music. A familiar type of modern painting is the one in which disjointed fragments are brought together to suggest the subject announced in the title. Surrealistic painters have chosen grotesque scenes and caricatures of people to suggest the absurdity of the world. Painters in many modern movements give their paintings titles that have so little correspondence to the content of the painting that they strike a viewer as absurd.

Modern forms of abstract art also have a foot in this camp. By painting shapes that represent nothing in the real world, abstract artists give us paintings devoid of rational meaning. It is possible to find delight and beauty in the designs and colors themselves, but this is not what most modern abstractionists have in mind. The failure of their paintings and sculptures to suggest anything in the world around us is an implied comment that the world contains no meaning. Faced with the failure of the painting to communicate a recognizable and definite meaning, the viewer has little choice but to conclude that in the painter's view, life does not make sense. Abstract art need not fail to communicate meaning, but in the modern era it usually has done so.

The quest for artistic expression of the felt meaninglessness of the universe has led some artists and composers to use randomness in the process of composition. Abstract painter Jackson Pollock would put his canvas on the floor and drip paint on it by chance. Musical composer John Cage would allow the toss of a coin to determine the notes he wrote down.

The Denial of Hope

With the loss of belief that the universe makes sense came a denial of hope. Modern art is characterized by a metaphysical and temperamental pessimism. There are several ways in which this pessimism shows itself.

It can be seen in the view of the person (traditionally called "the image of man") in modern art and literature. Until the modern era, the Christian and classical traditions generally agreed on certain assumptions about people. They agreed that people, despite all their faults, have a capacity to be good as well as bad. They have within their psyche a reasoning faculty that can control their appetites, emotions, and physical impulses. In this view, people are morally responsible beings with the power of choice. Most of the art, music, and literature produced within this framework of belief portrayed people as significant beings, capable of courage, love, heroism, and other virtues.

Modern art changed all that. Its prevailing spirit is called naturalism. Naturalism is a view of people and the universe that is pessimistic and deterministic. It believes that people are the victims of four types of determinism—cosmic, societal, hereditary and psychological. Given these types of determinism, people do not have a significant power of choice. They are the victims of their environment and their glands. Modern literature repeatedly portrays characters carried away by self-destructive and irrational impulses.

One scholar has described the image of people in modern art thus:

> We no longer speak of the moral nature of man. We talk about his reactions. We do not think of human nature as something equipped with ideals of justice, of hope, of truth, of mercy, of retribution; we equip it with social attitudes, a psychological slant, endocrine glands, and a set of conditioned reflexes.[18]

Edmund Fuller's description is similar: "Unlike the great tradition of man as individual, responsible, guilty, but redeemable, this despairing disillusionment sees man as collective irresponsible, morally neuter, and beyond help."[19]

Naturalism is also a theory of the universe. It pictures the universe as hostile, cruel, and impersonal. There is no God in this universe that victimizes people. The people who inhabit it are essentially isolated figures, powerless to control their destiny. Naturalism posits a fourfold alienation: people are cut off from other people, from God, from their natural environment, and from their true selves.

Even the subjects that modern artists choose to portray reveal a denial of hope. Modern artists have singlemindedly agreed that ugliness, violence, and human misery are what art today should portray. Everywhere we turn in modern literature, music, and art, we are bombarded with this type of subject matter. In the contemporary section of a typical art gallery, we have no choice but to stare at contorted human forms, despairing faces, ugly city landscapes, and tawdry objects from modern life. Much contemporary music concentrates on dissonance instead of harmony, disorganization rather than pattern, anguish instead of peace. Modern literature seeks by every means available to convince us that the rose bush in front of the house is much less real than the garbage can behind the house.

A Christian Assessment

Enough has been said to suggest how widespread the denial of meaning and hope is in modern art, literature, and music. Christians cannot avoid some contact with such an outlook because it is everywhere in our culture. How, then, should they view the phenomenon?

They can begin with an awareness that these works of art embody attitudes really held by large numbers of people in the twentieth century. It is not an insigificant phenomenon but one that Christians need to understand. If the value of the arts in our day is that they state the problems to which the Christian faith has the answers, then we can accept modern art as "primary data" for defining the problem.

The Element of Truth in Nihilistic Art

Another reason why Christians should not make a simplistic rejection of nihilistic art is that it contains an element of truth. Christianity postulates a threefold view of people and the world: perfect as created by God, fallen and therefore partly evil, and capable of restoration through Christ. The tradition of nihilism expresses part of this truth, though not the whole truth.

According to the Bible, life lived apart from God and biblical values is meaningless. This is the theme of the book of Ecclesiastes, for example. So Christians can begin their assessment of nihilistic art on a note of agreement. Ephesians 2:12 speaks of unbelievers as "having no hope and without God in the world." What does that condition look and feel like? For an answer, all we need to do is read some modern fiction and poetry and visit an art gallery and listen to some modern music.

The Untruth of Nihilistic Art

The agreement between nihilism and Christianity soon ends, of course. This tradition of modern art is guilty of falsifying reality in several ways.

It is false first of all by its concentration on the ugly and violent aspects of life. If sentimental, wish-fulfillment art is a false view of reality, so is nihilistic art. There is a realism of grace as well as realism of carnality. The rose bush in front of the house is as real as the garbage can behind the house. The art of nihilism and despair presents an incomplete vision of what is real.

Plausibility has always been a criterion for judging the truthfulness of art. Although we should grant the right of the arts to heighten their subject matter, we all have an inner gauge that tells us when the artistic portrayal of experience has crossed the line into implausiblity. Naturalistic art often crosses that line. Addison Leitch once criticized Flannery O'Connor for distorting reality by choosing atypical characters for her stories and acting as though they were representative of humanity. He wrote, "One gets the impression that in order to make our total depravity plain, she makes too many of her characters bizarre.

For example, in one of her great stories a woman with a wooden leg and a Ph.D. is seduced by a Bible salesman. That is not the sort of Reality I run into with any great frequency, which makes me wonder if that's the way it really is."[20]

Naturalistic art also falsifies reality by giving the impression that ugliness and depravity are the whole story about human potential. The Bible, I have noted, depicts human life in a threefold manner—perfect, fallen, and capable of redemption. Modern art is truthful in its depiction of fallen experience, but it is untruthful in its implication that this is the whole picture.

The nihilistic viewpoint also contradicts basic doctrines of the Christian faith. An important aspect of the biblical view of people, for example, is that they are capable of moral and spiritual choice. The deterministic premise of naturalism directly contradicts this view of people.

Christianity is ultimately a vision of hope. It is based on the Good News, not the bad news. This point has been well stated by Hilda Graef, who begins her book *Modern Gloom and Christian Hope* with the premise, "Our point of view is solely that of the Christian, for whom hope is one of the theological virtues and despair a sin."[21] I noted in the previous chapter Francis Schaeffer's theory that Christianity is based on a minor theme and a major theme. The minor theme is the fact of evil and despair in the world and in the lives of Christians. The major theme is the redemptive awareness of God's forgiveness and the hope of eternal life. Judged by such a doctrinal framework, we can reach a somewhat paradoxical assessment of nihilistic art as being partly truthful without telling the Truth.

The Revolt against Artistic Form and Beauty

Yet another manifestation of the nihilism of modern art is the deliberate rejection of artistic form and beauty. This is the purely aesthetic side of the general denial of meaning that I have noted.

The anti-art impulse is strongest in the visual arts.[22] The French artist Marcel Duchamp's work *Fountain* consisted of a commercially produced urinal exhibited in a gallery. Robert Morris exhibited bits and pieces of thread, mirrors, lead, copper, steel, aluminum, and asphalt sprinkled randomly on a large canvas on the floor of a New York gallery. Another painter in New York exhibited works made from human excrement. Numerous sculptors have used junk for their materials.

Musicians have done similar things. Some have taped noise from a street or factory. Ben Johnston's "Knockingpiece" consists of two performers hitting the piano case irregularly with wooden mallets for eleven minutes. American composer John Cage's work entitled *4-33* calls for a pianist to sit at the piano with hands suspended above the keyboard for 4 minutes and 33 seconds, after which the pianist closes the score and leaves the stage.

Writers of literature have been less drastic, but here, too, we can discern some specifically aesthetic aspects of nihilism. One of the most persistent literary impulses through the centuries has been the incarnation of human values and experience in heroes. In modern literature, the hero has been replaced by the anti-hero—the protagonist characterized by traits that are the exact opposite of the traditional hero. Instead of being talented and successful, the typical anti-hero is inept, immoral, and unsuccessful.

Or consider the anti-novel of contemporary literature. Instead of following such time-honored narrative principles as chronological sequence, beginning-middle-end construction, and causal coherence among episodes, the anti-novel is a collection of fragments. By its very formlessness it denies the meaning and order implied by the conventional novel. Its style is typically direct, flat, and unliterary, and its stance toward the subject matter detached and nonevaluative.

The anti-art movement has also invaded literary theory. Its most prevalent form is to deny that literature is a distinctive type of discourse different from other forms of thought and writing. This is a modern version of a very old tradition that values literature only for its didactic ("teaching") content. What both old and new versions have in common is the disparagement of literary form as an artistic achievement. To make a poem or story identical to a philosophic, scientific, or psychological discourse, one has to ignore its meter and rhyme, its structure and poetic texture, its purely artistic element that it shares with painting and music. This is equivalent to making all trees identical by cutting off their branches.

Carried to its logical conclusion, this theory ends up without a definition of literature. Standards for literary excellence disappear as critics apply their analysis to traffic signs and comic strips. A recent survey of contemporary literary theory ends with this rejection of literature as a distinctive artistic phenomenon:

> We must conclude, then, that this book is less an introduction than an obituary, and that we have ended by burying the object [that is, literature] we sought to unearth. . . . The present crisis in the field of literary studies is at root a crisis in the definition of the subject itself.[23]

With no artistic definition for literature, the author can only propose that in the future critics might choose to discuss the Muppet show and the portrayal of women in advertisements and the rhetorical techniques of government reports.

A Christian Critique of the Anti-Art Movement

We should be under no illusions about the nihilistic undergirding of the anti-art strain in modern painting, music, and literature. The attack on artistic form is part of a broader assault on traditional beliefs and values. It is not, in other words, the result of uncultured ignorance or an uneducated lack of appreciation for art. The movement comes from the very people who are specialists in art and have lost their belief in its value.

I can find no Christian justification for the attack on art and form. My best evidence for that position comes in earlier chapters on what the Bible says about the arts and on the value of artistic beauty. We know from the creation itself that God values beauty and form. The world that God created and declared to be "very good" stands as a model for the type of things that artists should create. Order, design, and beauty are norms for art, rooted in the very nature of God's creation and human creativity.

These norms apply to the audience of art as well as to artists. Jesus told us to "consider the lilies of the field" (Matthew 6:28). It is possible to see a whole theory of art in that great aphorism. What, after all, do we see when we consider the lilies of the field? We see a natural beauty so captivating that "even Solomon in all his glory was not arrayed like one of these" (vs. 29). Artistic form and beauty have value because God gave them to the human race. The modern disparagement of artistic form is at odds with a Christian attitude.

Because created objects have integrity for what they uniquely are, any attempt to rob them of that integrity is misguided. It should be obvious that a painting uses a different medium of expression from an essay. A poem or story is different from a sermon or textbook. The contemporary critical attempt to get rid of the distinction between the arts and other forms of communication is really a disparagement of art. But in a Christian scheme of things, we do not need to rob things of their created properties in a futile attempt to make them "respectable." They have value for what they are. In current literary theory, literature itself becomes expendable, but for the God of a thoroughly literary Bible, it is not so.

The Assault on Christian Morality

> Contemporary literature as a whole tends to be degrading.
>
> T. S. Eliot, "Religion and Literature"

Along with the assault on traditional notions about the meaningfulness of human life in this world, the attack on traditional morality has been the most troublesome aspect of modern art. The relation between art and morality is complex and much misunderstood, and it will require patience to untangle the threads.

Defining Some Terms

Let me say at the outset that in discussing immorality in modern art and literature I am not talking about censorship. Censorship is what a society decides to do about immoral art. My concern is to discuss theoretically how to determine whether art is immoral.

The morality of art should not be confused with its intellectual truth or falseness. Morality has to do with human behavior, especially between one person and another. Applied to works of art, this involves the behavior portrayed in works of art and the effect of works of art on the behavior of its audience.

Morality enters the artistic enterprise in three ways. In an ascending order of importance, they are the subject matter portrayed in works of art, the perspective toward that subject matter embodied in works of art, and the response of an individual to works of art, literature, and music.

It is easy to define what constitutes moral and immoral art. The difficult issue is determing what works of art fit the definitions. Moral art is art that recommends moral behavior for approval and that stimulates an audience to behave morally. Immoral art offers immoral behavior for approval and influences an audience to behave immorally.

Realism in the Bible

When we talk about immorality at the level of subject matter we usually mean realism. Realism is the explicit portrayal of human depravity in all its sordid forms. Modern realism has not shrunk back from portraying the full range of immoral behavior.

Thinking Christianly about realism begins with an awareness that the Bible affirms the necessity and legitimacy of realism as an artistic technique. The Bible depicts the full range of human depravity and as such adopts the basic strategy of realism. Stories of sexual immorality in the Bible include the stories of homosexuality in Sodom (Genesis 19); the rape of Dinah (Genesis 34); Onan's interrupted intercourse with Tamar (Genesis 38:1-10); Samson and the harlot of Gaza (Judges 16);

the "concubine at Gibeah" incident, in which sexual perverts were placated with the concubine, whom they abused to the point of death (Judges 19); the adultery of David and Bathsheba (2 Samuel 11); and the incest of Amnon and Tamar (2 Samuel 13).

Realism also includes the portrayal of violence. Stories of violence are everywhere in the Bible, especially in the Old Testament. Ehud's assassination of Eglon in Judges 3 is a good example.

The presence of realism in the Bible lays down a basic premise for art and its audience: Realism itself is not immoral. If we did not need it, the Bible would not give it to us. As a religious book, the Bible does not escape from life. It uses the technique of realism to tell us something that we need to know, namely, the sinfulness of the human condition and the misery of a fallen world.

The presence of realism in the Bible refutes a common misconception that works of art automatically encourage approval of everything they portray. This is a totally untenable position. Art has two main themes—life as it should be and life as it fails to match that ideal. As with the Bible, much art portrays things that the artist wishes to reject and denounce. The only way to offer a negative perspective on something is to portray it in a negative light. But notice in the meantime that artists have to portray evil before they can show their indictment of it.

In some Christian circles it has become fashionable to reject all forms of artistic realism. I recently saw an interview on national television with a high school student who had won his battle to be exempt from reading Aldous Huxley's *Brave New World* in a literature course. He expressed the belief that this was a victory for God. I doubt that this is so. *Brave New World* is not an immoral book, and its realism is essentially no different from what we find in the Bible.

Legitimate Realism in Modern Art

We can infer from the example of the Bible that one function of art is to present human experience as it really is. If modern life is ugly and depraved and perverted and violent, we can expect modern art to be the same in the subject matter that it portrays. By itself, such realism is not immoral, even though it may be distasteful. Whether or not it passes the boundary of morality depends on how the artist treats the subject. The modern painter Georges Roualt painted prostitutes in such a way as to reveal the devastation and emptiness of sin.

In appropriating what is legitimate in modern realism, Christians may have to put up with some objectionable subject matter in order to gain whatever positive benefits a work has to offer in terms of insight and the enlargement of our sense of compassion. We should make a distinction between subject matter and theme in art. The subject matter is the outward or obvious content of the work—the setting, objects, characters, and actions. The theme is the perspective that the work offers toward that content. My claim is that a Christian may find it useful, some of the time, to overlook offensive subject matter—profanity, explicit portrayal of sex, violence—in order to benefit from significant perspective or insight.

This will surely require a willingness to assess artistic works as wholes. We cannot judge the morality of a book, for example, only by a few isolated passages of realistic description. In one of the best discussions of the topic, Harold C. Gardiner writes that the effect of objectionable passages "has to be judged against the background of the whole moral import of the work."[24] Someone else has written that "to learn how to read a dirty book is to learn how to see the book whole."[25] The question that a Christian must therefore answer is, Does the moral or intellectual significance of a work exceed in value the possible offensiveness of any of its parts? The answer will vary for individual Christians with individual works, and it will even vary for the same person from one occasion to another.

The Immorality of Modern Realism

Although realism is not immoral in principle, much modern realism raises moral problems for Christians. I have said that the Bible affirms realism in principle, but to say only this obscures an important point: The realism of the Bible is realism within definite bounds. Modern realism frequently differs from biblical realism in the following ways:

- The Bible does not contain a preponderance of depravity in its account of human exeprience. It does not leave the reader with the impression that degradation is all there is to life, or that there is no alternative to ugliness and depravity.
- The Bible does not dwell on the sordid details of sexual immorality. It avoids dramatizing profanity by using narrative summary instead. It does not share the clinical or descriptive approach of so much modern literature and art in the portrayal of sex.
- The Bible never condones the evil that it depicts. A majority of modern art and literature, however, portrays immorality as a normal and inevitable part of human behavior.

The Bible probably does not fix the limits for the kinds of art and literature that we can consider moral. But biblical realism establishes a pattern that Christians can trust. As a model, the Bible strikes a balance. It gives us realism within certain bounds. Biblical realism serves as a reliable model to guide Christian artists and consumers of art.

When we look at modern realism through the lens of the biblical model, we find much that fails to measure up to that moral standard. Four types of realism are particularly troublesome: (1) art or literature that delights in the immorality that it depicts, or that encourages the audience to approve and emulate that immorality; (2) pornography, or art that elicits lustful thoughts and actions; (3) art or literature that is filled with profanity, blasphemy, obscenity, and sacrilege (ridicule of the sacred things of the Christian religion, including God or Christ); and (4) the explicit and unrestrained portrayal of violence. All of these are prominent features of the modern artistic landscape, as they are of modern life. By Christian standards of morality, they are examples of artistic immorality.

The Realistic Portrayal of Sex

Several things are objectionable about the detailed portrayal of sex. We can object on artistic grounds, first of all.

Edmund Fuller thus argues on literary grounds that pornographic literature is guilty of "the error of confusing cumulative detail with interpretive insight."[26] Fuller adds,

> Many writers are deluded into thinking that a four-letter-word vocabulary, carefully detailed scenes of undressing, and clinically direct anatomical descriptions add up to a profound study of the relations between men and women. . . . This is quite . . . fantastic. The criteria for every detail about sex in fiction should be: What does this illumine? What does it reveal that was not known before or that cannot be left as tacitly understood? Does this add anything to our understanding of character that was not already clear? (pp. 83-84).

We can also object to the realistic portrayal of sex on broadly humanistic grounds, as Roland Frye does when he argues that "the primary objection to glandular fiction . . . is simply that it belittles man."[27]

But there is also a moral objection that Christians must have the courage to make. Pornographic art and literature fill the mind with lustful thoughts. They make people preoccupied with sex and lead them to start viewing others as sexual objects. What goes through a reader's or viewer's mind when he or she reads a passage or views a scene that depicts the physical details of sexual activity or portrays the naked body? The range of responses is as follows: (1) embarrassment that sex, a private experience, has been dragged out into public, making voyeurs out of readers or viewers whether or not they wish to be; (2) repulsion at the lust being portrayed; (3) fantasizing about sex; (4) allowing the stimulus to lead to immoral sexual activity.

None of these responses gives Christians a compelling reason to have contact with such literature or art. There might be occasions when a Christian will have limited contact with art or literature in spite of such descriptions, but not because of them.

There is a great difference between art that uses reticence in portraying sex as part of a thorough analysis of human experience and art that lingers over the details of the human body or sexual activity. The Bible portrays sex in the former but not the latter way. Immersion in art and literature that portray sex in the clinical manner usually does what such art was designed to do, namely, inflame the audience's sexual appetite. At the very least it fills the mind and imagination with sexual images, making voyeurs out of an audience. Jesus extended lust and adultery to include a person's thought life when he condemned the mental act of lust in one's heart (Matthew 5:28). Modern psychology claims that there is an element of possessing in the act of looking at something intently and habitually.

The Hedonistic Impulse in Modern Art

My criticism of realism in the portrayal of sex needs to be qualified. It is eventually harmful to see too much sex portrayed in art. The results are a general coarseness of attitude toward sex, a blunting of the reverence and mystery that should attend sex, and a tendency to reduce sex to the level of a physical act or appetite.

But what bothers a Christian sensibility even more is the prevailing hedonism or abandonment to appetite that we find in modern art. It is one thing to portray sexual activity, and quite another to encourage viewers or readers to indulge their own appetites. Modern art generally elevates the liberation of impulse to the highest value. C. S. Lewis has described the pervasive hedonism of modern culture and art in terms that are confirmed in our lives nearly every day. "The contemporary propaganda for lust," writes Lewis,

> [makes us] feel that the desires we are resisting are so "natural," so "healthy," and so reasonable, that it is almost perverse and abnormal to resist them. Poster after poster, film after film, novel after novel, associate the idea of sexual indulgence with the ideas of health, normality, youth, frankness, and good humour. Now this association is a lie.[28]

No person can claim to be immune from the seductive appeals that art and the media make to us to indulge our sexual appetite. The arts and media have created a cultural obsession with sex. Will Durant has written that "our ancestors played this sexual impulse down, knowing that it was strong enough without encouragement; we have blown it up with a thousand forms of incitation, advertisement, emphasis and display, and have armed it with the doctrine that inhibition is dangerous."[29] The "compulsory sex scene" has become a fixture in modern fiction and drama.

The encouragement that the arts today give us to "let go" is not limited to the sexual appetite. Almost as common are songs and stories that give vent to our impulses to express aggression, anger, violence, and greed. Here, too, we become the sum of our indulgences. The effect of the hedonistic bias and encouragement to unrestraint that we find in modern art has long been an immoral influence in our society. Christians and moral people in general have reason to be alarmed.

Profanity, Sacrilege, and Obscenity

Christians also have standards of purity and morality in regard to the related phenomena of blasphemy, profanity, sacrilege, and obscenity. If we keep in mind that the Ten Commandments in the Old Testament are not simply particularized prohibitions but that each commandment implies a broader moral principle, we can see that the third commandment, "You shall not take the name of the Lord your God in vain," speaks about the sanctity of God's name and being, and that the seventh commandment, "You shall not commit adultery," asserts the sanctity of human sexuality and the human body.

Profanity, blasphemy, and sacrilege violate the command not to take God's name in vain (though of course the command includes much in addition to blasphemy). The seventh commandment prohibits obscenity, since obscenity defiles the sanctity of the physical body and human sexuality. Obscenity may be one of the things proscribed by the statement in Colossians 3:8 to avoid "foul talk," and it is certainly what is in view in Ephesians 5:4, which prohibits "filthiness" and "silly talk" (the New American Standard Version translation is "filthiness and silly talk, or coarse jesting"). There are, incidentally, vulgarities that may violate a standard of good taste but which fall short of what I am here calling obscenity and profanity.

What is so bad about contact with these things in works of art? Stop to consider what they do to us when we encounter them. They offend a Christian's sensibility and the Holy Spirit who lives within the believer. Only masochists go around looking for occasions to have their sense of rightness assaulted. The opposite response is also possible: contact with these things might lead a person to acquiesce in them or take them lightly, and this is to compromise one's integrity as a Christian. As we read the gospel accounts of the life of Christ, do we get the impression that he would have regarded blasphemy and sacrilege and obscenity as morally indifferent matters?

Christians are responsible for the furniture of their minds and imaginations. What they take into themselves is not morally neutral. It is like food that they digest and that becomes part of them. Some food is poisonous to the system. So are some forms of art, literature, and music.

"Sincerity" Does Not Make Art Moral

It is fashionable in the secular world to condone pornography and blasphemy in art because the artist is serious or sincere in the portrayal of depravity. Harry Blamires subjects this popular view to scrutiny in his book *The Christian Mind*. He attacks "the current superstition which sets such a high value on seriousness." In the process, he rejects

> the idea, virtually unquestioned just now, that any discussion or literary exploitation of sexual matters, perversions, or aberrations, is good provided that it is serious. . . . It is regarded as healthy to describe or represent intercourse, promiscuity, vice, homo-

> sexuality, lesbianism, sadism, and the like, if you do so seriously. . . . The increasing obsession with sexuality and vice in literature is defended today by an irrational and emotive exploitation of words like sincere and authentic which carry spurious "moral" overtones.[30]

In fact, to portray immorality seriously may make it more, not less, blameworthy. A scene of illicit love may be portrayed "sensitively," but its sensitivity does not mitigate its immorality and may actually increase it.

Many artists have defended the unrestrained portrayal of human depravity on the criterion of verisimilitude or lifelikeness. If it happens in life, runs this argument, the artist has a right to portray it. But verisimilitude can never become the moral criterion for art. The fact that something happens does not make it morally good either in life or art. Furthermore, art is a conscious activity where we are free to select and control what we put into works of art or what we take into ourselves as an audience. Morality in art involves the exercise of the same moral restraints that we exercise in life. Madeleine L'Engle observes that the root meaning of obscene is "off-stage; that which should not be seen on stage."[31] Traditional artistic and literary standards have agreed that some forms of human behavior should remain "off-stage."

In the long run, we become the sum of our indulgences, including the pictures at which we look and the stories we read and the movies we view. If we habitually fill our minds with images of sex or profanity or violence, we can become that type of person. The strategy of art is to give form to our own feelings and impulses. These inner impulses are a mixture of good and bad, waiting to be encouraged or discouraged by outward stimuli. The effect of some artistic subject matter is to awaken the wrong impulses—impulses toward hatred or violence or sexual license, for example. And the influence of other types of subject matter is to encourage good impulses—toward honesty or courage or self-control or compassion and many other virtues. Even artistic subject matter, therefore, can become a moral issue.

Perspective as Moral Determiner

The length at which I have discussed subject matter as a determiner of artistic morality is somewhat misleading. More decisive than what artists choose to portray is how they portray it. I have placed realism—the detailed portrayal of human depravity—into the category of subject matter, but there is a sense in which it could be regarded as a matter of perspective—of how an artist handles the material. The arts take all of life as their domain. Sex, violence, and evil are not themselves immoral topics for artistic portrayal. It all depends on how the artist treats them—in other words, on the artist's perspective. The crucial moral determiner in the portrayal of sex and evil is the degree of reticence and distance with which the artist portrays the experience.

We must remember that, as Harry Blamires puts it, "there is nothing in our experience, however trivial, worldly, or even evil, which cannot be thought about christianly."[32] Moral art is not art that avoids evil as a subject but that finds ways to discredit evil and encourage good. Calvin Seerveld has written that "art is Biblically Christian when the Devil cannot stand it. If the Devil can stand it or would hand out reproductions, then there is no Biblical Christian character to it. . . . The Devil cannot stand exposure of sin as sin, dirty, devastating misery for men; it unmasks him."[33]

How, then, does art (especially literature) embody an immoral perspective toward its subject matter? Essentially it does so by offering an immoral attitude for the audience's approval. The means by which it does so include these: making immoral acts attractive; leaving goodness "bereft of its proper beauty;"[34] generating sympathy for immoral characters and actions; belittling characters whose actions and attitudes are moral; omitting models of morally good behavior that would serve as a foil to immoral models and thereby offer the audience an alternative; treating immoral acts in a comic tone, thereby prompting a reader to refrain from moral judgment; portraying immoral acts as something people have no choice in rejecting.

By contrast, a work of art possesses a moral perspective whenever an artist constructs it in such a way as to recommend moral behavior. Here, too, there is a wide range of techniques: making the good appear attractive or ultimately satisfying (even when there is a price tag attached); displaying models of morally good behavior in such a way as to make an audience wish to imitate them; generating final sympathy for morally good characters and actions; exposing the self-destructive nature of evil; including foils to immoral behavior as a way of showing that people have a power of choice to resist evil.

The example of the Bible shows that subject matter by itself does not determine the morality of a work of literature. The Bible portrays experiences that are realistic, sordid, and evil. Yet the overall effect of reading the Bible inclines a person to be moral in behavior. It is not hard to see why. The perspective from which evil is portrayed in the Bible is a strongly moral one.

Audience Response as the Final Determiner of Morality in Art

Thus far I have explored the role of subject matter and perspective in determining the morality of a work of art. Both of these are tendencies in the work. But more important in determining the morality of art is something that lies outside of the work, namely, the individual viewer, reader, or listener. No artistic response is automatic. The same work of art produces far different moral responses in different people. Even reading the Bible does not automatically produce moral behavior in readers.

The ultimate responsibility rests with the individual reader, viewer, or listener to be moral in his or her response. When we read a novel or look at a painting or listen to the lyrics of a song, we do not need to be victimized by the perspective embodied in the work. What, after all, happens when a moral reader encounters literature that recommends immoral behavior? The most common response is to be repelled by the immorality that is commended and to have one's own moral resolve strengthened.

If a moral person can assimilate a work of art in a positive way contrary to an artist's intention, the reverse is also possible. Immoral readers can twist a work's inherent moral tendencies, or seize upon isolated scenes that portray immoral behavior, in a perverse way. People who want to do so can treat the Bible as a pornographic book, or can use it to rationalize immoral behavior.

Christians can begin by scrutinizing their own moral responses to works of art. Just as all education is ultimately self-education, the only effective type of censorship is self-censorship. Christian consumers of the arts need to be aware of how they are being affected morally by what they read and listen to and view.

Works of art are moral and immoral persuaders, but we are not persuaded against our will. If the effect of a work of art is one that pushes us toward immoral attitudes, feelings, or actions, the antidote is simple: we can either cease contact with the work, or exercise a stronger moral control over the influence that the material is exerting. The moral controls on art rest ultimately with the individual.

The Christian and Modern Art

> So long as we are conscious of the gulf fixed between ourselves and the greater part of contemporary literature, we are more or less protected from being harmed by it, and are in a position to extract from it what good it has to offer us.
>
> T. S. Eliot, "Religion and Literature"

The problems posed for the Christian by modern art are so complex that the general tendency has been to adopt simple responses. These fall into three categories. One is wholesale endorsement of modern art, combined with the attitude that anyone who finds modern art offensive is an ignoramus. Another is wholesale condemnation of modern art. And then there is the desire to resolve the issue with lists of approved and disapproved works. My belief is that the issues must be handled on a much more individualistic basis. The general principles that we establish must be applied by each person in connection with every particular work of art.

I believe simultaneously in the necessity and danger of a Christian's contact with modern art, music, and literature. This view of the arts is expressed in kernel form in the epigraph from T. S. Eliot quoted above. Eliot speaks of the potential harm that can come from modern art, the good that modern art can offer to a Christian, and awareness as the key to insuring that the effect of modern art will be positive rather than negative.

The Necessity of Contact with Modern Art

Christians need modern art because it expresses the mind and soul of their own culture. That mind and soul are not predominantly Christian. I am not asking Christians to approve of the contemporary arts. But the most profound and articulate expression of the modern spirit can be found in the arts.

The media claim to tell us what is happening in our culture, but they are terribly superficial. They bombard us with facts but ignore the meaning of those facts. By contrast, the arts lay bare the inner movements of our own time. What Henry Zylstra said about literature applies equally to art and music:

> If you really want to get at the spirit of an age and the soul of a time you can hardly do better than to consult the literature of that age and that time. In the novels and stories and poems and plays of a period you have a good indication of what, deep down, that period was about.[35]

This means that we should have contact with modern art, not necessarily because we enjoy it, but because we recognize it as a necessary way of keeping abreast of our own culture.

Furthermore, one function of the arts (though not their only function) is to present human experience and reality as they actually exist. Truthfulness to reality is one of the reasons for art. We have no right to avoid the truthtelling impulse of modern art. By presenting human depravity and misery for our contemplation, modern art, at its best and most responsible, aims to increase our understanding of the human predicament in the modern world. One function that such art can fill is to open the eyes of Christians to the needs of people whose physical and moral plight they might otherwise comfortably avoid.

We must also remember that modern art embodies the attitudes really held by large numbers of people in the twentieth century. Modern art records contemporary people's quest for meaning, even when it portrays persons who search for it in such vulgar ways as sexual license and violence. Christians cannot sweep aside the views espoused in modern art as being unimportant, for the fact is that they are important in the culture in which we live.

Moreover, contact with modern art is a way of achieving a sympathetic understanding of non-Christians. Someone has written that "if we truly want to communicate with our contemporaries we must understand them; and there is no more readily available way of understanding them than by reading what they have written for us and for each other."[36] In a similar vein, Roland Frye comments that if "we are to see clearly the ultimate problems of man's life for which Christian truth must have relevance if it has value, we can scarcely do better than to study man as his lot is clarified through enduring literature."[37] One of the lessons that modern art can teach the Christian is that persons who deserve our moral condemnation should at the same time elicit our pity and compassion. We can also be reminded that people who live without hope in the world do not usually enjoy their despair.

The Dangers of Modern Art

Along with some good reasons for making sure we have some contact with modern art, there are some dangers that we should not minimize. To begin, the arts influence us both consciously and subconsciously. As T. S. Eliot writes,

> The fiction that we read affects our behaviour. . . . When we read of human beings behaving in certain ways, with the approval of the author, who gives his benediction to this behaviour by his attitude toward the result of the behaviour arranged by himself, we can be influenced towards behaving in the same way. . . . The author of a work of imagination is trying to affect us wholly, as human beings, whether he knows it or not; and we are affected by it, as human beings, whether we intend to be or not.[38]

If the prevailing intellectual and moral spirit in modern art is as hostile to Christian values as I have suggested, the influence of modern art on Christians is always potentially harmful.

I said earlier that art covers the whole spectrum of life and that we should not run away from what actually exists in our world. But if, in art and life, we cannot completely avoid the depraved end of the spectrum, we can avoid most of it, particularly in art. There is usually no good reason for Christians deliberately to seek out art that assaults their morality and beliefs. For mature Christians it is not primarily a matter of being swept into immoral behavior or untruth. It is much more likely to be a question of the good use of time. If in life no good comes from deliberately jumping into mud puddles, in the Christian's spiritual life not much good comes from jumping into the cesspool of much modern art.

I firmly believe that Christians must know what is going on in their society. But this argument is less convincing as a rationale for immersion in the modern arts than it is sometimes made out to be. How can people not know what is happening in society if they watch television and read magazines? How much modern art must a Christian encounter in order to know what lust or hatred is like? Probably none at all. Frank Gaebelein once wrote, "No Christian is obligated to reside in the brothels of the mind in order to know the world in which he lives."[39] The question we must keep asking is, How much contact with modern art is required to make our awareness full?

Christian standards of holiness go far beyond the standards of a secular society. Society at large is concerned with external behavior only, which partly accounts for the difficulty that our society has in dealing with pornography. It also tends to equate what is moral with what is legal. The prevailing ethic on which modern society operates is that "you can't go to jail for what you're thinking."

Biblical morality, by contrast, goes far beyond what is merely legal. It is preoccupied with the inner life, not only with external actions. The classic text on this is Christ's comments about the law in the Sermon on the Mount (Matthew 5). Here morality includes the ideal of personal holiness and extends to thoughts, attitudes, and emotions as well as overt actions.

What this means in practical terms is that we are responsible for the stimuli to which we expose ourselves. Furthermore, we become, in significant ways, the sum of our indulgences. Christian readers are responsible for the images and thoughts that fill their minds. The arts are one of the chief sources of such images. The English poet William Wordsworth expressed the ideal of a mind that is "a mansion for all lovely forms."[40] Christians should not settle for less. After all, Paul pictures the Christian mind as a habitation of thoughts that are true, honorable, just, pure, lovely, gracious, excellent, and worthy of praise (Philippians 4:8). It is the goal of art to refine our sensibilities, not to blunt them as so much modern art tries to do.

Wherever an individual Christian draws the line, he or she has to draw it somewhere and leave some works of modern art untouched. Christians are accountable to God, not to a code or a fellow human. But in some Christian circles there is an unwarranted assumption that God's standards of holiness and purity are less strict than human standards. Spiritual reality has not changed since Jesus proclaimed that it is the pure in heart who will see God.

The arts are affective and infectious. Hedonistic art usually does what it is designed to do—inflame the appetites and passions. Christians are not exempt from the seductive powers of hedonistic songs and paintings and novels. Similarly, nihilistic art aims to get an audience to share the artist's despair. Immersion in such art produces predictable results, and they are the opposite of the living hope that the Holy Spirit promises to produce within a Christian believer.

We must also remember what art is for. Truthfulness to reality is one of its functions, but not the only one. It also exists to refresh and recreate a person. We do not push ourselves into an encounter with art as though it were a duty to which we are slaves. Modern art is not like paying taxes, something we have to do regardless of our interests. To be repelled by evil as depicted in modern art is a Christian response, but on what logic can it be argued that a person should spend leisure time seeking out ways in which to be repelled?

Finding a Balance

Our final stance should be a middle-of-the-road attitude that both affirms and rejects modern art. We must affirm its importance as a force in contemporary culture and therefore our need for it as a means of understanding our culture. We can affirm the necessity for some contact with art that portrays evil in a realistic manner since the presence of realism in the Bible leaves us no option on this score. And we can agree that art is intended to be not only a source of artistic pleasure but also a truthful reflection of reality.

On the other side of the ledger, I find myself questioning the value of a Christian spending great quantities of time on modern art. Much of this art condones and even glorifies the depravity that it depicts. In the words of Tom Howard, "It not only points to the stew. It stirs it. It jumps in."[41] Its view of people, reality, and morality is distorted. If allowed to have its effect it will fill one's mind with images of despair and violence and coarseness and sexual activity, in violation of biblical comments about what ought to constitute the furniture of a Christian's mind and imagination.

But whenever we find ourselves wondering about the legitimacy of Christian contact with modern art, we should stop to consider that we cannot run away from our own society, that we must face its art and values, and that the Bible itself insists on our contact with realism in art. We are left walking a tightrope between the extremes of total rejection and total affirmation.

A sense of balance is what a Christian needs. People who are inclined either to immerse themselves in modern art or to avoid it completely probably need to check their inclination.

A Checklist

To summarize the general drift of my comments about the necessity and dangers of modern art, I offer the following questions as a helpful checklist to guide a Christian's encounter with modern art:

1. Does this work of art call my attention to something about either reality or modern culture that I need to know?

2. What is the precise nature of the gulf between this work and my Christian beliefs and values?

3. Does my contact with this work have a negative effect on my Christian beliefs or on my moral behavior?

4. Does the overall cultural or intellectual significance of this work exceed in importance the offensiveness of some aspects of it? Can I minimize the impact of these negative aspects in order to appropriate the larger benefits of the work?

5. If I do not enjoy this work, is there a reason why I should encounter it anyway?

6. Does my contact with this work make me more capable or less capable of being God's person in the society in which he has placed me?

SUMMARY

There is much in modern art, music, and literature that is hostile to Christianity. Such trends as the idolizing of art, the isolation of the artist from ordinary life, nihilism, the revolt against form and beauty, and the assault on Christian morality are ultimately alien to Christian standards, whatever occasional truth one might find in works of this type. This does not mean that Christians should totally avoid modern art. While never relinquishing their own standards of truth, beauty, and morality, Christians should take modern art seriously as an expression of the prevailing values and attitudes of modern culture.

Further Reading

Edmund Fuller, *Man in Modern Fiction* (1949).

Gilda Graef, *Modern Gloom and Christian Hope* (1959).

Nathan A. Scott, Jr., ed., *The Climate of Faith in Modern Literature* (1964).

Richard Ellmann and Charles Feidelson, Jr., ed., *The Modern Tradition: Backgrounds of Modern Literature* (1965).

Herschel B. Chipp, ed., *Theories of Modern Art: A Source Book by Artists and Critics* (1968).

H. R. Rookmaaker, *Modern Art and the Death of a Culture* (1970).

John Van Zanten, *Caught in the Act: Modern Drama as Prelude to the Gospel* (1971).

Jacques Barzun, *The Use and Abuse of Art* (1974).

Chapter 8, Notes

1. A good book on the subject is J. Hillis Miller, *The Disappearance of God* (Cambridge, MA: Harvard University Press, 1963).

2. T. S. Eliot, "Religion and Literature," as reprinted in *The Christian Imagination: Essays on Literature and the Arts,* ed. Leland Ryken (Grand Rapids: Baker, 1981), p. 153.

3. Francis A. Schaeffer, "Some Perspectives on Art," in *The Christian Imagination,* ed. Ryken, p. 87.

4. Gustave Flaubert, letters to Louise Colet, in *The Modern Tradition: Backgrounds of Modern Literature,* ed. Richard Ellman and Charles Feidelson, Jr. (New York: Oxford University Press, 1965), pp. 195-197.

5. Matthew Arnold, "The Study of Poetry," in *Criticism: The Major Statements,* ed. Charles Kaplan (New York: St. Martin's, 1964), pp. 403-404.

6. C. S. Lewis, *Christian Reflections* (Grand Rapids: William B. Eerdmans, 1967), p. 10.

7. William Wordsworth, "Preface to Lyrical Ballads," in *Criticism: The Major Statements,* ed. Kaplan, p. 309.

8. See Roger Lundin's review article, "Modern Poets, Modern Madness," *Reformed Journal,* June 1984, pp. 16-20.

9. Hans Hofmann, excerpts from his teaching in *Theories of Modern Art: A Source Book by Artists and Critics,* ed. Herschel B. Chipp (Berkeley: University of California Press, 1968), p. 539.

10. C. S. Lewis and E. M. W. Tillyard, *The Personal Heresy: A Controversy* (London: Oxford University Press, 1939, 1965), p. 105.

11. William York Tindall, "Exile," the opening chapter in *Forces in Modern British Literature, 1885-1946* (New York: Alfred A. Knopf, 1947), p. 3.

12. T. S. Eliot, "The Metaphysical Poets," in *Criticism: The Major Texts,* ed. Walter Jackson Bate (New York: Harcourt, Brace and World, 1952), p. 533.

13. John Donne, "Meditation 17" in *Devotions upon Emergent Occasions.*

14. William Wordsworth, "Preface to Lyrical Ballads," p. 305.

15. Oskar Kokoschka, "On the Nature of Visions," in *Theories of Modern Art,* ed. Chipp, pp. 172, 174.

16. Albert Gleizes and Jean Metzinger, "Cubism," as excerpted in *Theories of Modern Art,* ed. Chipp, p. 214.

17. Eugene Ionesco, as quoted in Martin Esslin, *The Theatre of the Absurd* (1961; reprint, Garden City: Doubleday, 1969), p. 5.

18. According to my notes, the quotation comes from Howard Mumford Jones, but all of my attempts to track down its source have thus far proved futile.

19. Edmund Fuller, *Man in Modern Fiction* (New York: Vintage, 1949, 1958), p. 12. See also Wylie Sypher, *Loss of the Self in Modern Literature and Art* (New York: Vintage, 1964); Charles I. Glicksberg, *The Self in Modern Literature* (University Park: Pennyslvania State University Press, 1963); and Julian N. Hartt, *The Lost Image of Man* (Baton Rouge: Louisiana State University Press, 1963).

20. Addison Leitch, "Reality in Modern Literature," in *The Christian Imagination,* ed. Ryken, p. 196.

21. Hilda Graef, *Modern Gloom and Christian Hope* (Chicago: Henry Regnery, 1959), p. vii.

22. My examples in this paragraph and the next come from Jacques Barzun, *The Use and Abuse of Art* (Princeton: Princeton University Press, 1974), pp. 14-15; and Nicholas Wolterstorff, *Art in Action* (Grand Rapids: William B. Eerdmans, 1980), pp. 62-63.

23. Terry Eagleton, *Literary Theory: An Introduction* (Minneapolis: University of Minnesota Press, 1983), pp. 204, 214.

24. Harold C. Gardiner, *Norms for the Novel* (Garden City: Hanover House, 1960), p. 41.

25. Irving and Cornelia Sussman, *How to Read a Dirty Book* (Chicago: Franciscan Herald Press, 1966), pp. 12-13.

26. Fuller, p. 90.

27. Roland M. Frye, *Perspective on Man: Literature and the Christian Tradition* (Philadelphia: Westminster, 1961), p. 64.

28. C. S. Lewis, *Mere Christianity* (New York: Macmillan, 1943, 1972), p. 92.

29. Will Durant, "Man Is Wiser than Any Man," *Reader's Digest,* November 1968, p. 68.

30. Harry Blamires, *The Christian Mind* (London: S.P.C.K., 1966), pp. 96-100.

31. Madeleine L'Engle, *A Circle of Quiet* (New York: Farrar, Strauss, and Giroux, 1972), pp. 168-169.

32. Blamires, p. 45.

33. Calvin Seerveld, *A Christian Critique of Art* (St. Catharines, Ontario: Association for Reformed Scientific Studies 1963), p. 52.

34. This phrase comes from J. R. R. Tolkien, "On Fairy- Stories" in *Essays Presented to Charles Williams,* ed. C. S. Lewis (Grand Rapids: William B. Eerdmans, 1966), p. 79.

35. Henry Zylstra, *Testament of Vision* (Grand Rapids: William B. Eerdmans, 1961), p. 5.

36. Virginia Mollenkott, *Adamant and Stone Chips* (Waco: Word, 1967), p. 81.

37. Roland Frye, p. 84.

38. T. S. Eliot, "Religion and Literature," pp. 146-148.

39. Frank E. Gaebelein, *A Varied Harvest* (Grand Rapids: William B. Eerdmans, 1967), p. 116.

40. William Wordsworth, "Tintern Abbey," line 140.

41. Thomas Howard, "On Evil in Art," in *The Christian Imagination,* ed. Ryken, p. 116.

Conclusion

Christian Readers, Viewers, and Listeners

The Role of the Audience

> Of course, it is the whole person who responds to a poem or novel; and if that person is a believing Christian, then it is a believing Christian who judges; one can't . . . pretend to be something one is not. . . . Literary criticism is as much . . . the product of a personal sense of life and value as literature itself.
>
> Vincent Buckley, *Poetry and Morality*

Current theories of art are based on the premise that works of art do not truly exist apart from the activity of the individual viewer, reader, or listener. Artists depend on the response of an audience to complete the meaning of a work. The colors and shapes on a canvas, the words on a page, and the sounds that strike the ear are only a potential work of art. What the French philosopher Jean-Paul Sartre said about the writer is equally true of the artist and musician:

> Since the artist must entrust to another the job of carrying out what he has begun, since it is only through the consciousness of the reader that he can regard himself as essential to his work, . . . the writer appeals to the reader's freedom to collaborate in the production of his work.[1]

A little reflection will confirm the accuracy of this emphasis on the role of the audience. Even when simply describing what they see in a work of art, people differ widely in their descriptions. And far more discrepancy emerges when readers, viewers, and listeners start to make interpretive comments. What aspect of a work is most important? Is a given detail in a work offered for approval or disapproval? What is the artist saying about reality and values by means of the work as a whole? Our answers to such questions depend not only on our alertness but also on our background of life experiences and our world view.

The common way to describe the subjective element in artistic response is "the hermeneutical circle" (or "interpretive circle"). We can diagram it this way:

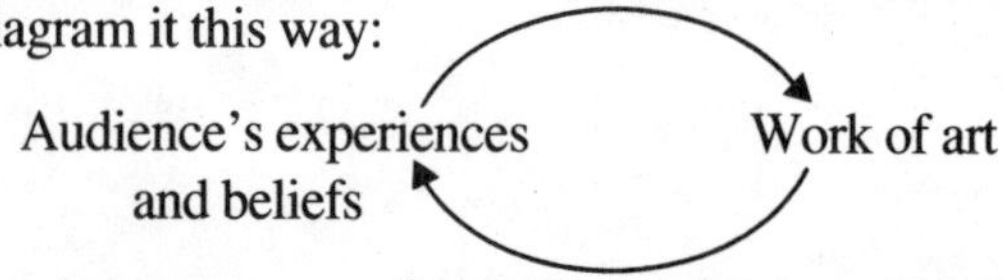

That is, we bring our own fund of experiences and beliefs to a work of art. What we see in a painting or poem is partly what our own personality and background (including previous contact with the arts) equip us to see. But the reverse is also true: Our excursions into art give us images and insights that we carry back with us into life. In the experiences of life, we are reminded of stories and lines of poetry and paintings and songs that codify and express our experiences of the moment. This is surely what happens when we read the Bible; it is no less true of our encounters with art.

Christians as an Interpretive Community

Artistic experience is a partly personal matter. But it is not wholly private and individual. Art is a public and shared experience as well. In fact, works of art are a major "bonding" agent in society. These shared responses to art occur not only because we are all members of the human race, but also because we belong to groups within society that have common sets of experiences and attitudes.

Modern artistic theory thus speaks of "interpretive communities"—groups of people who share a set of beliefs and interests and who interpret art in terms of that framework. Members of an interpretive community have their own "agenda" of interests and attitudes as they interact with works of art. We should be clear that everyone belongs to one or more interpretive communities simply by virtue of his or her outlook on life.

This means that everyone's encounters with art are based on a fund of presuppositions. One scholar comments in this regard that

> there can be no "presuppositionless" interpretation. A biblical, literary, or scientific text is not interpreted without preconceptions. . . . Where do we get our presuppositions? From the tradition in which we stand.[2]

Christians are an "interpretive community." They share a set of assumptions that inevitably affect how they experience and interpret works of art.

Christians are not necessarily better readers, viewers, and listeners than other people, but they have their own agenda of interests and beliefs that they bring to their artistic experiences. Like other audiences, they view art through the lens of their own world view. They are sensitive to certain aspects of artistic works because their Christianity gives them the "antennae" to notice and resonate with them. We can diagram the situation like this:

Christian audience → Christian world view → works of art

Christians do not need to apologize for having a value system and world view through which they interpret works of art.

The Presuppositions of a Christian Audience

What, then, characterizes this "Christian audience" of art? What are the presuppositions that Christians bring to the enjoyment and study of art, music, and literature?

The most basic of all presuppositions is the Christian view of authority and truth. The only authority for belief that all branches of Christianity accept is the Bible. Christian involvement in the arts begins with the premise that the Bible will furnish basic principles that determine how we should regard art itself. The Bible also provides the doctrinal standard of truth by which Christians measure artistic assertions about God, people, and nature.

Using Scripture as their foundation, Christians begin with the premise that this is their Father's world. God's creation (including the people in it) have meaning and importance because God made them. As the products of people made in God's image, works of art have a claim to the Christian's attention and love. People are significant, and their artistic attempts to discover and express their humanity are likewise significant. Nature, too, is a leading subject of art, and Christians approach the artistic rendition of nature with respect. In short, the doctrine of creation allows Christians to be open and receptive to the world of art.

Christians come to art convinced not only of the worth of God's creation but also conscious that the creation is fallen. Evil has left no corner of art untouched. Since the subject of art is human experience, the fallen nature of human experience is something that Christians expect to find portrayed in art. They do not turn away from the realistic portrayal of human depravity in the name of "niceness." The Bible itself provides a model for encountering evil in art.

The doctrine of the Fall also makes possible the perversion of art. Christians are not naive or undiscriminating in their approach to art. There is a sense in which they are "looking for trouble" as they encounter works of art. They know that every painting, every story, every song has a potential for error as well as truth, for inducement to immorality as well as virtue, for coarseness as well as refinement.

But Christians are not only looking for trouble as they journey through the world of art. They are also looking for innocent delight, God-given beauty and artistry, and moments of truth. They know that art can be a means of grace—a source of truth and beauty, an occasion for feeling close to God and realizing something of the perfection for which God created us.

Christians, moreover, can approach art in the freedom bestowed by a belief in common grace. God's truth and grace can be expressed by unbelievers as well as believers. We do not need to inquire into the personal orthodoxy of an artist before we are free to affirm the truth and technical excellence of a work of art.

Christians also approach the arts with a philosophy of leisure. They do not feel guilty about time spent enjoying creativity and beauty. Their stewardship of time leads them to choose enriching forms of leisure pursuits, including the arts. A Christian attitude toward pleasure opens the door to the enjoyment of legitimate forms of entertainment free from utilitarian-induced guilt.

CULTIVATING GOOD RESPONSES

> Art [is] the embodiment of man's response to reality. . . . The [Christian's] response to "reality" is his response to God's creation.
>
> John W. Dixon, Jr., *Nature and Grace in Art*

> Art as such needs no justification; rather, it demands a response, like that of the twenty-four elders in Revelation who worship God for the very act of creation itself (Revelation 4:11).
>
> H. R. Rookmaaker, *The Creative Gift*

Is there a unique function that the arts should play in a Christian's life? The framework under which I will consider that question is simple but important: The arts provide the occasion and materials for Christians to cultivate good responses—to God, to culture, to the world.

Art as the Human Response to the World

We should recall first that art itself is always a human response to the world. Even to choose a subject for artistic portrayal is a comment by the artist about what is real and significant in life. The way in which an artist then proceeds to treat the subject is an interpretive response to the chosen subject.

The arts are humankind's most accurate record of their affirmations and denials, their longings and fears. The arts are a picture of the kind of world people aspire to create and of the fallen realities that keep thwarting those aspirations. We do not ordinarily know how biologists feel about the natural phenomena that they study, but we do know how poets and painters feel about a landscape.

The arts deal with the same subjects (God, people, and nature) as the natural and social sciences do. But the arts differ from the sciences by focusing on the human response to those subjects. The arts express how the human race has felt about the facts of existence. Art is the record of people's involvement with life. It deals not simply with the facts of life but with things as they matter to people.

By participating in artistic responses to the world, Christians can cultivate their humanity to their own advantage, to society's benefit, and to God's glory. God created people to respond to him and his creation. He does not wish us to be unmoved by the beauty of a flower or the misery of human suffering. One function of art is to give form to our own experiences and responses. The artist is our representative, expressing what we want to say but doing so in a much richer way.

Responding to Culture

Involvement in the arts allows Christians to respond to their surrounding culture. Christians are responsible to be a redemptive influence in their culture. That responsibility begins by understanding their culture, including its artistic expressions. The Russian novelist Fyodor Dostoyevsky wrote that "man has no right to turn his back and to ignore what is going on in the world—and there are supreme moral reasons for not allowing him to do so."[3]

There are a number of good responses to one's culture that contact with the arts can foster. These include a sense of community with one's fellow humans, an enlargement of compassion, a sense of justice about what is wrong in the world, an affirmation of moral virtues, sensitivity to common human experience, and tolerance for the sheer range of human experiences and attitudes. At its best, art confirms one poet's claim that "poetry helps us remember what's brave and beautiful and sensible; to forget it is to have the life go out of us. . . . It guards our sensibility."[4]

Responding to God

For Christians, artistic experiences can foster right responses to God. For one thing, the arts have always been a part of worship.

The Bible itself is artistic. Our worship services include music and visual symbols. We make music, poetry, and visual art a part of our religious celebrations.

Christians can carry this same sense of worship into their artistic experiences outside of the church. Freed from the idolatry of worshipping art itself, they can worship God with their artistic experiences. In the presence of great art, Christians have someone to whom to be thankful, knowing that God is the ultimate source of truth, beauty, and artistic creativity in people. When Christians encounter an artistic celebration of what is good in creation and life, they can channel their celebration into praise of their Creator. When confronted with the artistic portrayal of the ugliness and misery of a fallen world, they can turn to God their Redeemer with both gratitude for deliverance and commitment to help others share in that deliverance.

The arts are not simply an aid to worship; they are the means of worship when Christians use them as the occasion to respond to God. Christians who scorn contact with art are missing a great opportunity to praise God.

Responding to the Truth

Because works of art make implied assertions they also elicit intellectual responses from an audience. The arts force us to agree or disagree with their viewpoints. It is virtually impossible to remain neutral in our contacts with art. By our very responses to characters in a story or objects in a painting, we engage in an act of interpretation.

To encounter works of art is to engage in thinking about the great issues of life. This, too, is one of the things God created us to do. Christians believe that their mind matters. They should welcome opportunities to have their thinking stimulated, challenged, and sharpened. Encountering the ideas and attitudes embodied in works of art is a form of stewardship of the mind.

As Christians look at works of art through the lens of their own beliefs, some viewpoints come into focus while others do not. This is to say that Christians encounter a combination of truth and error as they assimilate works of art. Sometimes their Christian world view leads them to complete a portrayal of reality that is left incomplete in a work of art. On other occasions, Christians intuitively use their Christian framework to correct what is incorrectly asserted in a work. Whether by agreement or disagreement, artistic works provide the occasion for Christians to respond to the truth that their system of belief affords.

THE IDEAL READER, VIEWER, AND LISTENER

> The experience of literature, far from being for the reader a passive process of absorption, is a form in intense personal activity. . . . Literature is . . . a medium of exploration.
>
> Louise M. Rosenblatt, *Literature as Exploration*

Once we grant that Christians should actively set aside time to participate in the arts, we can begin to formulate a theory of how to interact with art. The brief outline that follows expresses the rudiments of such a theory.

Encounter

A key element in any theory of what happens when we read literature or look at art or listen to music is summed up in the word *encounter*. What, specifically, do we encounter? We encounter people—characters in a story or painting or song, and the artist who created the work. We encounter human experience—love, death, nature, human emotions, in fact, the entire range of human experience in the world. We also encounter the physical world of nature and civilization, and the moral world of good and evil, virtue and vice. We encounter ideas, as expressed by characters within a work and as embodied in the work as a whole. And we encounter the artistic side of a work—the beauty, the form, the technical mastery.

If art represents this type of encounter, the corollary that follows is that as an audience we must be prepared to meet a work of art halfway. We need to be alert, as we are when we meet a person of note or attend an event of importance. We should not be passive spectators. We should, as it were, engage in an ongoing dialogue—a give and take of response—as we assimilate a work of art. Any successful encounter depends on the interaction of the two persons engaged in the encounter. Our artistic encounters are no different. Experiencing art is a transaction between the artist and the audience, with the work of art serving as the meeting point.

Discovery

Another key element in a good theory of artistic response is the word *discovery*. Whenever we sit down to read a book or visit an art gallery or attend a concert, we embark on a process of discovering what a work of art stands ready to reveal.

We discover many things on such occasions. We discover insights about human experience. One of the tasks of the artist is revelation—revelation about life and the world and God. We also discover the properties of the work itself—how it is made, how the parts fit together, what unifies it. Pondering a work of art is directed creation. Works of art are constructed to lead an audience to discover what the artist has revealed. To limit "doing art" to the creating of new works is a gross misrepresentation of what happens when a person actively participates in great works of art from the past. To scrutinize a work of art closely is a creative act, and it allows an audience to make many of the same discoveries the artist made while composing the work.

What are the implications of looking upon our encounters with art as a process of discovery? Primarily, it imposes on an audience the obligation to be alert, to be creative, to be active in looking. Audiences should never be ashamed of staring. They should approach art with the openness, the receptivity, the curiosity, the expectancy that characterize every true explorer.

Recognition

We also experience recognition when we encounter works of art. At the level of subject matter, art gives us forms for our own experiences, feelings, and beliefs. Our own impulses and fears, some of them hidden or subconscious, are projected onto fictional characters or painted scenes or musical patterns. When we see what is inside us projected and named, we recognize it. Dorothy Sayers has written that

> when we read the poem, or see the play or picture or hear the music, it is as though a light were turned on us. We say: "Ah! I recognise that! That is something which I obscurely felt to be going on in and about me, but I didn't know what it was and couldn't express it. But now the artist has . . . imaged it forth . . . for me, I can possess and take hold of it and make it my own, and turn it into a source of knowledge and strength."[5]

Novelist Walker Percy has said that "in art, whether it's poetry, fiction or painting, you are telling the reader or the listener something he already knows but which he doesn't quite know that he knows. . . . What the artist does . . . is simply to validate the human experience and to tell people the deep human truths which they already unconsciously know."[6]

Art is thus a mirror in which we see ourselves. This is a prospect that Christians should find attractive, since the Bible is so full of warnings against self-deception and hypocrisy and of encouragement toward self-knowledge. Someone has said that we go to art "primarily to discover ourself—above all, perhaps, to discover what St. Augustine refers to as the dark corners of the heart."[7]

Self-Revelation

Another word that summarizes what happens when we encounter art is self-revelation. We usually think that an audience judges works of art. They do, of course, but the reverse is also true: Works of art judge their audience. Someone has written that "books (sacred and profane) read the reader. . . . Books draw out what is in a man."[8] Our responses to works of art are self-revealing. They are an index to what we believe, feel, and have experienced. In responding as we do, we are making intellectual, moral, and emotional choices and revelations.

For our artistic experiences to be fully beneficial, therefore, we need to ponder our judgments and responses. We need to notice the types of artistic subject matter, the types of fictional characters, the kinds of music and pictures that attract and repel us.

Interacting with works of art can make us more self-aware and more self-critical. It can be a way of discovering things about ourselves, especially about our values and morality. We should pay particular attention to the types of art, literature, and music to which we gravitate when left to our own tastes. T. S. Eliot had Christians specifically in mind when he wrote that "for literary judgment we need to be acutely aware of two things at once: of 'what we like,' and of 'what we ought to like.'. . . The two forms of self-consciousness, knowing what we are and what we ought to be, must go together."[9]

Interpretation

A final activity that we do as artistic audiences is interpretation. To interpret a work of art is to decide what the work means, both in whole and in its parts. We engage in such interpretive activity continuously as we interact with a work of art. Even to react with sympathy or antipathy to details in a work is to make an interpretation.

Once we acknowledge that an audience always makes big and small interpretations, we also notice that people do not always agree in their interpretations. They disagree partly because they respond to art in keeping with their own experiences and beliefs. As Christians look at the field of art from their Christian perspective, they can organize the landscape into some broad categories.

Most works of art portray something that we recognize as true to our own experience. I call this the art of common humanity. Since art is the portrayal of human experience and external reality, much of the art we encounter fixes our attention on life as we know it, with its longings, its anxieties, its enduring elements.

A smaller category of art is Christian art. Art can fall into this category simply at the level of subject matter by being about such obviously Christian topics as God, Christian doctrines, or Christian experiences like conversion and prayer. More often, the Christian element in art consists of the viewpoint or slant on the subject, regardless of what that subject is. In either case, Christian art gives substance to the truth about reality as we find that truth revealed in the Bible and the example of Christ. It is one of God's richest gifts.

If we take art as a whole, we find that most of it has not affirmed a Christian vision in any thoroughgoing way. I call this the art of clarification because it clarifies the human situation to which the Christian faith speaks. Such art views life from the perspective of the world views and attitudes that non-Christians hold. From a Christian perspective, the light in such art falls from the wrong angle. But such art clarifies the values and world views (for example, materialism, hedonism, pessimism, determinism, humanism) by which people continue to live. Such art identifies where people seek for ultimate meaning when they do not find it in God.

Why Christians Need the Arts

> Art increases our state of aliveness by expanding and deepening our state of awareness. Art discovers, heightens and refines life experiences. . . . Art intensifies man's involvement with life. . . . Art makes leisure time and all time a thing of interest and beauty.
>
> d'Arcy Hayman, *The Arts and Man*

The arts serve many potential functions in the life of a Christian. Since the subject of most art is human experience, the arts heighten our awareness of life. They enhance our perception of both the world around us and our place in it. They sharpen our senses and emotions. The arts make us more conscious of the problems of life, the good in the world, and the diversities of life. They are one of the chief means by which people assimilate and grapple with reality.

The arts are an expression and record of the human meaning that people have found in this world. Music, literature, and visual art are humankind's testimony to its own experiences. For us as individuals, therefore, the arts give shape to our experiences, feelings, and beliefs, thereby satisfying our urge for adequate expression. The arts express our longings and fears, our affirmations and denials. By participating in the arts, we celebrate life.

The arts do more than name and intensify our own experiences. They actually expand the range of those experiences. Literature, music, and art enlarge our being by admitting us to experiences and worlds that we would otherwise never have known. In the process, they extend our interests, our knowledge, our sympathies, our consciousness. The arts also add beauty and color to the world in which we live.

The arts are a great organizing force in society and our personal lives. In art, the amorphous flow of life is temporarily halted, defined, and given pattern so we can understand and relish it. The imagination, moreover, organizes the confused pieces of our existence into a coherent picture arranged around archetypes (master images). The arts clarify life and focus a society's attention on its values, fears, and longings.

Because the arts interpret as well as record reality, they engage our intellect. The arts offer a diagnosis, definition, and explanation of the human condition. Artists make value judgments about human actions, thoughts, and situations. By means of these implied assertions about life, the arts force us to think, to ponder alternate viewpoints, and to commit ourselves to our own convictions of truth. Works of art thus provide both the occasion and materials for us to exercise and expand our own angle of vision.

Along with all these useful functions, the arts exist to refresh us. They are a form of recreation, entertainment, and enjoyment. They enrich our leisure time and add to the joy of life. The arts are the signature of humankind, setting people off from other creatures with whom we inhabit this world. Art affirms the humanness of humans.

These are the gifts of art to the human race. They are especially important to Christians because to the human reasons for cultivating art a Christian can add an even more ultimate rationale—the glory of God. I would call this the appointed consummation of the arts. When pursued with an awareness of God as the source and end of all creativity, beauty, and truth, the arts become a means of Christian growth and praise.

SUMMARY

Much of what ideally happens when Christians have contact with the arts can be summed up in the formula that works of art encourage us to have good responses—to human life in the world, to our surrounding culture, to God, to truth, to beauty. "Doing art" is not limited to the work of writers, composers, and artists. It also includes the creative participation of readers, listeners, and viewers in a process of encounter, discovery, recognition, self-revelation, and interpretation.

Christians need the arts. The arts enhance our sense of the richness of human life. They can activate us to thought and feeling. And at their best, they refresh us and direct us to the ultimate source of truth and beauty—God.

Notes to the Conclusion

1. Jean-Paul Sartre, *What Is Literature?* trans. Bernard Frechtman (New York: Philosophical Library, 1949), p. 46.

2. Richard E. Palmer, *Hermeneutics: Interpretation Theory in Schleiermacher, Dilthey, Heidegger, and Godamer* (Evanston: Northwestern University press, 1969), p. 182.

3. Fyodor Dostoyevsky, as quoted by Marc Slonim in his "Introduction" to *The Brothers Karamazov* (New York: Modern Library, 1950), p. xiii.

4. John Tagliabue, comment in *Poetspeak,* ed. Paul B. Janeczko (Scarsdale, New York: Bradbury Press, 1983), p. 138.

5. Dorothy L. Sayers, *Unpopular Opinions* (London: Victor Gollanz, 1946), pp. 39-40.

6. Walker Percy, "Walker Percy, the Man and the Novelist: An Interview," *The Southern Review,* n.s., 4 (1968): 279.

7. Simon Lesser, *Fiction and the Unconscious* (Chicago: Chicago University Press, 1957, 1975), p. 253.

8. Stanley Fish, *Surprised by Sin: The Reader in Paradise Lost* (New York: St. Martin's, 1967), p. 84.

9. T. S. Eliot, "Religion and Literature," as reprinted in *The Christian Imagination: Essays on Literature and the Arts,* ed. Leland Ryken (Grand Rapids: Baker, 1981), pp. 152-153.

Scripture Index

Subject Index